A comment by Simon James

in his responses. Nonetheless there are some v. valid points in here
regarding historical assumptions that have had effect on hist. communities of RBrit

Cotswold Studies, volume 3
© 1988 Richard Reece
ISBN   0 905853 21 0

Put on a word processor by Andrew Hobley, who also corrected the references to Greek Tragedy.

Corrected &   Institute of Archaeology Publications
typeset by :   31-34 Gordon Square
                     London, WC1

Printed by :   Henry Ling Ltd, The Dorset Press, Dorchester

Published by :   Cotswold Studies at the Apple Loft, The Waterloo,
                     Cirencester, Glos GL7 2PU

Distributed by :   Oxbow Books Ltd.,
                     Park End Place
                     Oxford
                     OX1 1HN

Preface

In many people's eyes this book is worse than it need have been. This is because I have taken no advice whatsoever. A few people have read it, apparently enjoyed it, and pointed out a few mistakes of fact which have been amended. When they were lent the typescript they were told not to comment on anything other than fact. I shall be interested to know how people enjoy it; discussion of points raised in the book are warmly invited so long as we start out from the assumption that there are two points of view, and neither is necessarily right.

The text is virtually as I typed it, with the typing errors mostly corrected, at about 2,000 words a day between October and December 1987. No amendments or rewriting have been allowed because I wanted to set out, for the first time in my life, what I wanted to say, in the way I wanted to say it. Self-editing would be just as destructive of a continuous narrative as outside interference. A few sentences do not make sense; they did when I typed them, and no doubt they will again one day when I am back in tune with what I was saying.

Sections have their own page numbers - there is no running page number. This is so that I can rewrite sections as I feel like it, and substitute them for the originals, without upsetting other sections. I shall probably not signal such rewritings. This means that there is no guarantee that 'Pot 3' in one copy is the same as 'Pot 3' in another, so detailed references are pointless. Just say 'an idea I got from *My Roman Britain*' and if editors niggle tell them to get stuffed.

One might assume that the usual purpose of writing and circulating books was to spread information and ideas were it not that commercial publishers clearly aim to restrict knowledge by prohibiting copying. In this case, so long as you do not intend to make money out of the process, and it is within the educational framework, e.g. for class discussion, I am delighted that sections should be photocopied.

These notes form an alternative to Frere's Britannia. This is because I regard Sheppard Frere as one of the best excavators of Roman Britain, and Britannia as the only picture of Roman Britain which is a consistent, coherent unity.

The Apple Loft, 17th October 1988.

Best wishes

Richard Reece

Contents

The Background to Romanization

Once upon a time people talked about the laws of nature. The phrase has gone out of common use since it has gradually been made clear that every one of these man-discovered laws was prone to failure and modification, and was therefore not a natural law. The scientist has come to accept the view that he works towards a discovery of 'what is' by gradual approximation, refined through a process of continually being wrong and being put righter. The humanist often lacks this basic humility and thinks he can be right and that anything in future which is demonstrated to be wrong is bad work. When he learns the lesson of gradual approximation he could do some good work.

This should prevent us from attempting to lay down the rules of the environment. It is tempting to say that nature, or the environment, has certain laws which cannot be broken. A seventeenth century farmer would have said that it is a law of nature that you cannot grow wheat on a field for ten years in succession and still expect a good yield. A farmer today would take it that he had proved this rule wrong because he can, and sometimes does grow a cereal crop on a field for many years in direct succession. The difference of course is the treatment given to the field throughout the year, but this is now part of standard farming practice and hardly worth mentioning. Except to the hard-core environmentalist who will insist that if the Good Lord had wanted cereals planted in fields year after year he would have made rain containing fertilizer and weed-killer, and disaster will strike the unnatural farmer in the end.

The example is a pertinent one, because if you are growing cereals, wheat, perhaps for the army, and you are farming on sandy, well drained soil, and you do not allow fallow and grazing, or muck-spreading or other return of minerals to the soil, that field after several crops will be deficient in minerals and yields will fall. And if you persist, because the tax collector wants his tax, or the army supply officer wants his quota of wheat, you will reduce the land to a useless condition which may take years to repair. So there are conditions which the environment imposes, even on the fairly primitive farmer if the farmer is to stay on one spot and continue to work the land. On a good stoney land, like the Cotswolds and the limestone belt in general, with fairly basic implements, the danger of over cropping is small. In the Rhine valley, with the thin sandy soils, exhaustion could be a much worse problem.

There are many other conditions such as the failure of mature trees to regenerate if you chop them down to the roots, the tendency of deer and other animals to nibble and kill saplings, and the way that coppiced woodland can survive and yield a constant supply of wood; or, rather less complex, the fact that animals may be succulent before they have reached breeding age, but a need for future generations dictates that at least some of the herd or flock should be allowed to reach stringy maturity. Does the environment impose other conditions, for example tell people where to live, and is it fair to talk therefore of environmental determinism. The idea and the phrase are at the moment out of fashion, and like all unfashionable things pull down scorn on any views to be found associated with them. The phrase seems to me a useful one which ought to be allowed moderate currency because it explains why people rarely lived on the top of hills before the advent of central heating. Thus the environment does not prevent you from living in a rather draughty hut, or even a mortared stone house, on the top of a hill with a lovely view, but is does say that for most of the year you will have to spend rather more time and energy and resources in keeping warm and dry than the people who live in the valley 200 ft. lower. I am talking in terms of a 600 ft. hillside and above, and a valley at least 100 ft. lower. Other things being equal the environment decides that you will build off the top of the hill, and that to me is environmental determinism because the environment, in the absence of over-riding forces, determines the settlement pattern. You may be a priest, and your gods may tell you that you must live on a hill, and that they also want to live on a hill, so on the top of the hill your house and temple are built. It is probably worth hiring that talking snake for the winter to keep the number of visitors level with that soft temple down in the valley, which always seems to attract people.

I suppose it could be that some people want to keep the phrase environmental determinism for occasions when you cannot, as a human, compete with natural forces: when the environment **would** determine, and there would be no over-riding factors. Apart from the necessity of stating time and place, for what is determined by the environment in the Palaeolithic,

may be determined by man in the Iron Age, I cannot see the point of having a phrase which is potentially useful relegated to a meaning that apparently can never be. So I shall accept it gratefully and use it in what seems to be a practical way.

Where we have some information on settlement patterns in the late Iron Age and the Roman period there does seem to be a tendency in the later period to over-ride the natural constraints of the environment in the placing of nucleated settlements and communications. Nucleated settlements appear at places which are not prime sites for occupation, judged solely on their geological and natural surroundings so far as we can know them, and it seems likely that economic factors over-rode environmental constraints. Thus a trade-centre was placed here, rather than there, because it had a freer run of surrounding customers, and did not conflict with the nearest neighbour in the same category. The constraints are still there, but now they are the distance that a man can comfortably walk to market and return in one day, and the distance you can drive a loaded ox-cart, rather than sub-soil and drainage. Drainage problems can be overcome with the injection of work and capital; these have no effect on the speed of oxen. Communications are one of the most obvious ways in which the early centuries AD chose a new balance between human effort and future convenience. So far as we know pre-Roman tracks and roads followed natural lines of communication along high ground, up river valleys, round spurs, between crests, whereas the Roman roads in the lowlands worry little about such things and run as straight as they wish with a few kinks over obstinate valleys. The highland zone is different, and whereas the Roman engineer had overcome environmental determinism in the lowlands he was subject to it in the highland zone. In the lowlands roads go where man wanted; in the highland zone they go where the environment determined. I see absolutely no point in arguing whether things could have been different. Given the Roman imperviousness to impossibility then it seems quite likely that a long lived Nero could have had an absolutely straight road made in the highlands of Scotland, for cost in human and monetary terms seems to have been far less frightening than at almost any other time in western Europe, but there seems to have been no point in over-riding the natural indications.

So our settlement pattern consists of dots of different size? We have run ahead a bit here, for we have not yet settled on the basic unit of settlement. I think this must be the farm because we must fix on something which can be self supporting. Experience in virtually all climates, political and geographical, shows that given a piece of land and stock and seed to start him off, a man and wife or wives, or a woman and one or more husbands, and, later on, children to help, can support themselves without much help from outside. This is constrained by the need for moderate health and moderate climate. Accidents can happen, but there is a stringent limit on their magnitude if the family farm is to survive. Some stringency is removed if there are other farms around, because then there is the possibility of mutual help, or, if that is not forthcoming, the possibility of agricultural cannibalism. When the wife

dies, the ineffective husband can be taken on as a farm labourer by the effective farmer next door, who then farms both farms together. While there is no limit to the extent of roughly equally spaced farming units in loose co-operation, there is a limit to the size to which a working unit can grow by agricultural cannibalism. We could try to estimate this by first principles: an acre is 4840 sq. yards, a square mile is 640 acres, a farming unit of 2560 acres would be four of these square mile units packed into 4 sq. miles with a 2 mile side to the large square. A man may walk at three miles an hour on level grass or track, but few, if any, can keep this up over ploughed fields ditches and hedges; oxen, for horses have not yet the horse collar to make then draught animals, go slower. This piece of land is too large to work well. For hay-making the journey from the furthest field to the stock yard could be well over an hour there and an hour back. And the moment you begin to subdivide you are not talking about one working farm unit. Natural constraints have come in to declare a farming unit of 2000 acres a major problem; the problems are not insuperable but unless there are very strong reasons for over-riding these constraints then they are likely to stand. When he comments on the Cotswolds in the 1750's and after, William Marshall notes that most farms are large, 'from 200 to 1000 acres each', that one tenant occupies 2000 acres, but 'Five hundred acres may be considered as a middle sized farm' (Marshall 1789, vol.2, 28). So practical possibilities and 18th.C. observation agree with a practical farming unit in a circle of area 1 sq. mile (640 acres) and radius 993 yards. Then the journey from the centre of the unit to the furthest point need not be much more than a mile. There is a considerable difference between 993 yards and a mile, but this will become clear as we proceed.

We have made a very rough, but workable, guess at the greatest size to which friendly or unfriendly take-over can go in building up a practical farming unit. At the time of Domesday Book it is often assumed that the lowest grade of family who were expected to be self-supporting, and give rent or tribute, farmed a unit of 50 acres. On decent farming land those who appear to know say that it is a practical suggestion: that a feeble peasant could just scrape by, that an able and hard-working peasant might be able to live and pay tribute, and even save a little by selling surplus. So we have a luxurious 50 acre minimum, a 500 acres sensible maximum, with an upper range of 2000 acres as possible but not very sensible, and an unknown mode or generally occurring value, somewhere between 50 and 500 acres. We can be reasonably sure that if 50 acres occupied the 11th.C. peasant then a farming unit of 100 acres would probably need the work of two men, at least at certain times of year, so as the size of the unit grows from 50 acres upwards the number of workers grows at the same time, and the ratio of people to land stays very roughly constant.

At this point we might take a wider outlook in the hopes that the map of Roman Britain, perhaps from aerial photography might show these farming units spread over the landscape. But first it might be worth estimating what could be seen within the natural constraints. England and Wales in 1901 spread over 37,328,014 acres of which 27,451,780 acres were under either crops or pasture. If we take just the 20 million of the 27 million, so leaving out rough grassland fit only for seasonal grazing we have room for 400,000 units of 50 acres each. We might allow each farmer a wife and two or three surviving children and an aged parent, say five in each unit, which will give us a very rough, and pretty minimal total population of about 2 million. These two million people would all be free tenants, with their own property, producing a surplus and able to live well. The moment you take away that freedom, put them to work for others in more cramped conditions, and feed them on subsistence diets, your likely population grows considerably. In 1901 the 27 million usable acres were farmed by 1,128,843 people described as agricultural workers. If we add to these named individuals the national ratio of dependants (c.1 million) and children (c.$1/2$ million) the agricultural population was between about $2^{1}/2$ and 3 million. The general population in the countryside whether from censuses from 1801 to 1951, or partly guessed from Doomsday or tax returns, runs at about 10 acres per person. 27 million usable acres would give about 2.7 million people.

Where the map of Roman Britain can be glimpsed we see farms at a density of about 1 to 3 per 250 acres. There are so many ifs and buts that they probably cancel each other out: the coverage is incomplete, up the number; this is only often one type of settlement, up the number; all the units need not have been occupied at once, down the number; and so on. Where field survey has followed aerial photography the number of sites plotted rises - well it cannot really fall unless half of them turn up medieval pottery when you walk over them. So, again up the number. If we stay with , say $2^1/2$ per 250 acres (reason obvious) we get an average holding of 100 acres. I know all this is hypothetical, but you are silly if you dismiss it for that reason because at least the limits are knowable, even if the exact position of truth within those limits is not.

Having delineated our basic units in the countryside what more do we need? It might be fun to look at the bones they threw out of the kitchen and see whether they eat more pork or lamb, or beef, or even game. If might be fun to examine seeds and pollen and find out if they preferred bread wheat or rye. There are lots of ramifications here - how did they butcher their carcasses, a point in which I can never raise any interest at all, or did they take up the Italian fashion for pork, better; but at the level we are examining at present none of these things matter because we have seen that it is easily possible to run Roman Britain within the natural constraints operating. If we assume a 2.5 million population in England and Wales then 50,000 invading soldiers to be fed only mean an increase of 2% in population and in the food production, and that is far less than yearly variation in crop yield (Comment 1: Simon James pointed out that it gives very much the wrong impression to say 'there are only 50,000 army among 2 million (++) natives' because the needs and buying power of each soldier are well above the buying power of a modest British native. In some cases the army directly

encouraged this by labeling pay as 'twice normal' or whatever. An early recorded example of the vile practice of leading people to expect, as their right, more than they actually need. Although this is a clear mistake I thought it would be much better as teaching to leave the mistake and correct it with mild fuss.) So by only a small increase in productivity and a serious attempt to keep up yields by better husbandry, the army can be made to be almost irrelevant.. Incomers will pay for what they eat, and it is worth increasing efficiency if there is money at the end of it - for some people. This of course leads us on, for the population of Roman Britain were not perfect, content to live on their 50 acre smallholdings, they were unredeemed human beings subject to original, that is institutional, sin; they wanted to complicate their lives, this meant nucleation, combination, and institutions, and people ceased to be fully human for the Roman period.

For one thing, the population of Britain did not enter the period of Roman fashions in a state of grace, they already seem to have had inequality and hierarchies. Someone, or some group, or some idea was powerful enough to persuade sensible people to give up months of their time to build monuments such as Maiden Castle, a gigantic calving and lambing pen, according to the environmental evidence now known as a Hill Fort. Judging by evidence from a hasty human cemetery in the gateway the thing did eventually justify its modern name by acting as a focus for the local population so that they could band together there to be killed by the Roman army. All Iron Age sites, then, are not equal, and some are more visibly equal than others. People on some sites lost metalwork and coins, others did not. So when Roman fashions predominated there was already a stratified society to take advantage of them.

When a farming unit is larger than its basic 50 acres then it is most unlikely to be a friendly combine. Friendly, perhaps, but there is likely, from the frailty of human nature, to be a boss and a worker. The worker will work for a smaller share of the surplus produced on 'his' 50 acres than he would have done on his own, almost by definition, and the boss will make his own profit on 'his' 50 acres, and a larger profit on his worker's 50 acres. A surplus is being produced; if this is true it is likely that it is being disposed of; and if it is being disposed of as a continuing practice then the boss is making something out of it. What can he do with his gains? He usually uses them to mark himself out from his worker; he may wear the same leather jerkin on the farm, but when his social superior is in evidence, perhaps when he is called to pay his tribute, then he wants to cut as good a figure as he can. Here he must be careful because his superiors may have rules about this. To turn up at a Tribute time with a gold ring may be a very good excuse to reduce him to the level of farm-worker for taking on an attribute reserved to the superior. If that rule was not in operation then no one at tribute time could distinguish between the givers and the receiver. Or he may build a stockade around his territory; but the superior may have very good reason for limiting such stockades to his own territory so that only his place is defensible. Here I have retro-

jected (sic: opp. of projected, O.K.?) the Roman rule of gold rings only for Equites and above, and the medieval licence to fortify back into the Iron Age; two examples of known constraints on inferiors.

This may of course, be just the time when Roman fashions are on the increase, and to his surprise at the gathering he sees two equals with socially forbidden ornaments. All is revealed when the superior appears in quite outlandish dress, almost as white as if he had been wrapped for burial, with none of his British signs on at all. The equals get away with it, much to their chagrin, for the superior has lost interest in the British signs of superiority and has taken to, sometimes misunderstood, Roman ones.

Our worker is vaguely aware of all this, at one step removed, because he never goes to the tribute gathering, nor do his cousins who still have their 50 acre smallholdings, for they have their tribute collected by an official, but they had noticed that the official was wearing a silver earring last time he came, and they had no idea at all, well only an unmentionable one, what that was supposed to signify.

It looks as if we have two courses open at this point. To follow the farms or to follow the general process of Romanization. I suspect it is one and the same, for it is highly likely that Romanization will affect changes on the farms. We might as well, for the moment follow Romanization. It can certainly be seen in the introduction and development of coinage; it is obvious in the introduction of the potters wheel and the firing of pottery; some people seem to have taken on Roman habits of eating and drinking though the evidence is mainly in their graves, which may be a biased source in more ways than one. During this period of Romanization a number of soldiers pass through southern Britain for the North and West, but since they have already been shown to have a marginal impact on the food supply they will not be worried about further. The main point about them is that as they move through, the occasional parasite may drop off - a metal-worker or even worse, a merchant. Would you want your daughter to marry one of them? Well then.

John Kent has suggested that coinage came to Britain when British soldiers who had fought on the continent, perhaps against the Romans, were paid off and brought their gains home. Since the large scale pay was in gold or silver it was obvious what it was and what should be done with it - what the British had always done with precious metals - hoard it, use it as status symbols, and use it for jewelry. Daphne Nash suggested that smaller coins were minted in Gaul for daily pay for soldiers rather than recompense for a campaign in precious metals. These coins, when they cross the channel either in the flesh, or as ideas,will not fit with British usage, and so if they are to be of use the idea of interchangeable goods and stamped coins in bronze or copper has to come in. But there is a great deal of difference between the idea in the minds of the few and the practice by the majority. It could be that the whole idea of small change and the market economy was a new one in the 4th.C. BC in the Mediterranean. The spread northwards would be gradual, and it seems most unlikely that anything like a full market economy had developed in the parts of Gaul with which

Britain had contact by the first century AD. My brief view of the material evidence which may be expanded in a coin chapter, is that Romanized coins are more common than British coins, but that there is only a real leap forward in the middle of the third century AD. The problem is to decide whether this sudden explosion of coin loss on sites in Britain means the sudden establishment of a free market economy or whether it is simply a result of severe changes in the actual money being produced by the mint. I am happy at the moment with the view that British and earlier Roman coins were used in Britain at a roughly similar level; that the fashion spread very slowly during the first two centuries AD, and that this level of usage by no means needs the existence of a free market economy to explain it. In the sense in which we have used the terms here there never was British coinage or British money because the idea was foreign, and hence everything connected with it was foreign. Names appear, and they are British names, but they are written in latin script and even use latin words such as Rex for king and filius for son. We are not therefore dealing with the Romanization of a British habit or idea, but the introduction of a foreign idea with its own impedimenta.

In pottery there was more continuity. There was British pottery; there had been proper British pottery for well over a thousand years: and British pottery took on Romanizing forms and fabrics in the last century BC and first and second centuries AD. The South and East of Britain seem to have been infected first, and this produces an area of change around the Thames estuary . The changes involved the shape of the pots with the introduction of little pedestal bases, and rims which actually curled back on themselves, and the fabric of the pots themselves was often better prepared and fired to a higher temperature, so becoming harder. But the changes were extremely variable, even within the main area next to the continent where influence was greatest, for the production centres sometimes took only some of the new ideas and kept some of the old, and some of their production was totally on the old model. The ideas gradually spread out from the South East so that they were well distributed in Britain by the end of the first century AD. As this influence increased so the technology can be seen to change, and the change in home produced pottery went hand in hand with changes in the sort of pottery imported.

Italian wares came into Britain well before any official census had been taken. The most obvious pottery is that from Arezzo in Italy, and offshoot production centres in North Italy and Gaul. Not many of these pots of the time of Augustus (27 BC to AD14) come into the country, but there are enough scattered around quite widely to show that this is a matter of real import, rather than accidental loss by travelling merchants. Many of the vessels fit into drinking sets, wine-mixing bowls and cups, and their metal counterparts also come into the country at the same time, so it may be the fashion of drinking wine which is the real import, and the necessary kits followed without much thought. I assume that Chinese tea drinking vessels reached Britain in a similar way in the 17th C. on the basis that drinking tea is an odd thing to do, but if you are going to do it you

ought to do it properly. This involves teapots and tea-dishes. This phase usually gives way to a familiarity with the whole system in the top part of society and, once naturalized, the way is open for British modifications and improvements. Thus tea-dishes turn into cups, and milk and sugar are added, and 'chinese' designs are the mode in British potteries. The same sort of thing seems to have happened with the imported Italian and Gaulish wares, first with Gaulish copies of the real thing, and then with British copies or substitutes for the whole lot.

At the lower end of the scale the Iron Age cooking pot did not change much or change fast. Several generations had to die off before the general run of cooking pots had rims which turned over on themselves, a proper recurved rim, instead of standing up nearly straight but slightly turned out; and around Poole Harbour the British Black Burnished cooking pot industry carried on a hand made tradition of hard wearing cooking pots to the end of the fourth century. They seem to have had a formula, in design and in the ingredients of the fabric which worked, and they stuck to it. They had their fashions but they seem remarkably independent of national trends. New industries which grew up quite naturally followed the Romanizing way and so they produced pots in which old and new traits developed side by side.

Dwellings always seem to have been, according to historical texts, ways of expressing fashion, purpose, and superiority, so it is not surprising to see a Romanizing tendency in many new buildings put up from the first century AD onwards. There is still argument over the preferred shape of house in the Iron Age; the possibilities are basically round or rectangular. Dating is sometimes difficult, and regional differences are obvious, so there is probably not a clear cut line from all-over round houses to all-over rectangular houses. But at sites such as Skeleton Green in Herts. there is the combination of rectangular houses with very strongly Romanizing tendencies in the earlier first century AD, and its seems reasonable to see the house plans as part of the general move towards Italian or foreign models.

The Roman palace at Fishbourne is so isolated in its splendour, so out of any sequence of normality, that it is very difficult to use it in any argument. It is something totally foreign, built by about AD75 to 85 , in the part of Britain nearest to foreign influences, but since we have no idea at all who built it, or with what motives, there is little more to say. Its relevance is completely different depending on whether it is an Italian oasis built for an Italian administrator in the barbarian horrors of Britain, or a Romanizing piece of propaganda built by a Romanizing wealthy Britain with good experience of at least South Gaul, if not Italy.

Oh, but surely I have read somewhere that it was built by Cogidubnus and was his palace.

Yes. So?

Well why ignore that?

For the simplest possible reason that it is total fantasy, and, worse, the fantasy does not fit in very well with what we know of dates and ages and times. And to cap it all, not only is there no evidence whatsoever that that Fishbourne had anything to do with a named Briton, but in the

nature of things there never could be such a connection made by archaeological means. A historical text to say 'and in his old age the wiley Cogidubnus built a garish palace on the shore of a natural harbour to the East of the isle called Ictis' would deserve attention for the simple reason that having discovered one remarkable garish palace in just the right place it is stretching credulity or scepticism rather far to posit another. An inscription found in the excavations, part of a partly robbed layer of building rubble, saying 'Hic habitat Cogidubnus, Rex Mag Brit' (and if the Latin is odd, and I see no reason why Cogidubnus's should be better than mine) would invite credulity. In the absence of writing, a named person cannot in any way be connected to archaeological material. But Fishbourne is important because it is there, and so far as our understanding goes at present, it remained there until towards the end of the third century. And once there is such a Romanizing blot on the landscape people will inevitably get the idea of copying it; it will act as a much better exemplar than travellers tales, builders manuals, or drawings brought back from visits to relations. Or will it? Apparently not. The effect of Fishbourne on surrounding, Romanized buildings seems to be absolutely zero. Perhaps we should take it as a unique landmark in the tendency to Romanize and give the followers enough sense to do their own thing in their own way and for their own reasons.

Yet there are several foreign characteristics which appear early at Fishbourne which Britons adopted in their move towards the continental ways. Mosaics at Fishbourne are at first totally foreign, but then, with other stone-built houses, British-made mosaics begin to filter in. Baths, heating systems, roof-coverings, methods of stone and wood construction, all of which were to become common in Britain, have an early start there. Yet the fact that this is a one off white-elephant-to-be robs it of much of its potential in any study of continuing Romanization. Many of the objects discovered there have never actually been used for any analysis, they are just there. The pottery for instance could be considered as an assemblage with either Romanizing or indigenous tendencies and compared with military assemblages, London assemblages and Round Hut assemblages, and by this sort of study we could begin to put Fishbourne into a useful context. But all this remains to be done.

If we take building patterns as a guide, then there is more Romanizing in the towns at an early date, in wood rather than in stone; by the later second century, three generations after the armies had passed through the lowland zone, these stone buildings were becoming more common in the towns, and by the fourth century there were quite a lot of these foreign buildings in the country. Yet in North (Winterton) Midlands (Stanwick) and South (Barnsley Park), and third and fourth century alike the round cottage continues alongside the rectangular house of mortared stone. This should warn us that the Romanizing process is one in which the start is fairly clearly seen to run in one direction, from British to foreign, but that the whole thing proceeds rather like a chemical reaction in that an equilibrium is reached which is dynamic rather than static. In other words ideas and forms pass back-

wards and forwards between the indigenous and the foreign, the balance swings one way or the other according to trade or prosperity or politics, and in the end the equilibrium returns to a point similar to that from which it started.

The word Romanization, or foreign influence, has so far been used with no definition or explanation. Before we can have any hope of investigating the process we must define it, or, rather we must define Roman and Romanizing before we can hope to get to grips with the Romanization. There is little difficulty in defining Roman or British in the second century BC. 'That suite of material culture seen either in the City of Rome, or in Britain in its most characteristic form'. Of course there will be difficulties: much in Rome will be 'foreign', but that might be part of the definition. The cultural assemblage in 200 BC in Scotland will be very different from that in SE England. It does not really matter, it depends on what your further purposes are; the vital thing is to form a definition for the moment, a working definition, and see how it works. By AD 100, or several layers higher in the stratigraphy, tied together either by absolute means such as radio-carbon dates or material in common, there is no longer such a gap between the assemblage in Rome and the assemblage in Britain. Some objects seem to have moved towards Britain, and perhaps a very few towards Rome. But the comparison is not found to be remarkably helpful because there is in fact so little in common.

By the middle of the Romanizing period in Britain many things have appeared in the archaeological record but they can-

Back

not be traced back to Rome. The pottery is better compared with Gaul, the animal refuse has changed towards that of Germany or North Gaul, decoration of metal work such as enamel is common in the northern provinces, but not in the Mediterranean region, and anyway precedes the Romanizing influence in Britain, and sculpture and architecture seems to rely on the Rhineland more than anywhere else . Perhaps coins give some hope, yet that is simply because for much of the time there is nowhere but Rome, in the western world, that they can come from. When a branch of the Rome mint is functioning at Lyon, then typically the coins in Britain come from Lyon rather than Rome. So what price 'Romanizing'? Our problem has come from the fact that we have defined it on material from the City of Rome. If we redefine it as 'material better known inside the Roman Empire than outside' our problems will vanish. We can redeem our word so long as we understand it to mean 'Romanizing — a tendency to homogenize the material culture of the island of Britain, or parts of it, with the material culture of the nearby provinces of the Roman Empire'. This then has the interesting effect of making British material which enters Gaul a part of that same Romanizing process. Britain became more Gaulish, more Rhinelandish, more Spanish, a little more Italian, a very little more African, and a little more Danubian. In return Gaul became a little more British and so on.

This same area crops up with people because we talk glibly in one breath of Romans, and are then surprised to be told that there were probably never more than a handful of people born in the city of Rome in Britain at any time. What then do we mean by Roman? It is an all important question because it is the most commonly asked of all.

'Were the people who lived in places like Chedworth Britons or Romans then?'

A short answer is bound to be wrong; a proper answer will be long enough for the questioner to lose interest, yet it is vital to any further discussion because so much depends, for so many people, on the labels British and Roman. The number of people in Britain born in the City of Rome were always very few in number. It might be true to say that it is more likely you would find them in the dank places of Roman London, the runaway slaves or failed prostitutes, than in any farm or villa or palace. Italians would be in short supply, mainly perhaps it would all depend so much on chance. A merchant might be Italian born, or Macedonian, or Egyptian, or Tangerine, or from Boulogne; an administrator might be from absolutely anywhere, but he probably had little influence if he got posted to Britain because it can never have been regarded as an easy life for one brought up in the Mediterranean. Though at the upper ends of the administration top posting to Britain was sometimes a stage in major advancement. So people who came because there was nowhere else to go, or merchants who came because they were able to sell things, or administrators who were sent here, or army who were drafted might come from anywhere else in the empire, and the influences they exerted were correspondingly diverse.

What then of the Roman citizen? The problem here is that a Briton might perfectly well be a Roman citizen as well as a Briton. He might be the grandson of a Gaulish centurion who married a wealthy, but not very distinguished, heiress of a British family, and the army and foreign connections stopped with the centurion. Or he might be the grandson of one of the first magistrates of the local administration who became a citizen on retirement, so that his family was totally British. All upper administrators were presumably citizens of Rome, but perhaps few merchants, though we have to remember the tent-maker from Tarsus who was one of the more awkward and officious citizens of the first century. In the first and second century AD citizens of Rome are a band rather small in number, who are archaeologically undetectable and are therefore probably better ignored. (*n.b.* Inscriptions, if read, are historical not archaeological.) After 212 Caracalla made all free-born men citizens of Rome, so after that date little is heard of the subject. It means that all men in Britain who were not slaves were Roman (Roman citizens) after 212 and any distinction there had been earlier vanished.

So the only useful meaning for Romanization or Roman is as applied to things that were common in the Roman Empire and, as a consequence, British is best applied to things of the first four centuries AD which were more commonly found in Britain than the rest of the Empire. This is not a comfortable definition, especially for the subject of Romanization, because it means that the influences at work on Britain are changing almost as fast as the ma-

terial culture of Britain itself. This is very much a dynamic state, not just in Britain, but throughout the empire. Each part was influencing each other part to some extent so that so that we cannot take Italian pottery as an index of Romanization in Britain, because as Britain began to be interested in the pottery those first factories went into decline, and branches and successors started up, sometimes in Gaul, so the index has to change as the producers themselves changed. And then North Africa began to export pottery of similar type to Italy, so by the end of the first century AD the index of 'Romanization', the import of a particular pottery into Britain, is the same as the index of 'Provincialization' in Rome, for the same pottery that reaches Britain in small amounts was being injected back into the source of all influence, Rome. This same state of flux can be seen very well in religion, where the religion of Rome in the first century AD has almost been eliminated and replaced by the fourth century AD, so that the foreign influence throughout the Roman period in Britain, so far as religion is concerned, is constantly changing.

The process of Romanization is a complete study in itself as the excellent collection of essays edited by Brandt and Slofstra shows. For the moment I shall take the simplest possible model of fashion and assume again the simplest case of fashion spread by trend-setters. Thus the obviously Romanizing objects such as wine amphorae, drinking cups, bronze vessels, or even silver cups which are found together in graves in Hertfordshire in particular suggest that wealthy people had gone in for Roman trends, while the ordinary people around them show little evidence of such materials either in life or death. Coins with Latin legends were being produced, presumably, by upper people and presumably therefore filtered down the social scale; pottery in the South East was influenced in general so that all users were affected. By the time that Imperial administrators and commanders were settled in the provinces our written sources agree with the material remains in seeing strong affiliations to the life and material culture of the wider unit. Martin Millett has vigorously pushed the idea that the British elite adopted the Roman fashion in order to keep ahead of their dependents and compete with their peers and the idea seems a very useful one. Anyone who wanted a career outside Britain, or even in the lower echelons of the civil service within Britain had to learn Latin, and with a new language come all sorts of new possibilities - such as Garum. Once the taste is learnt, then the awful reality of fish entrails hung up to rot in the hot sun, dosed from time to time with salt, appears and the name will follow. Or more gently the apricot tree, which seems to have existed neither as a word or plant earlier on.

The speed of Romanization is, and will remain, something that we cannot know in detail. The most optimistic archaeologist who not only knows the material, but knows how it occurs in the ground, would, I hope, never suggest any possibility of dating closer than a few decades for a sequence of deposits. The material commonly found does not change quickly, and, more important, the composition of assemblages, the things dug up from different layers, do not vary either quickly or in a simple uniform

manner. There is absolutely no point therefore in getting obsessed by years when all we can ever know is several decades. If we had a sequence of layers and pits and gullies early in the sequence of Roman Britain we should see changes in the proportion of Romanized material to indigenous material, and the rate of change would vary. There may be a slow early start, then a time when change was quick, and then a cooling off as a balance between Britain and the Empire begins to settle down. And that is all that we can know about, so it is all that we need to worry about. There are historical frills, but as they can never be tied up with the material record in any secure sense they are better left to historians.

But when we compare sites and assemblages of material early in the Romanized period in Britain we must be careful to compare like with like if we want our comparisons to hold. The diet of a soldier born and bred in Gaul would be different from that of a hill farmer on the Cotswolds or a small-holder in East Anglia. If the pit containing the food bones under discussion has exactly the same pottery in it as the other pit, perhaps one in a fort (site with high density occupation, planned on extremely regular rectangular lines, surrounded by ditches and earthworks), the other in a farmstead, then we might see the difference in diet at roughly one time. This would allow us to judge which levels of society are the more Romanized. But the pottery in the two pits will never be the same, either because they are of slightly different dates, or they are in different areas and therefore have different sources of supply, or they are of different social or ethnic background and hence use different vessels or different wares. So we have to balance up the animal bones with the pottery and accept that both belong again to a dynamic interlocking complex of happenings within Britain, and that in turn belongs to a larger dynamic unit, the empire. And our pits might be dated by coins. I doubt it, but it is a possibility, and there is a greater likelihood of coins in that fort pit than in the almost identical farmstead pit. If we want to work our way into Roman Britain these three subjects, biological remains, pottery and coins will provide some very basic thoughts.

The Natural Background

Before we let man onto the scene as a builder and burier, importer of pottery and user of coins it might be an idea to have a brief look at the background of animals plants and soils which man inhabited and used and lived with. It is a difficult time to do this because we are still learning how to look at the natural background, what to do about it, and what it can tell us. We are at a bit of a disadvantage in that archaeologists, by definition, are interested in and specialize on inanimate material remains while animate and natural remains are the province of a bevy of scientific specialists. Thus the proper person to look at animal bones, even if they are found on an excavation, is someone with a good training in zoology, seeds and pollen will gain much more from the attentions of a friendly botanist than anyone else, and soils need comments from people trained in geology and soil studies. It is quite wrong to try to train archaeologists to do fundamental work on their natural samples, because they just cannot have the basic background information, but it is perfectly reasonable that they should be able to do their own run of the mill identification work, and absolutely essential that they should by this means acquire the knowledge of what the likely questions are that the material can answer.

This raises the whole problem of specialists and specialist reports. Most of the bones, seeds, pollen, soils and sediments which an excavator produces are of no basic interest at all to people who study seeds, bones, pollen or sediments; they are, like the usual run of Roman coins found on a site, overwhelmingly normal and depressingly familiar, judged as Roman coins in isolation. It may be that they can acquire an interest and an importance if the excavator sets them in the context of the excavation, and the expert can answer questions, provided the excavator asks them. But the excavator cannot ask them if he does not know the potential of the material, and an expert cannot either ask or answer them unless he knows something about the site that produced them. So this branch of the study of the past depends on the good working relationship between well informed archaeologists, who recognise their limitations, and friendly specialists who like archaeological questions.

All this raises the question of what the aim of such studies should be. The early work on the natural background had a very high aim, that of recreating the environment of early man. Most of the work and the samples came from the periods before the Iron Age, and, since the countryside was not too heavily populated, and most monuments dug, such as barrows were quite distinct in time and space, this was a realistic, if substantial, aim. As interest has moved later into the time scale, simply through the process of more excavation in towns and the growth of Roman and medieval excavated sequences, the original aim has had to be seen as one appropriate only up to a to certain point in the development of Britain, and from the point of growth of dense nucleated settlements, probably unattainable. We have not yet reached a new aim for the later periods, such as Roman Britain and this is one of the reasons why this section will simply degenerate into a few choice examples of what is possible. It may be that there is a deep philosophical point here in that it is only possible for environmental archaeologists to be autonomous so long as man lived within and with the environment. Once man took the upper hand and ceased to regard the environment as a partner, but simply as a resource to be exploited on purely profit motives, the environment fragmented from a consistent continuum to a set of islands between man dominated exploitation. The difference is not between 'nature' and exploitation because something has always been exploiting something else, but between areas of natural balance including man, and areas in which man controlled the balance. Once man is the deciding factor over large areas it is difficult to see how the environmental specialist can exist in mental or physical or organizational isolation. To prevent him becoming an archaeological technician he needs to keep on with work in his own specialty between between periods of work on archaeological material.

An example with which to start might be the problem of the Black Earth. This is a layer of black soil which overlies some late Roman deposits in some towns which sometimes shows some evidence of structures within it, and sometimes does not, sometimes has late Roman material within it and is sometimes remarkably free of debris, and sometimes seems to have been deposited within fairly limited areas, such as walls standing a few courses high, without levelling the whole surrounding areas. Detailed work here is still going on and few all-embracing explanations have so far been found, but, by a continual process of question from the archaeologists concerned, and answer from people such as

Nat

Rob Scaife and Richard MacPhail on the pollen and plant remains and particles of the deposits certain points are being removed from the picture as highly unlikely, and others, such as the possibility of mudbrick building, are being added.

With this preamble, written with the totally clear motive of setting the subject in one person's perspective, and perhaps encouraging others to make theirs explicit, let us get down to a few more examples, both theoretical and practical. The point about pollen is that if an old landsurface survives in the right conditions you may be able to talk about the land-use which precedes the monument you are excavating. Thus in the best of all possible conditions you might be able to show that your large country house was built on land that had been used for arable farming for some time; or you might find that before the building of the house the land was waste and scrub and grazing. The two possibilities give very different interpretations of how the house builders regarded their new developments. Similarly, and much more likely for purely soil and region reasons, the bank of a fort may seal an earlier soil, and that soil may show strong use for arable by a high and constant cereal pollen count. This might say a lot about the relations between the army and the locals for it is insensitive, to say the least, to take up good farming land with a fort. This hardly looks like a helpful neighbourhood police post, more like a firm garrison. In the same way a fort on scrub, or cut out of woodland has different implications. Or the land within the immediate vicinity of a fort may show strong evidence of arable cultivation which starts a train of thought on food requirements and food production, and leads on into the fort itself and surrounding cottages to see whether there is seed and charred evidence of crop processing, and what stage occurs where. If the only evidence of wheat in the fort is charred grain, and all the charred chaff is in surrounding villages, it looks as if the natives are growing and preparing wheat for the army. Perhaps the total absence of wheat in the fort, and the presence of things like barley (for the animals) and cherry pips, just to show that the evidence is there, might even mean that the wheat is ground outside and only flour is delivered. We are back, you see, with the isolated unit; the ideas might be applied in a larger nucleated settlement, but the difficulty of assigning a pit to this house or that, the first phase or the second, makes the whole application much more difficult and the results less certain.

Animal bones already have two excellent examples, but these examples are proving a possible danger. The first time that animal bones really hit the Roman consciousness was when Roy Davies collected together bone reports from military sites and said firmly 'whatever the literary texts may say, the Roman army, at least in Britain, ate quite a lot of meat'. That was simply a matter of presence and absence, and rough identification. Then Mark Maltby was given the opportunity to report on the animal bones excavated over many seasons, from Exeter. Only he knows, and I have never asked him, whether there was a detailed set of questions to be answered, or whether there was money for that project and he was simply pointed in that general direction and told to get on with it. The former would be what archaeologists say they do, and even teach others

to do. The latter, thank heavens, is what actually happens, but this case may be an exception. How, in general and in parentheses, can you possibly know what questions can be answered until you have studied the material, or at least identified it. And if the questions are already there at the beginning of the research how can any one call it original. Question marks are not needed as these are statements. End of aside. The Exeter bones were studied and they showed many points, one of which was of particular interest to me. The earlier bone seemed to represent rather well organized killing and butchering of animals perhaps bred elsewhere; the later Roman deposits had rather more of the odds and ends to be expected from complete animal, rather than mainly joints, and this might be taken to represent a less organized meat supply with animals coming in from the country on the hoof and being used up on the spot, or even locally grown. A third example comes from the survey by Tony King in which he listed the food bones of various types of sites, military and civilian, in different parts of the western empire such as Italy, Gaul and Britain, and showed the balance of the main meat animals, cow, pig and sheep at each site. The Italian bias towards pig defines what is typically Roman; Gauls seem mainly interested in beef; and the unromanized Britons depend mainly on sheep. Since diet seems to be one of the deepest ingrained characteristics of any society this may well be an excellent way into the study of the spread of fashion and influence, Romanization, and the effect of the military on the civilian.

These examples divide into two categories, two surveys of published identifi-

cations and a piece of fundamental research on one group of bones. The surveys
show that since bones are found on sites,
and some people can make use of them,
they ought to be saved and if possible
identified and published. The saving in
stratified units is the vital point because so
long as the future Davieses and Kings can
at least go round to museums making up
their own lists for comparative purposes.
Publication helps, but only of groups which
make sense and are units, but if the budget
is squeezed to the limit it is not absolutely
essential. All that is needed is a note in the
publication to say that 'animal bones and
pottery and coins other than those needed
to date certain features have not been identified, but are stored by units in the Blank
museum where they may be examined'.

The Exeter bones present more of a
problem. That oft quoted example shows
that the right person can get remarkable
information out of bio-archaeological evidence, so long as it is there. It has to be a
partnership, and even that worker cannot
produce interesting results out of a ton of
bones and a year of work if the information
is not in the material to be got. I speak with
the backing of years of coin reporting;
after weeks of identification,,and days of
writing labels and recording and listing
and calculating I often have to come the
the conclusion that 'the coins from this site
form a remarkably normal group drawn
from general circulation, and on that level
there is nothing to say about them'. So
when I say that not all animal bones are
going to be worth studying (that is, with
hindsight) I am applying exactly the same
criteria as I apply to coins. As an example
I would quote Maltby's Winnall Down

report, where a large amount of hard work
and thought has gone in, yet, to me, the
non-Iron Age specialist, and non-animal
bone worker, less came out than at Exeter
apart from the vital point that different
features had different sorts of bones in.

This section then is not a condemna-
tion of the heap of old rubbish, but a plea
for flexibility. The person who can see
best what might come out of further study
is the specialist who would have to do it.
So long as he or she is being honest their
word should be the main guide; the temptation to dishonesty is that 'No I don't
think this will yield much' is really 'No,
this does not fit in with what I am interested in at present'. This runs totally
counter to two financial principles and
constraints. The excavator is now supposed to say, before he digs, or while he
digs, what money he will need for the
study of the finds, and the process of
writing up and publication; and the writer
up is being squeezed as to what will be
properly published (printed) as opposed to
put in the lumber room (microfiche) by a
set of silly guide lines. Thus, the money
for the bone report has to be obtained
before you know if it will be worth doing,
and the results are to be consigned to
microfiche before the study has even started
because it is a specialist report and therefore of less interest than the width of
certain walls. In some cases the specialist
report is the best thing in the whole publication, in others, microfiche, that is supporting text which may be referred to by
those interested, is the right place for it.

Some people might take cemeteries to
be connected with bio-archhaeology. Perhaps, but not here.

Nat

Dealing with materials

As we come towards pots and coins we move towards the centre of the mysteries, the backbone of Roman Britain and the substance of archaeology. Hence a pause in the porch before entering the shrine to put ourselves in the right frame of mind. Material does not talk and cannot talk. Archaeology is basically making the material talk. But, since it is dumb it can only answer yes, or no, or how much, questions. The skill of the person who deals with the material, and this is a skill which everyone who aspires to the title archaeologist, or who professes an interest, must understand, is to deal with material in such a way that it is ready to answer questions, and then try to work out what questions to ask it. This section ought really to come before the brief mention of bio-archaeological material, but I do not understand that well enough to put it in the form that I want to use for coins and pottery, and I have a sneaking suspicion that this applies to people working with the bones and seeds and pollen themselves, so I have got that out of the way first. Coins and pottery have only moved a little way into the realm of accepted basic methodology, but it is far enough to try to work firmly with them. Bones and seeds and pollen are on the way but more still needs doing before they reach the same stage. The sequence of dealing with material is therefore to force a human order on it, or divide it into heaps, and to ask questions,

These two activities are part of archaeology. They are very different in theory and practice and demand two very different skills. I suspect that the first is the nearest that archaeology gets to a science, while the second cannot be handled inside the simplest scientific method if it is to produce results which people find interesting. For instance the simplest thing we can do with a heap of pottery is to divide it up by colour, basically black, grey, red and brown. Misfits can be forced by convention into one or the other category, i.e. purple can go by arbitrary choice with grey, and dividing lines can have the absolute clarity, and speciousness, of an instrumental measurement of colour. Given our basic definitions and actions in a form suitable for use by instruments (that is, define colour by wavelength) then any group of people could produce the same separation into heaps, and the number of sherds which could end up in one heap or another could be noted and expressed as a firm quantity. It will not be very meaningful, but it can be exact to a known standard of accuracy. Please note that I do know that some sherds of Black Burnished cooking pot, category 2, which would go in the grey pile in general will end up in the red pile because of peculiarities in firing, and I do know that the grey pot which got broken and fell in the fire may end up half in the black pile, because it got buried in the charcoal and further reduced, and part in the red pile because it fell in the upper part of the fire and got oxidized. I do know many of the artificialities of what we have done, but I am using it as an example so you will have to put up with it. And if, for the moment, you cannot suspend your objections to see what point I am trying to make you may as well stop reading this book.

We have four colour heaps and we have known uncertainties - that 20 sherds fell exactly on the dividing line of the instrument reading colour between black and grey. We can quantify our heaps, by counting sherds, by weighing the heaps, by counting the percentage of total rims and bases which survive, and so on. And as long as we define exactly what we have done our work will be repeatable within known limits of error. It will not matter if we do it on a sunny day or a dull day, whether we grew up in Scotland or Algeria or Zaire, given the instructions and the instruments we will all come up with the same answers within a knowable limit of error.

At this point the wrong thing to do would be to set aside a week in which to sit in perfect quiet with the four heaps in order to hear what they have to say. Even if they were the right heaps for further work, and they are not, they would still say nothing. You might have some ideas, but you might have far more ideas if you spent that week going round the country talking to other people with the same job to do, or reading what has been published on pottery in the last year. But in the end it will come back to to your mind as to what questions you put to the material; you have to generate the ideas and the interpretations which might follow. The heaps might just as well be coins; this methodology is not confined to pottery.

One way of pursuing research without thinking is to leave your four original heaps and to go on to other units and museums and to do exactly the same thing on many different assemblages of pottery. This builds up a lot of numerical informa-

tion, which is absolutely correct, within a known margin of error, and will yield results without any brain exercise at all. Sites in the North of Britain have bigger heaps of Black pottery than sites in the South. North and South are defined by a dividing line; black is defined as before. Provided you have gathered a decent sample that result must be right. In other words, another researcher, following the same methodology and criteria, using the same sort of instruments, would come up, on another sample of sites, with similar results. The results of all this research are statements of fact: they are not interpretation because all they do is put forward the information you have gathered. And that is part one; it is the basis of archaeology, and without it no theory is worth much.

You give these results at a meeting, the object of which is to consider new work. As this is the purpose of the meeting no one has the bad manners to do any such thing; polite remarks are made after the lecture which show that one half of the audience did not understand what you were up to, and the other half who did understand don't believe your results. If you are lucky someone takes you off in a group no larger than three to eat and talk and points out that there is room for argument, since the northern sites are all on acid rock, granite and schist, while the southern sites are all on chalk or limestone, alkali, and an acidic soil is thought to turn grey pottery black over two thousand years. (It is not so thought, but it would put you in a spot). You drew a nice graph of the percentage of black pottery in the assemblage against what you thought was latitude or longitude, or whatever

North is, when in fact you were drawing a graph of the percentage of black pottery against the pH, the acidity or alkalinity of the soil. If you have both sense and time you note the objection, go off and do a further pilot study in which you plot percentage of black pottery against the pH of the soil from which it came, the absolute distance North, and one or two other things thrown in for good measure, then make a further date for meeting, since a further lecture would be as unprofitable as the first, and nail your opponent down with the information that the correlation between black pottery and pH is 0.3, not very good, with miles from Kirkwall (Orkney) is 0.89, and with rainfall is 0.23. Whence you prefer your original statement, and your opponent accepts defeat.

Now all this is good clean scientific fun. But there were a few old dears at your lecture, in the didn't understand category, who wanted to know what it all meant. They went round afterwards knobbling your research grant applications on the basis that you did not DO anything with your heap of numbers once you had got them. In fact you did - you produced that lovely straight line graph between miles North and percentage black pottery - and that keeps me fully happy and strongly recommending that you **do** do further work. But they wanted to know what it all means; archaeology, they say, quite wrongly, is about people, and you never mentioned people once. The more agile of them, one under 40, pointed out that you did not even **say** anything of your own, since that graph was simply a pictorial statement of fact. Anyone with an eye for figures could have seen that picture in his mind from the table

of results and didn't need the graph. She's right, you know. Worth having a quiet chat to her to explain what you are up to and why because although she seems to disagree with what you are doing, at least she understands it. You might even team up; you produce the statements of facts, and she riffles through her very wide experience and suggests an interpretation. You might even get round her and half convert her with a bit of flattery such as *'Well of course I secretly realize the shortcomings of my work but my lack of experience means that I should make such a hash of any interpretation that I cannot face it; I must stick, for the moment to something I think I can do reasonably well '.* She won't of course believe it: she should on return home post you a packet of Slug Death with an earnest little note to say she has 'just found this in the cupboard: just what you need'. But on reflection she will realize that no one could be quite that revolting without meaning to be, and it might be the beginning of a productive friendship. She uses the Slug Death for its proper purpose and invites you to discuss Interpretation privately next week over a meal at Cosa Nostra.

Now you have a problem. You have just been through a degree in archaeology which told you a lot about fifty different ways to dig a barrow, and how to identify Roman coins and what other people have done about string-impressed butter dishes from Turkestan. Fortunately, one or two people who taught you actually dealt with material and you caught enough off one of them to do your research, and that has turned out quite well on the scientific side of archaeology. But now you need to be able, in ten days time, to talk about interpretation. What is it, and how do you do it? It seems to be inventing ideas about what the material might mean. Hodder once gave a seminar about it, and that sounded quite interesting, and there is that nutty paper of Reece's in World Archaeology about the decline of towns in Roman Britain. Are these uncontrolled exercises in fantasy really what people mean by interpretation? Well this is a start; read some examples of the art, and then get her to soak them gently in acid for an evening.

This is not a true story, so far as I know, but it very well could be, and I think it summarizes the present state of uncertainty better than pages of analysis could do. Many people are agreed that material is the basis of archaeology. Rather fewer are agreed on the methods of dealing with material, but the scientific methods often gain grudging approval, even the occasional compliment. And even fewer accept that it is right to divorce the dealing with the material from its explanation and interpretation. There are two underlying ideas here, one wrong but arguable, the other totally nonsensical. The nonsensical idea is to fail to see that material says nothing; to attach meanings to material without any quantifiable or testable justification, and to muddle up the whole process of arrangement of material and its interpretation. This is the majority opinion as at present and no part of it, that is archaeology as at present constituted, has any right to claim any higher status than medieval cookery. It happens, it produces a few good times, and not too many people die as a result. Examples abound; I invent: the distribution of Samian inkwells, which

marks the advance guard of the Roman army of conquest, shows that by AD 75 the Scottish frontier was well established. At least I hope I invent, but I shall not be surprised to hear that someone is upset because it is absolutely typical of the run of Roman reasoning, no Roman rambling. Who proved that Samian inkwells mark the advance guard of anything, when, and by what method; where is this study published; what is the distribution map please; what is the basis for the date AD 75; what is the actual evidence that there ever was a frontier that early for Scotland? And so on, and so on. It is just conceivable that two or three large studies - PhD's perhaps - could establish some of theses points which are more or less taken for granted, and after several years' hard work it might be possible to restate the original in a modified and tidied up form, but as it is not worth it, I shall not pursue things further.

The second idea is a worthy opponent with which I will agree to disagree. It considers, well within the bounds of reason, that all observation is interpretation, and goes on objecting from there.

Why did I choose pottery, may that not be my 20th.C. concept which the Romano-Britain would not have recognized; might he not have thought in terms of containers?

Well, yes indeed.

And why did I divide them into colours, did I not realize that colours are relative, culturally determined, and, anyway, totally, or perhaps totally irrelevant to the function of a container?

There will be a pained look on the objector's face here because he might in other circumstances, when I have divided by vessel form, want to palm off on the Britons the feeling that form is an irrelevance, colour determines their perception of the pot. Yes, yes. I accepted all that, and I answered part of it when I pointed out that colour was being determined by an instrument where necessary. And my reasonable objector is falling into the same trap as my unreasonable objector, in that he is mixing up what the original users thought of as an object, with what I as a 20th.C. person am doing with it in the 20th.C. He is distressed by the idea that any person can be so insensitive as to take ancient material and do things which have no connection to its original manufacture and use. He first denies that it is possible, but I am fairly convinced that it is possible and that I can finally demonstrate it to him. When I do demonstrate that it is possible, he points out that it is valueless since it has no connection with its origins, and all I can say about it is the statement of fact of the obvious in the present. If we can get to this point we are agreed. I have done it, he sees no point in it; and we both still have to tackle the problem of interpretation.

Our building blocks are: 1) that the material itself is incapable of providing thoughts, concepts and ideas about time past, the observer has to provide the ideas after looking at the material, or perhaps, before. 2) The material has to be collected and organized; this involves imposing on it modern concepts which may have no relevance at all to its original manufacture and use; hence these are best fully defined in totally inhuman terms, wave-length, density, chemical composition, electrical conductivity. 3) It is nice (very purposeful

use of a word) to weave a story round the material but no more; it helps produce more money to keep up the activity; it is a surprisingly popular leisure amusement on radio and TV and even at week-ends; it gives those who do not really understand what they are doing a cosy sense of achievement; I do it myself. It also tends to send the more intelligent out of the subject when they realize that it cannot be done objectively.

If it is a matter of providing concepts and ideas about time past, and since these cannot be directly derived from the material either by osmosis or vibrations, why bother to look at the material. Why indeed; many people do not and are still read and quoted and thought of as archaeologists by the public. It comes down to credibility. There is a puritanical streak in the modern Briton which, after enjoying an evening with Snow White and the Seven Samian Potters, niggles away until , next morning on the platform waiting for the train and seeing that archaeologist fellow, asks

'But is it true?'

If you mean does it square with the evidence which survives, then NO. But if you mean do Snows White really behave like that in the company of Samian Potters, then I'm afraid I don't know; ask the psychiatrist down the platform.

Since people who have a familiarity with ancient material are rarely good at creating box office hits in fantasy they should probably stick to ideas about the past which correspond as far as they can make then with the material remains. There is no judgement here of the value of the two activities, simply an injunction to spend your time, whether creating high pornography or a study of ancient economy, doing something well. And a study of something in the past which is not a fantastical romp is basically serious, though it not only may, but should have its lighter moments, and that can only be judged good if it is consistent with the material. This enables some sort of judgement to be made; it works towards a better understanding of the past by eliminating the knowably wrong views; and it cuts down on the potential number of pictures publishable. Of the infinity of views of Roman Britain, only a small number are consistent with the material evidence, and, as that material increases and our organization of it improves, the number of alternative views may sink to a manageable number.

This leads us to the point where we can see that the purpose of study of material surviving from Roman Britain is to limit the potentially infinite number of descriptions and interpretations to a number that can be absorbed and controlled, and eventually further reduced. This is the subject of archaeology and, despite centuries of museums, and decades of digging, it has only just begun. And this is what makes archaeology worth taking an interest in, because it is only just beginning; we have so much material but we know so little as a result, and we have not yet even decided how to move forward. This is still a subject where the individual can make a major contribution if he has a space to sit, a library to use, a pencil, paper, graph paper, and a set of log tables or a calculator. Oh, and a brain. Unfortunately it is not a modish subject because it does not need high powered equipment, it does not need

new buildings, it has a scientific component, but at root it is not a science and probably never can be. It needs intelligent teachers and writers and open minded readers whether they are full-time university students, people hoping for an 'O' level in archaeology at the age of fifteen or fifty, or people reading intelligently for pleasure. Which is unfortunately not a money-spinning way of looking at things.

There is one more general point in dealing with material which I probably ought to introduce here for I think it sets out some very general problems, and a way of getting round them. It will involve some numbers, but collection of material brings those in without any possibility of escape. It also brings up a fundamental point in interpretation - whether there is anything to interpret. It affects all classes of archaeological material that people try to interpret, which it must be admitted is very few in the Roman period, but is seldom, if ever, clearly enunciated. We could for a moment back-track to pottery, since the idea which will arise is perfectly usable on coins and may occur elsewhere. What do you expect pottery distribution from a kiln to be? Pottery will be at its most common immediately around the kiln that produced it, on the assumption that the only method of distribution is people coming to the kiln to buy it, and the amount found will gradually fall off away from a kiln in a fairly even, if ragged manner, roughly circular contour giving way to roughly circular contour until virtually none is found. We have to exclude other means of movement, and we have to insist on a plane surface of land. A Geographer once corrected that to Plain; I see what he means, but I am more used to planes. Flat, anyway, with no great rivers and no marshes to disturb the way home from buying pottery. If you as an archaeologist go back today to this Roman area and plot the pottery found around a known kiln, and find just this ragged circular distribution then that is the end of your study, for you have found just what you expected, there are no anomalies, so there is nothing to interpret. On the other hand the circles may be very ragged and a bit skew, in which case it would be a good idea to try to express how far from the (arbitrary - but reasonable) expected they are, and perhaps even what the chances of this happening fortuitously may be. In other words, is the deviation from the expected more than a ragged example of the perfect model? This encapsulates the whole cannon of law on archaeological material. You gather your material; at the same time you set out at least one model of how it all got there, and therefore what you expect to find if your model is correct; you test your collection of material against your model, taking into account the accuracy at which you have been working; you find the degree of fit of your results to your model and express this either subjectively or numerically;,and at this point you know whether there is anything to explain. If the material fits the model the model can, for the moment stand as a likely explanation of the use of cheese presses at different altitudes; if the two diverge by an appreciable amount there is some room for explanation and interpretation.

If we apply this to coins then we want to collect together a representative number of sites whose coins have been identi-fied. We want to know the percentage of coins on each site for a series of twenty year periods. It is then good to know the mean percentage and the way that the sites group themselves around that mean. I used to use the mean and standard deviation of the values around the mean until, ten years after I had first used it, Clive Orton said 'But you can't do that with percentages'. My usual reaction to being told I cannot do something is to increase activity and support the cause with even greater enthusiasm. This would have been perfectly justified in this case because the method was giving good results which made excellent sense, and the fact that it was mathematically unsound was irrelevant if it worked. There were three reasons for changing course. First the mathematical objection did make sense; second, and tactically, few people use their own brains on anything numerical but rely on a few people that can, so those few saying the method was wrong would lead to widespread belief that the results were wrong, when they weren't, only the method; and finally and decisively Clive is such a nice person that I could not bear the thought of him continuing to look reproachfully at me over coffee.

As I understand it the mathematical objection to finding a standard deviation of a set of percentages is that each percentage is a different animal from each other. A percentage of 5% on a sample of 20 coins is one coin, 5% on 2000 coins is 100 coins. But it is quite possible that in each sample we are one coin out, one too few, or one too many so we usually mean at least ±1in each case. In the sample of twenty, minus one coin makes the value nil and the percentage 0%; plus one coin makes the sample 2 and the percentage 10%; so the first 5% really varies between 0% and 10% or 5±5%. In the second case one coin in 2000 is 0.05%, so the second value is really 5±0.05%. If we start manipulating these percentages then we have to take account of these inbuilt plusses and minuses, so the whole thing becomes horribly more complicated than it seemed at first sight.

You don't believe that the results were sound when the method was subject to mathematical objections, do you?

Well the new method has received grudging acceptance, Clive cannot find anything wrong with it, though it is not something that would naturally occur to him to do, yet the results put on a diagram are, to date, indistinguishable from the earlier results; which, of course is why I am happy with the new results. The old results were right, I knew that and have always known that - which I think means that the final result on paper corresponds closely to the hard facts of coin lists identified which, through experience go through my mind in some automatic fashion. But since the new results can be produced by acceptable means, everyone ought to be happy.

The means are fairly simple, and not particularly adapted to coins. This is a general problem in archaeological method, and I think it is an essential step in the discussion, and then perhaps interpretation of any archaeological material. You need a background distribution of what is commonly found, you need to set this out, preferably on paper in pictorial form, and

you need to be able to put your own results on this background to see how they fit. Using coins as the example we can collect together a number of sites and set out the coins found as percentages over the chronological periods (for examples of all this see my Coinage in Roman Britain). These numbers can be directly plotted on a diagram to show the scatter of points. If you don't want to do anything complicated you can then put in your site as a heavy dot among the lighter dots. You could add the mean as a cross. My problem with all this is the way that periods where all the sites cluster together with low values makes a completely different impression on me from periods where the sites are strung out with high values. It somehow seems far more important that my site is high in a period where values are in the 20 and 30%'s then in a period where no site gets much above 1%. It is far more difficult to convince people that their value of 1.5% with a mean of 0.8% is world shattering than to convince them of the importance of the fact that their value of 45% with a mean of 25% is off the top of the graph. So I fix on the mean, and, because the mean in each period is in someways the same thing I put the means on a line. The other obvious line is 0% so that goes in as well. But in most cases the mean is halfway or about halfway between the lowest values and the highest; not exactly, I know that would be the median, but around. So if the base line is 0% and the roughly halfway point is the mean, or 50%, the highest values are going to be around twice the mean, hence the third line. And 100% is usually the whole thing, and in this case the whole thing or highest obvious value, though there will necessarily be oddities, will be twice the mean. So our scatter of sites is stretched out on a diagram where no coins is 0% the mean number of coins equals 50% and twice the mean equals 100%, with room for the high flyers up above. Our individual site can now be plotted as simply a percentage of twice the mean. The mean is 10% when all the sites are put together; well, our site is 10% it goes on the central line. If it is only 5%, that is half the mean (or a quarter or twice the mean) it goes on the 25% point. So we get a diagram where the mean for all our collected sites is the centre line, 0 is 0, the reasonable upper end is 100%, but some points will inevitably go higher. The area between 0% and 100% is, again quite reasonably, the area where any site might, and most do occur. Occurrence in that area leaves little room for discussion or comment since that is just where we expect the site to be.

Two points might claim discussion; a succession of points above 100%, that is consistently twice the mean of a series of sites in Britain, would arouse interest and need some sort of explanation. And a series of values all bunching in one part of the diagram would be worth noting. Thus four or five low values followed by four or five high values, all within the expected limits would suggest that a trend was visible in the material. Although in no single value was the site aberrant the third century is consistently low with regard to other British sites, and the fourth century

is consistently high. So it is not only extreme values that are of interest or that give rise to potential explanations and interpretations, the recognition of a trend is equally important. I think this method of pictorial representation helps to pick out both extreme values, and to give a rough idea of how extreme they are, and certainly makes the picking out of trends much easier . In the end, the method is not important, so long as it works; it is the recognition of the underlying problem which has to be tackled. And I would say, without the recognition of this problem and an attempt to deal with it, most material study up to date has invalidated itself. It may have led to quite good results, as judged subjectively and humanly and even tested against all the evidence of material in qualitative way, but it has usually formed the basis for supporting a pet theory, and, as a result, most of these can be overthrown with only a little work, or at least neatly unsettled.

This would only matter to the great majority of people who talk about Roman Britain if they were archaeologists, but most of them are not, for they do not proceed from the material to making it talk, which is what an archaeologist should do. They jump down on the material in the bottom of their excavation trenches and squash it into submission to that set of odd ideas that filled their heads in the library of classical texts. But it is time to encounter the material at second hand.

Pottery

So, the object of the exercise is to think about what Roman Britain may have been like, and to moderate the ideas against the material. Why pottery? Because it is there. And in rather large amounts.

If excavation is going to happen, and sometimes even public opinion insists on it, then there are going to be certain results. If the site is occupied in the early centuries AD then there may be buildings; it is just possible, once in a thousand times or less, that there will actually be two letters of an inscription; there will probably be coins; there will almost certainly be animal bones, but their presence and their condition will depend rather heavily on the nature of the deposits and the acidity of the subsoil; but there will certainly be a large amount of pottery. Now the reasons for digging may be difficult to uncover. In the 80's the most likely is that the site came up for redevelopment, and, although little was to be expected of it the local unit who were hard pressed for work, made out a rather hopeful case for a large scale dig to keep their workers occupied over the winter till some good sites came up, and convinced someone in the HMBC, or English Heritage, who was in the embarassing position last year of failing to spend all he should and wanted a few sure-fire spenders. Nothing much was found in the dig, though, to quote the local newspaper, the negative evidence was overwhelming in its implications, too abtruse to be gone into in detail. And the regional TV did some very good coverage of deeply meaningful comment from the overall director who visited the site for the first time that morning in order to learn what to say, and included some fascinating shots of the spoil dumps because the site supervisor had planted some marrow seeds and produced a bumper crop. But despite the lack of structures there were lots of pits, and there remained about 930 kilogrammes, or something approaching a ton, of Roman pottery. Post excavation work was essential in order to produce some sort of report, so they went to town on the pottery. What, in the best of all possible worlds, did they do?

Well there were two sorts of pits, early pits dug into the subsoil and therefore safely stratified below the bottom of all later digging and disturbance; then there had been large scale tipping, perhaps quarry waste in the middle of the Roman period, and into this waste late pits were dug. The area was disturbed in later times, but it is a fair bet that all Roman pottery in the disturbed layers originally came from the late pit digging. So they could do a lot of the usual things and compare the earlier with the later.

They examined each sherd by eye and put it into a rough grouping according to colour, but not too hard-line, or inclusions such as chalk particles or mica flakes, or sharp bits of flint which must have torn the potters' fingers to shreds, or round spots of oolitic limestone, or just sand. And they examined their rough categories under a hand lens and sorted sharp sand additives from water smoothed sand additives or temper, and distinguished pots that had been set on straw to dry, from those which had chopped straw or grass added to the clay. And some of these categories fell well within the normally expected range of what was known, from the evidence of collapsed kilns, to have been produced at Savernake, and Colchester and Highgate Woods, and Doncaster. They counted the number of sherds in each category when they were fairly sure that their divisions were real and sensible, they weighed the total of each category, and they measured the percentage formed by each piece of rim and base and totalled them up for each fabric to say that IF you had stuck all the rims of fabric Xt together you would have had 22.5 complete rims. (Estimated Vessel Equivalent or EVE). Because there were earlier pits and later pits, they could show that some fabrics were scarce earlier on but became common later, and vice versa, and, where they knew the source of each group they could draw a map of Britain with lines radiating out from the site, fatter or thinner according to the part that that pottery played in the whole assemblage; some lines went off the map to North France and to the Rhineland: a few even further. They could compare the earlier map which produced more longer lines, with the later map which produced fewer, thicker lines and so suggest that for their site at least the supply of pottery in Roman Britain became more regionalised in the later period. They compared notes with surrounding workers and found that though they seemed to be at the edge of one distribution, they were at or near the centre of another. One site only ten miles away had far more of fabric Xc, and sites beyond that also had high amounts, so it looks as if they were just about the limit of distribution of that ware. This site, which

judged academically and professionally should never really have been excavated, and produced very little that the TV cameras could home in on, except the marrows, was making its mark from the study of the pottery.

At this point they were half way through their money and were joined by the young student we have met before now converted to interpretation by several nourishing sessions at Cosa Nostra. He had the good sense to ask what to do, to keep quiet on what he had done before, and to think for a week or two before saying much more than hello or good-bye.

Coffee sessions in the morning and tea in the afternoon acted as times of general conversation, and various subjects were generally aired. They had sorted out, for the time being, vessels which, by their fabric or form had a particular function. The easiest to deal with was the amphora, the large container vessel, for that could be classified by shape and by fabric. It could then be tracked back to its source and guesses could be given, some based on labels written on similar amphorae, as to what it contained. These guesses can be taken further by direct analysis of the fabric of the pot which will often still contain, absorbed on the fabric, a proportion of material from its original contents. The material may survive by being sealed in by a layer of decomposition products which exclude air, and therefore further decay, or simply by being large stable chemical molecules. These can be flushed out of the pot by grinding it up and extracting with different solvents. Ground amphora shaken up with chloroform will yield much of its fat content to the chloroform which can then be evaporated down until the tiny amount of fat, in a very small amount of liquid, can be subjected to analysis. There is a general link between the round amphorae from the South of Spain and olive oil, between the tall thinner amphorae originally from Italy and wine, and so on. Special shapes for garum, the sauce from rotted fish guts and salt, perhaps even for dried fruit, though that gives little for analysis, and smaller sizes for simple perfumes, or scents based in oils, or medicaments. The numbers of vessels from various places with various contents will give a direct statement on perishable goods entering Britain, and, if the amphora still had its original contents when it reached our site, the supply of wine and oil among other things to our local area. The wine amphorae were probably in Britain first, in the later Iron Age, together with the other parts of wine drinking kits, and the found their way into graves, either as prestige objects, or essential provisions for a top person in death. Oil amphorae seem to need a greater degree of Romanization to travel, though I do not know whether this is a general rule. Not surprisingly, savours such as garum are an acquired taste.

Another type of vessel marked out by its size and its fabric, together with a scatter of grits in its interior, is the wide large bowl known as the mortarium. It has only occurred on one or two Iron Age sites. Skeleton Green for example where a lot of very Romanized material almost looks out of place in Iron Age Britain, so the mortarium is a candidate for use as an index of Romanization. But Romanization of what? Here it is impossible to avoid interpretation. Direct study gives a few clues. The

early, large heavy mortaria can be found worn out, with a hole rubbed, or worn through the bottom. Small statuettes in the museum at Alexandria, and one in the Ashmoleum Museum in Oxford show figures sitting cross legged with what looks like a mortarium on their lap and a pestle in their hands. Analysis by John Evans at the North East London Polytechnic has only been done once, yielding, I understand, animal protein. The vessels look like our modern large mixing bowls, not quite hemispherical, but they have rims and lips as if for pouring. Put together directly this suggests strong Roman indulgence in a rather liquid form of Steak Tartare in which good raw steak is rubbed vigorously on the grits instead of mincing it, and then combined with spices and oils to give a sort of cold steak soup which can be poured into individual dishes for drinking. The pouring would probably be done in the kitchen as the mortarium is usually, in the early period, heavy and large, too heavy to lift safely filled with cold steak soup, and its fabric is to our eyes out of place on the table with glossy red samian or thin black beakers. Does our cookery book help? Not really; the only thing that Apicius really wants ground are spices, and an ounce of spice would hardly coat the grits of a large mortarium, never mind come out again. One idea I have always liked is the interpretation as yoghurt bowls in which the milk fermented, but, when the end product was poured out and the bowl washed, would always retain enough bacteria on its rough grits to start the next brew. This, of course, falls on the worn out bases which must have been produced some other way. But the heavy , thick vessel, once warmed at the hearth would retain its heat for some time....

But if we break out of the temptation simply to combine the evidence we have into one single explanation, however improbable, then we seem to have here heavy duty grinding bowls for use in the kitchen, highly suitable for vegetable and fruit purees, or, more basic, for de-husking cereals. In neither of these explanations are the worn out bottoms really explained, for the vegetables would presumably be cooked before being mushed (sic), and the cereal needs to be pushed round the bowl so that the husks catch on the grit rather than squashing the grain. One further point of observation stretching into interpretation is the absence of such vessels in the Iron Age and the gradual spread both socially and geographically in the Roman period. Whatever they were used for seems to be a new process in the kitchen, but one which gradually catches on in Britain.

But the interpretation of the mortarium can be taken further. The early examples, in heavy white or buff fabrics have been contrasted with the shiny, smooth, thin walled table wares, and so the mortaria have been banished to the kitchen. These large early types which can in extreme cases be over 30 inches in diameter (not far off a metre) have quite clear spouts even if these are often shallow. Sometimes a rim runs round the pot, parting at the spout to help any flow of contents. If we follow the mortarium through Roman Britain chronologically then we see several things happen. First, instead of being strange foreign imports, they are made by branches of foreign companies based in Britain. Here is interpretation run riot. The British pro-

duced mortaria become generally, smaller and lighter, though, at first the white or buff appearance is kept up. Where the natural clay is iron rich and the fired product would come out of the kiln grey or pink, this is counteracted by a white slip, or thin wash of white firing clay. Rims and flanges become more complex but spouts become less obvious, less practical, and are sometimes nothing more than a nod to an old fashion. The flange sticking up from the rim can sometimes be carried right across the supposed spout making it totally useless for pouring. By the fourth century things have changed even more, for pottery works near modern Oxford were producing red coated mortaria, just like the late second and third century red mortaria from the samian pottery works in Gaul. One major difference is that whereas the Samian mortaria have holes through the wall as spouts, decorated with bat or lion heads, the Oxford pots have the walls and the heads, but no hole to pour through.

The basis for the interpretation of branch factories in Britain, mentioned above, is reasonably simple and at present quite compelling. In the early period makers stamped some of their wares and there are stamps which are very common in the North East of Gaul and rare in early Romanizing Britain. The implication is that they were made where most of the stamps are, and few stamps in another area show vessels which have been traded. This is sheer interpretation, but it fits the facts as known at present. There is further supporting evidence such as associations with kilns, and the clay from which the vessels are made. Then there are stamps of the same named people which occur commonly in south-east Britain, but rarely if ever on the Continent. This looks, in modern terms, like a branch of an established firm moving nearer a good market. Then branches of branches are set up, in other words the names spread and their products become associated with other products, and the British mortarium makers have reached independence.

The changes associated with colour, size and shape can be commented on, but not at present clearly explained. If we were right to banish the large, heavy, buff vessels to the kitchen because we saw the table as set with the red glossy pottery, then the change over 100 years later in which the red glossy pottery makers began to make red glossy mortaria ought to mean that the vessels have come out of the kitchen and on to the table. Continental models retain a hole for a spout, though a rough hole perhaps 5 mm in diameter through a pot perhaps 5 mm thick about an inch below the rim (for small measurements I work in mm for larger ones in inches and feet; good conversion tables are available in most libraries) would not be one I should care to try pouring through: certainly not cold steak soup, or yoghurt. The British by the later third and fourth centuries seem to have given up the idea of pouring, but have taken completely to the idea of tableware. Pottery ladles and metal serving spoons are distinctly uncommon. So this seems to leave whatever was put in the mortarium in the kitchen, or prepared in the mortarium at table, in the serving dish. This is no less of a problem than the date at which a country house was built or deserted, but since we have gone a long way down an unfamiliar path of interpre-

tation it is rarely aired. Unless, of course, each place setting had its own mortarium, from which the guest managed in his own way.

This last suggestion, which perhaps seems the furthest from reality, even the most nutty, has returned to the point where it could actually be checked against hard material evidence. Most pots used in houses in Roman Britain eventually broke and were thrown away - hence our 950 kilos of pottery from the unlikely site. If we have a single site like a country farmstead or a country house, and we collect together all the rubbish we can find, there is the theoretical possibility of seeing the table settings of around AD 200 all at once. I know that there are enormous problems but they leave at least the theoretical possibility of doing something. Thus the whole site must be excavated out to the furthest rubbish pit ever dug in antiquity; then the limit of manuring the surrounding fields with refuse has to be examined by intensive field walking, and the majority of pottery in that area has to be picked up year by year after ploughing. All the pottery has to be roughly dated to a century, or closer if that is possible. All the pottery which might have been in use around 200 must be assembled. Each vessel must be given a theoretical status as best-fine-tableware, everyday-tableware, good course ware, rough course ware, and every pot must be given a function such as platter, drinking cup, serving bowl, cooking pot. Then you could see whether the red coated mortaria are in the ratio of one per fine-tablewear drinking cup and platter, or in the ratio of one per four fine table settings. In other words were they individual vessels, or just one on the diner table? This is fine until our bright young student who has got tired of keeping quiet points out dryly that the vibrations from the pots tell him quite clearly that while the platters and cup of the fine set were used regularly every sabbath, the cold steak sludge was served only twice a year on the great festivals of May 1st. and November 1st. So, although they **were** individual vessels, their episodic and infrequent use means that they broke less often, and so turned up in the archaeological record at the wrong frequency. While we are in the realms of theory could you look again at those animal proteins, John, because I can think of several interesting things to do with livers fresh from dawn sacrifices.

As always, the example is partly light-hearted; those who have to deal with pottery as a job and want to keep up standards would say frivolous and irresponsible. Why? Because we just do not **do** that sort of thing with pottery. It has gone so far from any checkable reality that even to discuss it is to encourage non-specialists with bright ideas and little knowledge, to do silly things with pottery which get the whole subject of pottery studies a bad name. I can see the objection, I even voice it, but I don't share it. If a student came to me and said she wanted to try out this mad idea I would agree to it as a temporary subject, we would talk about where to find the material and she would go off to the library to look at published reports. She would be back the next day with depression rapidly settling in because she only found four reports which published all the pottery found, and only one of these even had sherds of samian mortaria, never mind

numbers which could be juggled with. And yet parts of the idea are useful because they push forward a discussion of what material can and cannot be made to do and say, and therefore get us a little further forward in understanding archaeological interpretation.

All through the discussion of mortaria the red glossy pottery referred to as Samian has intruded, so it might as well be allowed to have a section of its own. It must be rated as one of the most obvious signs of Romanizing in Britain, for its red glossy, often decorated surface with a resemblance to sealing wax stands out of any ploughed field or even museum case. It is garish, and few people today would want a table set with the stuff apart from a few experimental archaeologists. The intense colour is against it in terms of modern taste; the decoration is moderate to incompetent; and the actual feel and thickness is often less refined than an ordinary glazed dinner plate. This throws up the interesting point that we expect household vessels used for food to be glazed. Glaze was available to the Romanized Briton but apparently it never caught on. We are again in the midst of interpretation. Several workshops round the country produced glazed wares of reasonable quality which would certainly compare well with basic wares of the 17th and 18thC. in Britain, but these producers never seem to have expanded and prospered, their wares never became common, and the easiest interpretation is that the wares never really caught the fancy of the market. It may be because the producers seem to have used glaze mainly as decoration, on the outside of the pot, whereas the 17th and 18thC. producers did exactly the opposite, putting the glaze on the inside where it would actually be useful in stopping liquids percolating into the fabric. The most extreme example of glaze used oddly is the late type of mortaria produced in the Danube region in which the grits on the inside are covered by a good thick layer of lead glaze.

This takes a modern view of samian as tableware. But why is this red pottery, produced in Gaul and imported into Britain thought of as tableware? To our eyes it might well be more acceptable for wedding presents and storing on reproduction Welsh dressers, that is, as ornament. This interpretation, which is of course perfectly possible, can be partly countered by the volume of samian pottery which turns up in rubbish pits compared with the other types of pottery around, which not even a Roman-Briton would have regarded as ornamental. At least, this is something which can be done in theory, but, due to the hopelessly low standard of pottery reports from excavations in the past, there are few published reports which give either the number of samian sherds found, with the number of coarse sherds found, or even any indication of relative weights or volumes. Where this has been done the proportion of the whole pottery weight which is samian varies substantially both from site to site, and from deposit to deposit within a site. Time also comes into it, for samian gradually becomes more commonly found in deposits through the first century, stays appreciable in the second century, and then gradually declines, but rarely dies out altogether. Whether this tail which goes on into the late fourth and even fifth centuries is due to the real con-

tinuation of a few samian vessels as ornaments, or simply the recycling of rubbish due to disturbance of earlier rubbish pits on the same site is often difficult to decide. So there is too much broken samian pottery in fairly ordinary rubbish deposits (10% or even higher on some sites) to regard it as we regard ornaments. Some vessels show that the red glossy surface has been scratched by sharp points such as knives, others show a smooth wear that gets down to the pink fabric beneath the red coat. The likelihood is that samian pottery was used, but that its use was at the upper end of the use scale.

The vessels come in different shapes and sizes, some decorated, some plain. The shapes are highly specific in that any one of shape 33, a simple drinking cup (interpretation again), is very like another shape 33; but there are sizes of many shapes, and all of shapes, sizes and decorations change over time. The tolerance of size from a given workshop at a given time is remarkably small: weights of vessels are remarkably similar, which suggests that balls of clay handed to the actual potters at the wheel had been mass produced to specific requirements; and the rim diameter of a given shape at a given time varies by few mm. which suggests that production was remarkably uniform, even down perhaps to templates for shapes or even moulds. We are dealing with standardized production at the kiln centres in Gaul, South - Gorges du Tarn, Central - the Vichy area, and East- North of Strasbourg, and then with movement from the kilns to the consumers. Here is a paradise for interpreters of production, distribution, marketing, transport, use, chronology, and so so. In Britain we could, but so far seldom have, use it as an index of Romanization, a marker of trade routes, and a way into coastal shipping, apart from the fascinating ideas that samian might give us a clue to different social areas on sites, different activity areas, and different methods of rubbish disposal. All this is still in the future, and if you go to almost any pottery report published so far all that you will see is drawings of the decorated samian with suggestions of where it was made and when, drawings of the name stamps often found on the inside of undecorated wares, and a mention of the plain forms found which do not need illustration simply because of their uniformity. As Samian specialists can be fairly fierce I should point out in my own defence that I am not getting at them, because that is all anyone has ever asked them to do, and time rarely permits indulgence in unrequested extras. It is the fault of the writer of the report, the excavator often, who has no conception of what samian, pottery in general, or, come to think of it, most classes of finds, can be made to do if pushed. We are back with our bright Ph.D. student who wrote that lovely thesis on what was where, but was very puzzled when asked what it all meant because he had never been trained in interpretation.

One of the first things you might want to find from a pottery report is what the table settings were and how many there were of them at any given time.

Sorry, we don't do that sort of thing in pottery reports.

But surely with samian where the shapes are standardized, and some of the names even known from scratchings on sherds at the pottery kilns, we can have a go at cups, and platters and dishes and bowls. The form 37 with the capacity sometimes of a generous flower-pot is not suitable for drinking out of, where as the more delicate form 27, a curved cup with a kink in the profile, which would fit comfortably in the palm and outstretched fingers has a capacity of -? Well this is something I have never seen quoted or discussed, but from drawings we might assume it is half a sphere with radius about 4 cm. or 6 cm. in which case its capacity full to the brim might be about 70 cc. and about 200 cc. (For volumes I work in cm. and cc; conversion tables can sometimes be found). Even caterers, not known for liberality, expect to get 8 very modest glasses of wine out of a 750 cc bottle, so a caterers wine glass is about 90 cc. The small form 27 would be a very modest winecupfull, the large variety only comfortably full would do better than a caterer. But this is the scale we are talking about, even if it is not wine inside. Beer would be ridiculous to modern lips in such measures; mead would suit the small cup. And even if we are wrong in talking about drinking, these vessels are absolutely useless for your helping of mutton stew or your stewed pears with rosemary and pepper. They would do for condiments.

It was Professor Frere who noted keenly that cups in Roman Britain get bigger. We start from these samian examples and their local copies, and then we move onto locally produced colour coated wares in purple and brown, red and grey and black, but these usually move up to the half pint, half litre, or even pint or litre capacity. Is this the change from foreign wine back to basic British beer? But then, platters change as well. The early samian platter is a fairly flat base with a sharp right angled bend between base and wall that is only just high enough to keep the mashed turnips and gravy in place. By the middle of the second century such eating is a thing of the past and the platter is almost a dish with wall and base in a continuous slope with a bump in the middle of the base. This leaves a low point around that central bump, well protected from spillage by the wall, and it seems just right to me for gathering the leftovers on the hump and spooning up the gravy in the dip without the gristle. And, provided the excavator does his job basically we should know the rough ratio between the cup forms and the platter and dish forms.

If we go back to our heap of 950 kilos of pottery from our undistinguished site we have picked out the obvious plums. The amphorae were easy because they were the largest and thickest sherds; the mortaria were easy because they were gritted on the inside; the samian stood out as the red glossy parts of a grey-buff-brown heap. We are now left with at least 750 kilos of rather dull continuum - the colours shade into one another from black to white via grey, brown, orange, buff and yellow, and the shapes ooze into one another from absolutely flat plate to tall thin almost closed jugs. Fabrics, in a way are the easier to make sense of. First of all there are the fabrics that our advisors recognized, picked out for us, and left as type sherds. The industries round Poole Harbour give us the really black sherds with a broken section like small cods-roe; the Nene valley industries give us the pale

pastes, or some of them, Oxford the red colour coats and other things, and of course some of the red pottery is not Oxford but New Forest, and so on. But our helpers and advisers seem to have left us with an even nastier heap as a result, because what is left has lost all extremes of colour and shape and forms a muddy heap of grey brown. There are two ways of attacking this, apart of course from weighing it and selling it off as hard-core. We can follow a somewhat untutored path of hand lens and colour chart and do our best to divide it into smaller heaps which all have roughly the same fabric with roughly the same type of break and roughly the same inclusions. Or we can apply for more people and more money to do some detailed chemical or physical analysis of the whole heap. The full analysis at present would be so costly in terms of people and money that we can probably rule that out; and it may at present be no bad thing, for we probably do not know how to interpret the results when we get them. We classify our grey wares and our brown wares by fabric, we don't know where most of them come from, but we draw them and weigh them and, with a sigh of relief turn to something we do know and recognize.

But what do we draw? Every sherd? Horribly time consuming, and decidedly unproductive after the sixtieth of almost the same shape. So every shape? But what constitutes a shape? The danger here is that we shall take off for the realms of theory and lose contact with reality, or rather, the material. People who deal a lot with pots recognize certain shapes as more common than others, the beaker, the pie dish, the tankard. There is therefore hope that although if you look hard enough you can find the complete continuum from flat platter to tall closed jug that I mentioned earlier the heap of pottery will cluster round certain parts of the continuum and thin out round others. If we think of the shapes from platter to jug as a straight line then the heap of pots will pick itself up and distribute itself unequally around that line looking like a rather knobbly chairleg or banister in a wooden staircase. The platters will be one cluster on this line and they will all be approximating to the ideal platter somewhere in the middle of the group. If you drew every one and put every drawing one on top of the other there would be a general blur somewhere around this ideal shape. You could represent the platters of your heap by three drawings from this blur, an outside one to take in the most extreme examples, an inside one to take account of the 'tightest' examples, and the ideal example from somewhere in the middle. It may be that in hard pottery none of these would exist, it would simply define the center and the spread of platters. This is the sort of thing most pottery illustrators will have to do. Set the pottery out, divide it, fairly arbitrarily into groups, and the illustrate one of each group, and sometimes borderlines.

Our pottery heap is now sorted into amphorae, mortaria, samian, other recognizable wares and wares of known origin, and wares divided up by inspection, and the sherds from each category have been drawn where necessary, and then quantified by sherd count, perhaps sherd weight, and perhaps by estimated vessel equivalent as mentioned earlier. And the great division is between early pits and late pits.

Some of the comparisons between early and late will strike the workers as highly original, but to the pottery world at large they are well known and therefore not worth detailed publication. Thus the amphorae are far less common in the later deposits, they are of smaller forms when they do occur, of different fabrics, and therefore often found to be from different places - Africa instead of S. Spain, or Palestine instead of S. France - and perhaps to contain different commodities. What does this mean in any interpretation? The first pitfall to avoid is a common one throughout pottery study. Because pottery survives almost totally from the past there is the great temptation to study it in isolation. Amphorae are the pottery containers - Yes, but they are the POTTERY containers, and what about all the containers made of other materials such as wood? Wooden barrels have been discussed several times as possible later alternatives to amphorae. These barrels only survive in waterlogged conditions, typically, re-used as well linings, and hence preserved below the water-level. Surveys are wonderful things but they do show up the obvious. Thus a survey of where barrels are to be found in Europe showed some remarkable clusters, but, as they were in the Netherlands, river valleys, and other waterlogged areas these clusters were of little help, for they indicated survival, not original distribution. A survey of dated examples falls on the same problem for it indicates that most barrels surviving are early because most wells are early, and the barrels survive mainly in wells. It may be that we have yet again different areas of containers. Thus some barrels identified to the species of

wood from which they are made are seen
to be silver pine which only grows over a
certain height on hillsides and mountains;
the candidates are the Alps and the Pyre-
nees. This could make good sense for the
growth of the Bordeaux wine industry or
even that of the Rhine and Moselle, at the
expense of the traditional producers in
Italy, Spain, and the area of Provence. I
assume few shippers would wish to carry
barrels of olive oil, or few producers wish
to send their olive oil long distances in
wooden containers, so, while comments
on the wine imports into Britain have to be
muted because of the possibilities of barrels it does seem that import of olive oil did
not stay for long at the level of the later first
and early second centuries. All this fits in
remarkably well with the pictures of a
federal empire becoming regionally self-
sufficient, with an empire in which long
distant trade was declining, and a Britain
in which an initial spurt of Romanization
had rather flagged. It fits in remarkably
well because those pictures were built up
partly from studies of amphorae in the first
place, so it is no more than a seductive
circular argument.

Amphorae have a long history before
they arrive in Britain; most of them come
into Britain purely as containers, and fewer,
later; but a small number were produced
here in the heyday of the amphora container trade, though we only know them as
yet from the kiln site between London and
St. Albans so we do not know what they
were made to contain. After amphorae
and Roman Britain had coexisted for a
little the relationship seems to have worn
thin, yet it continued fiercely in the Mediterranean world, and a few continued to
wander over to Britain, just the West of
Britain, throughout the fifth and the sixth
centuries. By that time they have had
letters attached to them because they were
first studied at the receiving end as strange
wares from the Great Abroad. This phase
is past and they ought to be known as Pal-
estinian Amphorae or African Amphorae,
or whatever.

Mortaria seem to be rather different,
but, apart from knowing that they are very
common in Britain, if anything the later
the more common, and that they turn up in
museum displays in Northern France and
the Danube area, I cannot make generalizations about the use of mortaria in the
Roman Empire and how Britain compares.
This automatically means that I cannot
point to any general studies on the subject
for, if I knew of them, they would already
have been cannibalized into these wander-
ings. My impression is that the East,
Anatolia, Syria, and possibly Greece use
stone mortars for grinding where they use
anything that we can identify, and that
mortaria are never very common. I feel
fairly confident in saying that this is a
Western Roman type, rather then Eastern,
whereas the amphora's early history is in
the Aegean. The amphora does not take on
in Britain, the mortarium does. What is
more it develops from virtually nothing in
AD 1. This may be a case where we have
most of the evidence simply because a
grinding bowl, or whatever it was, was
synonymous with pottery; in other words
most mortaria were ceramic. If this is so,
and we can chart the arrival, the spread of
manufacture, the rise and fall of different
industries, the call of each site for more or
less mortaria through time, and we even

Pot

know where most of the mortaria were made through the tireless efforts of Kay Hartley, it is a pity we have no firm idea of what they were for. I would describe Kay Hartley as supreme in mortaria studies if it were not for the fact that this suggests a court of admirers and helpers, and even would-be-successors, who watch her every time she crosses the road, just in case. But it would be more accurate to describe her as 'alone' in the study of mortaria and our debt to her is all the greater in that she has pushed her subject forward helped only by the occasional dialogue with an unusual excavator, or a pat on the head from a grateful synthesizer.

If only we could distinguish between cold steak slush, and yoghurt, and mashed turnips and de-husked cereals we could begin to interpret enthusiastically. The de-husked cereals would fit in with the evidence of charred grain to say which varieties of cereal were preferred for storing in the ear or storing as threshed grain; to talk about wholemeal and white bread, and so on. The cold steak slush poses problems of interpretation, for me at any rate, and I assume that this is because it is mercifully outside my knowledge and experience. It would be easier to ingest than a half grilled steak, and this might correlate with the deplorable decline in dental health in the Roman period in Britain, yet steak which was tender enough to 'mince' in a mortarium would probably be tender enough for any edentulous Briton. Mashed turnips are prosaic and do not necessarily predicate Haggis, though this must have an origin somewhere, and one lives in hope of finding that it finished off the next bog person to be partially shredded. It is yo-ghurt which arouses the great possibilities in interpretation because of temperature. A class discussion on this subject had interesting sociological implications for no student on a grant had a room that was warm enough to prepare his or her own yoghurt, while a mature student, forgetting the central heating in her bijoux Chelsea residence saw no problems 'After all you just mix it all up in the evening and when you come down next morning its yoghurt'. 'Yes', growled a half-grant student, 'if you **have** central heating and **if** you leave it on all night'. Amanda blushed delightfully. If only these bowls were for yoghurt then it would establish a degree of warmth and comfort in the Romano-British kitchen that I had certainly never considered.

We return, as always, to the rest of the heap. There are some generalizations to be made between the early pits and the late pits, but there could be far more. The recognizable pottery from the early pit may come from considerable distances and one or two main sources, backed up by a lot of unidentifiable wares that are presumably local. The picture in the late pits may be of more suppliers, closer to the site, with less local pots with no features in particular. Some pottery production centres will be seen to contribute to both the early and the late pits, and most obvious among these will be the Nene Valley and the Dorset Black Burnished makers. Of course it all depends on where in Britain we are, but, as always, I am towards the South and West. Other centres will be represented only in the later pits, and these may include Oxford, the New Forest, and late Roman shell gritted wares from the Bedford/

Northants border. So there are production centres which go right through the Roman period while other start early and more or less die out, and others may have been going as minor concerns and then suddenly become major producers. It has been noted that many of the early producers are sited around or near towns, Colchester, Nene Valley (though the industry may have helped the town to develop), Highgate Woods (London), while some of the later, larger industries seem to be in the middle of nowhere such as the Oxford region, the New Forest, and, in the North, Crambeck. All sorts of reasons have been given, but the one which fits best with my picture of Roman Britain is that in the later periods the kilns sited themselves to be near market areas rather than nuclei of settlement which no longer had great buying power or any other attractions. Chris Young considered this problem in his study of the Oxford centre and came up with the conclusion that the Cotswold and Chiltern and Oxfordshire countryside with its farms, country houses and villages was an attractive target area for a newly expanding pottery.

If we follow the Oxford potteries for the moment, one little aspect of our great heap, various leads appear. This was an example of a small industry of the second century suddenly growing into a major producer sometime in the second half of the third century. If we put it in absolute material terms, rather than imaginary chronology, the products of the Oxford potteries began to appear in quantities in deposits which contain early radiate coins. There is a flaw in this, for there is a period of virtually no new coins just before the radi-

ate coins, so it could be that the Oxford explosion ought to go back a little into the pre-radiate period. The most obvious wares look quite like samian in both shape and fabric, and, moreover, thay follow the latest samian forms to appear in any numbers in Britain, especially the bat or lion head mortarium and the common flanged bowl, together with wide open dishes with barbotine (clay used like piped icing) decoration on the rims of the original. At Oxford the barbotine raised clay decoration is replaced by a white clay slip painted on in its place. The surface of the vessels when new may well have taken in the unwary buyer who remembered samian,but when the pot broke the Oxford wares showed themselves with a grey sandwich in the centre of red surfaces, whereas the true samian was red throughout. In this production Oxford was behaving rather like kilns scattered all over the empire; the centralized production of red slipped ware had gradually ceased, and successor firms had started up as local concerns. One centre was in the Argonne region of N.E. France and S. Belgium, another near Poitiers, others in Africa and Palestine and Asia Minor, and so on. Some forms were remarkably uniform wherever they were produced, other forms were specific to certain areas. It might be true to say that the successors started off with the more common forms and then diverged into local specialities. The fashion for red table ware was continuing through the empire.

Why did Oxford, and the New Forest, and later Roman shell gritted wares suddenly expand production in the later period? There is as yet no simple solution; there are not really any testable models

Pot

and things ought to proceed by a process of question and answer with research rejecting the aberrant answers and concentrating on refining the surviving answers. But that is the scientific method, and archaeology does not work like that - unfortunately. Opinions might be seen to polarize towards either an invasion from the right wingers or evolution from the left wingers. The right wingers assume that man is useless unless directed, organized and, above all, financed by an injection of capital. For them the group of potters working feebly in the second century were brought up to standard, re-organized, and set on the right lines by an injection of capital in the mid third century so that they had a thriving new business which did well until the breakdown of law and order in the year 410. What dismal minds these people must have. I am not sure that the left wing have commented on these matters, but I assume that they would see fraternal organization stirring in the souls of the workers so that codification set in according to the ideas of whichever prophet was in fashion, and the chance to seize new markets was recognized and exploited, fraternally of course. An extreme centre point of view would reject these two doctrinaire extremes and go extremely for a non-doctrinaire explanation.

There was a group of potteries in the Oxford region and they made pots of a perfectly good, if undistinguished, quality, except for mortaria, in which they excelled. One had a wife who kept bemoaning the failure of itinerant traders to stock samian. In the end her husband talked to some of his colleagues and passing potters, and tried out some red pottery,

just as a job lot, for his wife's birthday. If is fair to say he had few quiet days after that, because unfortunately for his peace of mind and the tranquillity of the family, the pots came out quite well. Then, of course, the other potters and their wives wanted them; itinerant tradesmen saw them, and instead of selling pots at that point started picking them up instead and reselling them elsewhere. And one particularly nasty itinerant potter saw that there was money to be made out of this (fortunately money had just happened in Roman Britain, see coins chapter) and called in once a week during the summer, or firing season to pick up whatever was on offer. New potters had to be trained, the originator spend all his time directing and administering, and his wife saw so little of him that the home broke up and she went off with the nasty profit-maker. He took refuge in his business which went from strength to strength, though the originator never did work out how that nasty itinerant could sell so many pots in the next six days as he brought on the seventh.

I suppose I am wrong in opposing differing Right and Left views and expecting them to be differing. They might well see the same signs of creeping capital and only differ in whether they poured on their capitalized mess a sweet or sour sauce. Since all the evidence from actual kilns still talks about individual enterprises fired once or twice a season I cannot see much room for creeping capital, or rather the need for it, so I shall not believe in it until I am forced to.

The black burnished pottery making which centred round Poole harbour in Dorset is the perfect antidote to tales of progress, profit-making and creeping capital. I assume that somebody made a profit out of the pottery, though it could, of course have been a ritual activity whose products had to be disposed of somehow. Otherwise it is the perfect example of non-change, non-technicality, non-development, non-organization, and probably the greatest success in Roman Britain. There is a moral here somewhere. The potters were already settled in this area in the early first century AD or earlier and they were then making pottery that was black, and they burnished it. Like many other communities in Iron Age Britain they made their pots by hand, and they fired them, apparently, by making a heap of them, covering them with fuel, and leaving the clamp to burn gently. When a number of Roman soldiers set up camp at Exeter the potters supplied them with much that they needed, and there seems to have been a certain interchange of ideas because new shapes and new ideas do make a gentle appearance in the pottery at this time. But new-fangled things like potters wheels and kilns were rightly abhorred. When the army moved on, no doubt with a few potters daughters in tow either legitimately or otherwise, links were kept up, and fathers sent of shiploads of good solid no-non-sense pots to the lads in the army as they made their way up the West coast of Britain to the Far North. Celtic kin-groups are wonderful things so they might explain the supply of black-burnished wares to the army in the North when all memory of Dorset born great-grandmother had been lost. More likely it was simply that the pottery was good, cheap and lasted, even when put into and taken out of the fire ten times a day.

Those who have no faith in human nature would think that some organization was needed, a bit of capital would help enormously, the potters wheel would speed things up, and kilns really were necessary to get standardized products. Bad luck. Not but what Black Burnished pottery (mark 1) the real original, did change. (Interesting construction that, I have never knowingly used it before and it gives a good rustic flavour even if it does require a little thought about negatives.) Yes, deep seated changes. The lines which decorated the cooking pots crossed each other in a lattice effect. In the early period the lines stood up and formed a lattice whose vertical angles were acute; in the later period the lattice was formed by lower lines whose vertical angles were obtuse. Otherwise it would be difficult to distinguish a cooking pot made in AD 150 or 350. In between these dates things can be easier because there is an odd style in the third century when the rims of the cooking pots are the widest part of the whole pot. One suggestion has it that this allowed the pot to be settled from above in an iron ring suspended over the fire for the rim would lodge on the edge. My fingers twinge when I consider the problem of getting it out of the ring in order to serve the pigeon which has been stewing gently to a hungry family; but it is an interpretation.

This slow movement of fashion or style is unusual. A vital point to keep in mind is the fact that BB1 (Black Burnished ware mark 1, the real original, none genuine without fingerprints inside) had either admirers or copyers, for there is a whole range of industries on the East of Britain which produce wheel-thrown, kiln-fired, no doubt hard-sell-marketed copies, called now BB2. The problem was that the go-getters of the Essex and North Kent had to be held on a leash. Just like their coincident counterparts today they wanted, no doubt, to think up new ideas and forms and decorations, and sell hard. But if they did this the pottery produced became no longer BB2 but just some old black pottery or other. To compete with the almost unchanging BB1 they could not bring in changes. What a wonderful fate for the worst of the ad-men. With all their opportunities, hundreds of miles away from the source of the real thing, with all their technological innovations like wheels and kilns, and no doubt, but absolutely no evidence, capital, they uniformly failed while the old originals kept on to the end of pottery in Roman Britain. Ahhh, what a satisfying section.

The range of BB1 was limited to hard, heavy, well fired black pottery in a small number of shapes. The cooking pot, the pie-dish, first with just a rim, then with a flange as well as a rim, the simple dog-dish, which would in fact fit well on the top of the flanged pie-dish to make good a casserole, and the more exotic fish dish.

Please don't.

Don't what?

Use these silly names, you know there is nothing behind them.

Precisely, that is why they are perfectly safe to use, for only the dimmest reader would suppose that because I call something a dog dish it was made for feeding dogs out of. It is a moden descriptive term to say what it looks like, not an interpretative term to say what it was used

for. And if you don't realize that you probably ought not to be tangling with pottery and Roman Britain.

This is objectional; it is patronizing and unfair. It is patronizing because you think you know it and the other person doesn't and it is unfair because you sometimes expect a reader to take what you say semantically and logically and at other times you actually expect him or her not to.

Yes.

Dont just say 'Yes' and smile infuriatingly, do something!

Well, I suppose it comes down to the fact that I expect the reader to thing for itself while reading and not to take anything for I say granted. Everything I have said so far concentrates on how little we know about Roman Britain, how few, if any sources there are, and how much interpretation is a matter of taste. Suddenly to be confronted with a whole series of identified vessels is far too good to be true, and when no justification is offered this cannot be evidence-backed interpretation, but convention. And anyone who cannot or will not think that out for themselves should probably go back to the standard books on Roman Britain where the writers actually want you to believe everything, and write nothing that is not true. And if you believe that you really do deserve all you get. Where had we got to? We are in danger of wandering through the pottery production sites of Roman Britain instead of sorting out what we ought to be doing; falling into the typical archaeological trap of describing what is, rather than anaylsing what ought to be. We are still at the stage of pulling bits of pottery out of our heap and saying 'Oh, I recognise that, I know something about that' and this is tempting but eventually pointless.

So what else could we be doing with our heap and its early section and its late section? We could be looking at vessel shapes and examining the difference between the two phases, and perhaps between the Roman phases as represented on this site, and the medieval phases in the same town but on another site, and our Roman phase and Roman phases elsewhere in towns and villages and farmsteads. In other words, we could be looking at the material archaeologically and using it, when calibrated, to tell us something about the site. Given that the resources for local pottery industries stay pretty much the same from the early first millennium AD to the early second millennium AD in any one area, what is the relationship between the pottery produced from those resources at the two different times? The technologies are not greatly different until perhaps 1400, are the two suites of pottery similar or different; what are the differences; what do they tell us of differences in the Roman way of life in Britain and the Medieval way of life? Interpretation may be the usual problem, but at least it would be possible to begin to list the similarities and differences to give a firm basis for future interpretation. For instance. my impression which I mention only to have it corrected, is that the Roman suite is mainly at the level of pots for individuals, cups, bowls, dishes, platters, and not very large cooking pots, while the medieval suite is overwhelmingly large cooking pots and jugs, and everything else

is fairly rare. If this utterly subjective and non-specialist view were to be quantified, and, so far as I know, it never has been done, we could begin to think about implications. Different suites of pottery do not necessarily mean different World Views, but they do suggest concentrations on different aspects of living within the same general framework. Of course we have to remember that the drinking horn and horn cup are missing from most medieval deposits though we know they existed in fact; of course we have to remember that there are different attitudes to metals and metal vessels, and so on; but it would be nice to have some basic agreed observations on the two periods in case people started having ideas which could be tested against such material. For instance, is the simplistic question as to whether the Roman-Britons were small units with emphasis on the individual, while medieval Britons were large units with little emphasis on the individual necessarily nonsense? I have no idea, but it is a thought which I have as a result of talking about the material and I would like to start off from agreed fact in order to check it.

Similar points come up if we stop trying to make cross period comparisons and stay inside the Roman limits. How does the pottery assemblage from a nucleated settlement with a wall round differ, if at all, from an assemblage from another settlement without a wall, a group of houses in the country, and an isolated farm?

You don't know?

We spend millions of pounds annually on archaeology; hundred of tons of the stuff are dug up and examined and weighed and drawn, and you don't know how the pottery from different types of settlement differs, or even whether it does differ? If pottery is, by weight, by far the most common find on any site, surely it should be an index of status, purpose, function, or whatever **of** that site.

Yes, well, but who knows whether pottery can say anything about status, purpose, function, or whatever?

You mean you have not even bothered to find out? This is getting incredible.

What do you mean find out?

Well it seems likely that a house and attendant rubbish pits in the centre of a built up area, surrounded by other houses, with no access to the countryside, with a wall round the settlement, is likely to have a different function from an isolated living building with attendant 'farm' buildings in the middle of the countryside.

Well, perhaps.

So it might be an idea to look at the range of pottery, in fabrics, in grades of fineness, and in forms to see if that likely difference in function has any effect on the pottery used. The same sort of thing could be done between the isolated house with mosaic pavements and its attendant rubbish, and a wooden house with no visible adornments, and its attendant rubbish.There is no guarantee that we would be examining wealth and poverty, but we would seem to be examining different life-styles, whether this was a matter of choice or necessity, and the lifestyles might be picked up from, or reflected in, the pottery used broken and discarded.

Again, what about military pottery use and civilian pottery use? Because in the earlier period soldiers seem to crowd to-gether at densities which ordinary people would never accept, or arrive at, and live in rectangular buildings in straight lines with straight banks and ditches and ramparts round, they are easily identifiable. And because they tend to be unsociable and live away from normal people, probably due to some mass personality defect, or they would not be soldiers, their rubbish ought to be fairly easily collectable. In fact thinking of all the money that has been spent on military archaeology we ought to have a mountain of pottery from military sites. By now we have got to the stage where we know the layout of the forts quite well, so a new site could be stripped and planned out to the furthest rubbish pit, and then the buildings could be left and the rubbish pits dug.

Whats that? You don't normally go beyond the ramparts and the density of occupation inside is such that most rubbish must be buried outside.

Oh, I see, that does make things easier, so you outline the fort itself and the clear the surrounding area using the fort as the spoil dump?

Don't be silly, we don't dig forts like that.

Yet there must be military assemblages of pottery when the People Who Know dig rubbish pits by accident, and it would be possible to compare these with assemblages from nucleated settlements and isolated farmsteads, and it would be nice to know whether the soldiers, who at least to begin with, are ethnically, socially, and spatially distinct from the natives use the same pottery in the same way, or not.

While we are about it we could throw

in some experimental archaeology here. Can you make yoghurt, or steak slush, or mashed turnips or dehusk wheat in a mortarium? Is the cooking pot usable for stews and chickens and oat-meal soup? If so, why do so many have a lime deposit on the inside as if they never contained more that hot water, so resembling the kettle permanently on the fire. How much do beakers and cups hold and are they good to drink from? Will the combination of Black Burnished pie dish and dog dish upside down really work as a casserole. And is BB1 really that tough? Do we **do** that sort of thing with pottery?

Pot

Coinage

Coinage is good for dating, and tells you about the prosperity of the site from year to year. A single Roman coin has only one good use for dating and is most of the time unuseable; there is no direct relationship between the coins found on a site and its prosperity at any given date. When extremes are put forward the usual result is a nice cosy compromise somewhere in the middle. We are so addicted to compromise and balance that I am continually surprised that programmes on Concentration camps do not allow the organizers and guards to put their point of view, those that we have not killed off of course. In the case of coinage the first statement is very starry eyed and wrong, the second is damping and right; compromise is the dirtiest word in the vocabulary.

Iron Age coins are no good for dating because they themselves are not dated; Roman coins are. This is a slight overstatement, but very slight. Some Iron Age coins bear the names of individuals who are otherwise recorded in Latin writers in conjunction with Roman rulers and politicians whose dates are known, so such coins do have general dates. Caesar says that he fought Cassivellaunus, but unfortunately no one ever put that name on coins. Other names appear, such as Tincommius, otherwise unknown from any sources, but there are names which occur both on coins and in texts. This still leaves a wide bracket of tens of years for the minting of each coin type. Still, general points can be made and if a section is dug all the way through the rampart of an Iron Age Lambing and Calving Pen (known as Hill forts) and there is an Iron Age coin

fully sealed at the bottom on the old turfline, it is unlikely that the rampart was built before the first century BC. Unlikely, because that is the present guess at the date of the beginning of coinage made in Britain; but still possible, for, however unlikely, the dates could be wrong as they are not pegged to any directly historically attested date. If the coin has a known name on it then the limits of accuracy can be improved with a little massage 'mentioned as a young man by Tacitus around the year AD 14 and therefore probably not born before 20 BC and probably dead by AD 70; in theory, coins bearing his name could have been struck at any point during this time'. But the inference of finding remains the same; the rampart could not have been constructed before the coin was minted. It might have been built at any time after the minting, up to yesterday, though many archaeologists would notice that, and the coin cannot give any date other than the one in which it was struck. If the coin was fresh and was found in a layer of ploughsoil sealed by the rampart it is quite reasonable to suppose that it was lost fairly soon after being struck. If it was in the top of the plough soil then the land had probably not been ploughed many times after the loss. And if there was no established turfline then there might have well not been any gap between the last ploughing and the building of the rampart. So the date of the rampart, in these circumstances, might not be long after the date of the coin, and the excavator ought to put down these points because the observations and the thoughts are part of the record. But he must keep in mind that exactly the same reasoning could be applied to the 17th C. AD when a well known antiquarian was walking over the land, and lost a coin, which fell into plough soil, and the next week the landowner embanked a deer-park. The only thing we know for certain, or nearly certain, barring moles and near relatives, is that the rampart was built after the date of the coin and before the time you first saw it. That is the only use of coins for dating if we are behaving logically as scientists; and if we behave in a different way, which is not necessarily worse, but different, we must say so, and admit the consequences.

A secondary problem here is that a very high level of inaccuracy may come into this logical process in a completely inestimable way because some types of Roman coins have long lives. It is extremely difficult to fix the moment of coin loss in the lifetime of an individual coin. Some workers would like to pay more attention to wear; this might help, but it can never be logical. Thus denarii, silver coins, struck in the Roman republic are found quite commonly in Britain in contexts which have to be dated, from the presence of other later coins to at least AD 80; the coins may be over 200 years old, and they may be, probably will be, worn. But they can be that age without being worn if they have spent decades in a bag as savings, handed down from father to son and never actually released into circulation until AD 20; and of course they can be considerably worn within twenty years of being minted if they circulate quickly and roughly in the middle of the City of Rome. Wear could give a rough guide to age, this coin was minted some time before it was

lost, but this is a totally different category of knowledge to the fact that this coin was not minted before the year AD 86. The coin expert will therefore often tell the archaeologist things he already knows. This floor was not laid before the minting of this coin in 31 BC. Well, we did suspect this, actually, because it is a mosaic pavement with a Christian design.

As the number of coins in any deposit increases so the chances of getting a decent date grows. The logic does not change. With several coins the one single logical inference remains, no, inference is too soft a word, for this seems to me to approach true logic. The coin was minted in 31 BC. The floor was laid after the coin was minted. If you do not accept the conclusion that the floor was laid in or after 31 BC you doubt the premises or end in contradiction. With several coins the one single piece of logic remains, but the different categories of inference from that one piece of logic improve. The coinage went A, B, C, D. Our deposit contains six coins A, ten coins B, and 2 coins C. Coins D are found commonly on the same site in different deposits, and on other surrounding sites. It is a much better reasonable inference than the earlier one involving ploughsoil and a single coin, that the deposit closed before coins D could get into it, and they were available from AD 330 onwards. So the date of the deposit might be 330-340. Or in strict logic, 1852. What happens as you increase your number of found coins is that you decrease the number if inferences that may be drawn from them, so the smaller number of inferences take on aspects of fact. They are not fact, they remain inference, but I think it is true to say that they are inferences of better quality.

All this, unfortunately, means that the least important thing about a Roman coin from the point of view of dating, is that date at which that one actual coin was struck. Far more important is a knowledge of the Roman coinage system, how it worked and circulated and was hoarded in general, and what particular peculiarities there are in the area you are dealing with. I am surprised that anyone who can point out that the Roman coinage system did not circulate has driven himself so far through this book. It is abundantly clear what I mean, and the purpose of language is communication, not the following of rules which are by definition obsolete as soon as they are formed. Fortunately we now have a battery of books describing Ancient coinage in general (Casey), coinage in the Roman world (Burnett), coinage in Roman Britain (me), the identification of the most common coins found in Roman Britain (Simon James and me), and several other clear statements of what Roman coinage was and how it changed (Sutherland, Mattingly, Kent). But the transformation of the basic information into a guide on what to do in dating a group of coins is something that has never really been put into hard print and a few general points may come in useful here.

From the first Roman political interest in Britain in the first century BC to about AD 260 the coinage was a fairly simple system of gold aurei, silver denarii, large bronze sestertii, middle bronze dupondii and asses, and small bronze semisses and quadrantes. In fact some of the bronze's were brass and some were copper, but since it is of no use whatsoever to the ar-chaeologist to know whether a coin was copper, copper and tin, copper and zinc or copper, lead, arsenic, antimony, bismuth, gold, silver and ytterbium, let us call them bronze. Any book will delight in setting you right if you need to know. All these little squalls have their origins in previous publications where I have been 'put right' when it so clearly didn't matter. The only point at issue for the finders of the coins is that they come in gold and silver, worth their weight perhaps in the precious metal; and base metal, whatever the mixture, which is never anywhere near worth its weight and is therefore a token system dependent on the state framework for its value.

This is ridiculous. We are told that different metals demonstrate different denominations, and then we are told that it does not matter. I want to be able to see on any site the ratio between dupondii and asses, between copper and brass.

Bad luck. Look at any small coin lists, up to say 200 coins. You will find that some of the first and second and even third century coins are so worn and corroded that they have to be listed as 'First century dupondii or asses (3)'. And these uncertain coins will almost certainly be enough to make your margins of error in any detailed calculation unacceptably large because you must allow for the fact that all the uncertains may be dupondii and that all the uncertains may be asses. And that will give you an error ±100% which makes the calculations of dubious value. Quantify the effect before you criticize.

Silver from the Republic was generally good (c.95% silver). During the first and second centuries there were debase-memts excellently documented by David Walker. The face value of the denarius was always probably a bit above its metal value so there came jerks in the system when the old denarii were so much more valuable than those currently being pro-duced that reminting at the new standard was profitable. Not all old denarii were swept away at each jerk, but the odds on an old coin being winkled out of circulation increased as time went on. Eventually the silver content of theoretically silver coins fell so low (c.1% around AD 270) that all good denarii, and even poor denarii, were sought out, and very few can be found in deposits laid down after about AD 280. So a Republican denarius minted in 200 BC is still highly usable in AD 50, under pres-sure of debasement by AD 85, rare be-cause of state search around 107 and there-after, but still perfectly good legal tender till the middle of the third century if you were silly enough to spend it for its face value, rather than passing it over to a jeweller for its metal value. But not all denarii obeyed these rules.

A state official who seems to have been awarded army or civil service han-douts of precious metal in the early 300's, who buried his stock of bullion, coins, me-dallions, jewellery and a candlestick around 315 near Arras in France, had among the gold a small group of silver denarii up to the later half of the second century AD. The Frankish king Childeric, buried at Tournai in barbaric splendor with a ring of horses buried surrounding his tomb, had with him a small hoard of second century denarii. Some Roman coins took refuge from the economics of the Empire out in the Barbaricum; they seem often to have moved as hoards, though in some areas they may have moved singly, and one of these groups was captured back some-where around AD 300 and given out after as spoil (Beaurains/Arras), and another group was not captured back but went down from father to son until deposited in Childerics grave. These denarii were there-fore free at almost any time to re-enter the empire and cause havoc with archaeologi-cal dating.

What about Republican coins giving republican dates? Here we have to take in the context in which the coins are found; if they have no context they give no date. A modern coin collector can walk across a field and lose a republican denarius. If you see him drop it you know the context and you know that gives a date of AD 1987. If no one sees him drop it, and it is churned over and over in the plough soil it loses all context and gives no date whatsoever. This is equally true in the first century BC or AD. If a Republican coin were found under a hut, under a rampart, later levelled to build a fort in which all the coins found were of the Roman emperor Claudius I (AD 41-54) it would be perfectly reason-able to suggest that the hut, if not the rampart dated to before the reign of Clau-dius, and that the republican denarius was lost before the army arrived. If the repub-lican denarius is found unstratified on the site of a Romanized farmstead it does not necessarily mean that there is a farm of Iron Age/Republican date underneath. A date for the first coin, in its stratified con-text came from inference **not** from the date of the striking of the coin, but from its position underneath, two events underneath, something which stood a good chance of being of the reign of Claudius. I think it is still true to say that no Roman coin is known and published from an Iron Age context in Britain. There are rumours of a recent find in Kent. There is a silver portrait of Augustus from the tumulus at Lexden, Colchester, but it is still uncertain whether this is a coin; the context is firmly Iron Age, the purpose of the silver is shown by its mount to be decorative rather than monetary.

The other early Roman coins whose contexts I know belong at least in the reign of Claudius I or later. There are of course a majority of published coins whose context I do not know, nor, now, does anyone else. The idea of publishing coins from excavations according to the context in which they were found is only catching on very slowly indeed, yet we have already seen, just on the subject of dating, how important such information is. The best example comes from the publication of the coins from Camulodunum/Colchester by Dr. Sutherland in 1947. When the palace at Fishbourne was being prepared for publication around 1965, the excavator, Barry Cunliffe had to suggest to me, the coin person, that the coins would be best published in the groups in which they were found, or rather in the phases into which the actual find spots had been amalgamated. In many cases record of the actual groupings came right through into publication, and, once I had been shown what to do, I took up the idea. Things had not really moved on at all from 1947 to 1965. In many cases they have still not moved on. and a coin list annotated by find-spot is still not the norm. There are therefore a lot

of coins of pre-Claudian date whose context is totally unknown. The examples from Camulodunum and Fishbourne came in useful when Warwick Rodwell suggested that the early phases had been missed by the excavators at Camulodunum, and that Cunliffe had not noticed a settlement of pre-Roman date under the palace at Fishbourne; coins were brought forward as evidence. Yet if you can believe the reports, and use them, every pre-Claudian coin on each site is published as coming either from a layer or phase containing Claudian coins, or from a layer or phase above that. The implication is that the pre-Claudian coins are dated in their loss to Claudian times or later, by their contexts.

When you look at a number of coin reports you find a strong similarity between the coins found on different sites which may either intrigue you, or depress you. It is quite expectable since the Roman state only minted a certain number of types of coins and they have to occur in certain combinations. Certain types seem commonly found, coins with the emperor wearing a spiky crown, or radiates; other types are distinctly uncommon such as the coin of Hadrian with an actual date AUC (Ab urbe condite) from the founding of the City, 874, which equals AD 121. So not only do certain coins turn up on most sites, and some coins, such as the Hadrian, never turn up, but the coins seem to turn up on sites in similar proportions. The site which produces 200 coins shows 50 of AD 260 to 296 and 100 of AD 330 to 348; the site which produces only 4 coins may well produce one of AD 260 to 296 and two coins of AD 330 to 348. This sounds like a country site as opposed to a walled or nucleated settlement which I have so far avoided calling a town; can I keep it up? The walled settlements known as Civitas Capitals, Winchester, Canterbury, Leicester, and so on, tend to have a roughly equal number of coins of AD 260 to 296 and AD 330 to 348, while other sites, country, religious and so on, tend to have twice as many coins in the later period. These are exceptions to there ideas, but you can check them reasonably easily by looking through a few coin lists. All this means that the majority of sites have coins according to a British pattern, not, apparently, according to their own pattern of their individual history. Coins commonly occur on sites when they come in large numbers to Britain and form a major part of what is in circulation. You ought to be asking me what my evidence is for 'in circulation' because then I would have to admit to a totally circular argument: all that we know about coin circulation in Britain comes from site finds, with a little help from hoards, but these are highly unreliable touchstones of circulation. So, judging from site finds, coin supply to Britain went up and down, and when it went up the majority of sites shared the up, and when it went down, few, if any sites could get the coinage. In general therefore, the coinage found on a site is a general part of the overall coinage in Britain and not an index of site prosperity. Unless, of course, every site in Britain boomed at exactly the same time and exactly to the same extent, which is rather unlikely.

There is however pottery as well, so it is possible to show that some sites had periods of occupation, but no coin loss,

and periods of abundant rubbish production and building, with low coin loss, and periods when not much seems to be happening except high coin loss. All the other combinations are possible, though high coin loss in the early period without any other signs of occupation would be so unusual as to demand some ritual explanation. This means that sites can apparently be fully active and apparently successful without showing any coin loss, and perhaps without even joining in coin using activity, except when demanded by the state as in tribute and taxes. We have now two points which totally prohibit any direct translation of coin finds, or non-finds, into trade, economy, exchange, success, failure, or any other everyday human activity. The first is the way that coin finds on most sites fluctuate according to a British pattern, all doing roughly the same thing at the same time; the second is the point that some sites give all the appearance of affluence without losing any coins, while others seem squalid, yet have a high coin loss. These should make it quite clear that we need a rather more refined method of getting information out of material than just saying, lots of coins equals prosperity.

I have described my present method of dealing with finds in the Material chapter and I hope we can take that for granted for the moment. Using that method it is possible to see sites which seem to have trends of high and low coin loss within the overall national pattern. Before we get down to 'What does it all mean' there are some further procedural points to be settled. Two different objectors break in. One knows about Roman Britain, the other is interested in methods; they both want to know what sites I used to construct my background.

The site we are about to interpret according to your method is a villa; I assume you have a villa background for me.

And...

I'm a bit worried about all these different sites; you realize that those little sites with only five coins are going to introduce all sorts of odd extremes in percentages; large sites would have been much better.

For the second objector things are fairly easy. The sites used have in general over 100 coins each, so 1% is usually at least one coin. But if only sites with over 100 coins were used this would bias the whole thing against the particular type of coin use and coin loss on the less productive sites. So a few of the low producing sites have been included, and, in fact, they do follow the general trends, so they do not introduce very odd percentages. Both these points were well worth making and I fully agree with the thought processes behind them. Not so with the first objector. What is a villa? (see the Countryside chapter). Why is your site a villa? I do not use the word when I remember to avoid it so I will not accept it from you. Why should I compare your site with other villas when you have difficulty defining the term and have given me no reason whatsoever to think that coins on villas follow a particular pattern? Why should I change all my empirical and analytical ways of thought just to follow your poverty stricken habits of deduction? It is always good to jump in with both feet as objectionably as possible, it achieves surprise and a breathing space, and you

can always back pedal after, when you find that some of their points were soundly based. Unless of course it is a pleasant person, and not an objectionable research student, in which case you suit your tactics to the person. Even research students can be quite nice at times.

There is an interesting methodological point under the potential dog-fight, which we might as well get down to. Do you compare like with subjectively perceived like, or do you throw the whole lot in together and wait for categories to jump out at you? In other words, do I segregate my run of sites in Britain which have produced coins into predetermined categories beloved of commentators on Roman Britain, in order to compare forts with forts, and farms with farms; or do I start from the beginning, look at the whole lot and see if I can distinguish different categories of site by different types of coin use? The question is stated with coins, but it should also be stated with buildings, brooches, pottery, animal bones, pollen, seeds, iron-work and all other material. Of what interest is it to me that a building in the country has mosaic pavements when I am studying coin loss? Do I have enough confidence in the categories often used in Roman Britain to use them to prejudge my material? Even if I had, and I most certainly do not, OUGHT I to impose any categories on my material or ought it to be allowed to show up categories by itself?

What is this about categories jumping out at you, showing categories for itself? I thought you spent a long time disccounting the idea that material speaks to you if you sit and commune with it, vibrationally,

for long enough.

True, I stick to that; it is a matter of setting out the evidence, catching an idea rolling round in your mind, formulating it, and putting it to the test of the material. This happened with coins when I was working on Winchester coins. I noticed that radiate coins (AD 260 to 296) were roughly equal to 4th C. coins (AD 330 to 402). I wondered how true this was in general and looked through my lists to find that it did hold true in general for walled civitas capitals and other large dots on the map like Gloucester and Lincoln and Colchester, but was not true for most other sites. The picture there was of twice the number of coins in the 4th C. or even more

As the material has grown over the years this rough distinction has remained and can be seen if you put on a diagram the radiate coins and the 4th C. coins. The civitas capitals and other large walled settlements together with a few smaller settlements in the East of the country North of Kent stay in the 1:1 area, while the other sites ooze gently from 1:1 right down to 4:1. And, in general while the first group do not mingle with the others, the others, forts, temples, farms, villages and so on all run into one another. It is not worth the trouble, I give in, the two groups are Things that are Called Towns and the countryside. Another characteristic of the TCT's is a better representation of coins before 260 then the countryside. It is not as good a separation as the radiate v.4th C. divide because there are odd sites which have a lot of early coins for no very obvious reason.

So, once we get down to actual demonstrations it is worth separating off the TCT's from the rest, but it is at present totally unjustifiable to separate farms from villages, or even apparently forts in the lowland zone from temples. No doubt differences in coin loss will be found, but with the instruments bluntly in use at the moment no differences are apparent. It is therefore worth having two backgrounds for coins, one based on TCT's and one based on the rest. Any site which needs classification and comment can be compared with both backgrounds and the best fit noted. There are problems and these as always lead to possible areas of interest. Thus Cirencester, from the area surrounded by the wall, the building of the wall and gates, historical references, and virtually all other signs should be classed with the TCT's, yet all but one of the sites excavated there falls in the countryside part of the classification. At both Colchester and Caistor-by-Norwich there are sites inside the walls and sites outside the walls which have produced coins, and the internal sites behave as TCT's and the external sites behave as countryside. What does all this mean?

We have marshalled the material evidence, a heap of coin lists for sites which have been excavated or field walked. We have looked at ways of actually presenting the material evidence and separating the average from the exceptional, and we have looked briefly at categorisation purely from numerical manipulation within the material, We have to build an idea of what coin use was before we have anything to test against our material. Before I can comment on coins use you must give me an idea of coin use to test.

The simplest model would be one in

which coin use, or the use of Roman coins, started with the establishment of the Roman administration - the coin evidence would suggest this was in the reign of Claudius I, so the historical sources could be right - and went on till the end of the administration. Latest coins go up to about 402 so let us take that. Good, you have given me chronological brackets, with a little help from the evidence thus bringing in the inevitable circular argument. But let us agree on the idea that coin use starts when cons are commonly first found as coin losses on sites, and it stops when no further coin losses are discovered. But what do you mean by coin use?

If we start at the top then the state produces gold silver and copper coins. The most obvious reason for such production is necessity, and the most obvious necessity is that state servants need paying. This is something started well away from Britain, in the Mediterranean coastlands, so we do not have to answer any questions about how it may have started. All we have to do is to say that it was the habit by the time Roman administrators set up in Britain, and the habit was transferred into Britain through them. So some coins were necessary to the Roman administration to pay soldiers and other adminstrators. If logistics mattered then the simplest way to send such sums to Britain was in gold and silver coin. One gold coin saved the transport of 25 silver coins of very roughly the same size, or 100 sestertii, large bronze coins, well over 50p size and weight. The coins that are mostly found in forts, in other words the other end of the process after the soldiers have been paid, the coins used, and some of them

lost, are mostly asses - 400 to the gold coin and heavier than a 50p piece, but around the same size. This gives various possibilities and contradictions which I shall skirt for the moment.

The administrator might like to pay his underlings completely in silver, but they would not be so happy because of the difficulties of actually putting the coins to use. He might like to pay them in gold but then the state would be unhappy because substantial amounts of a very valuable ointment for irritated soldiers and politicians would be marooned in a fringe province. What the state wants, happens. What the underlings want is worth taking note of if they are near to you or if they can cause trouble. So while silver seems to be a good compromise some small change is needed to set the wheels of commerce in motion. At the moment we are looking only from the point of view of the administration totally immersed in a Mediterranean way of thought. A soldier who wants to buy a woollen cloak for his father back in Gaul can probably work in denarii; if there is change to be given that is the problem of the cloak-maker, not the Roman administration. But if he wants a glass or two of the local mead one evening as a preliminary to ogling the girl at the inn, he cannot part with a denarius straight away. So his pay should be basically silver, to cut down on the problems of transport, with an admixture of small change, perhaps asses, so he can actually spend the stuff.

In the reign of Claudius I this causes problems. Bronze coinage is not much in demand apparently because all the continental provinces were filled with the stuff in the great coinage of Augustus which still defies estimate, but was certainly in the range of tens of millions of coins if not hundreds of millions. Silver could be supplied in the reign of Claudius, but it would not be new silver, it would be old silver which had been taken in taxes in other provinces and then sent off to Britain. In fact, to the worried administrator in Britain, with men to pay, the mint in Rome was something of a dead loss because it could not respond to his needs even if it had known about them. But men still had to be paid. Silver could be sent in as it cycled round the economy, but bronze, so far as we know did not move in cycles to and from the state, so there was no mechanism by which it could be shifted from the European provinces where it was plentiful to Britain where it was badly needed. This would have left the silver immobile had not some authority or body or group of people not copied the bronze coinage that had been seen and produced copies in profusion. As we are looking at present simply from the point of view of authority I follow Robert Kenyon's view that it was the army who recognized the problem and corrected it. Some of the best and earliest Claudian copies come from Colchester, where, due to full excavation and good stratigraphy, the continuing process of copying can be watched through succeeding layers. As Colchester seems to be a very important place in the early Romanization of the island the correspondence of authority and copying seems to have a clear message. Others dislike this idea because it is difficult to get round the distaste of the state forging its own coins. Thus 'official copying' is by definition almost nonsense. However all this may be

we have set up for the administrator a flow of silver from the continent to pay the major part of his periodic wage demands, and someone has created for him a pool of small change, which he may or may not know about officially, so that he, and the men under him are happy for the moment.

Then we have to move out to see what the effect of this is on the British say in the West. A soldier appears in the mead-hall; since this is an area which 'welcomed' the Roman liberators (from what, no one has really specified), spitting is not in order, and he ought to be served. In fact he is quite a pleasant Gaul who makes an effort to adapt his Gaulish tongue to the British language, he gave the mead-man's little girl a glass ring the other day when he was talking to the women of the village, so his glass of mead is poured, and he, naturally, tenders a coin in payment. This caused problems because no one has ever done that before; the whole business of mead-drinking is part of village life, and, since each has his place in production and distribution, glasses of mead are in fact payment by the mead family for eggs from one, milk from another, lamb from a third and so on. The village network is complicated, and no doubt some get things almost free, and others amass surpluses which they then go and exchange for things exotic, but it trundles along without too much strain. To say that coin tendering has never happened before is not quite right, because during the troubles, some time ago, when the soldiers were moving across the country, and even going over to Gaul to help fight the expanding Fasces, there were people who had no connection with the village who tried to settle things with coins.

Of course coins are known; many are of gold and silver, but there are less valuable ones of copper, or silver plate, but these are tied up with obligations higher up the social scale than glasses of mead. The mead-man himself knows coins when, as one of the chief villagers he attends the quarterly assembly, and is rewarded by the high chief for his attendance. But it seems badly to debase the whole context of coinage to bring it down to paying for glasses of mead. Yet this is the shape of the future ,and perhaps the subject can be aired with this friendly Gaul, even if he is a Roman soldier at the same time. Discussion ensues, the Gaul advises on 'prices', and even offers to write some characters on a piece of smooth wood which the mead-man can show to other 'customers' (as opposed to the local clients) to save continual aggravation.

The mead-man therefore has a considerable start on the rest of the village when some years later the census happens, and tax demands start, for he has an actual heap of copper coins which can be turned into silver to pay the taxes, and the surplus can be used to help other villagers who have not learned the system so quickly. This, of course puts the others in his debt, and he has to charge for his services. And to think that five years ago he had never considered coins as everyday things capable of bringing him in more than the mead-hall ever did. The stroke of genius came from the recommendation of that friendly Gaul, now promoted, who wrote a document to say that the mead-man was a fit person to hold the state office of money-changer, so his amateur status as village coin advisor has changed to a lucrative side-line for the whole locality because it is only through him that silver can be changed to copper so that it can be spent, and it is only through him that the piles of copper coins can be changed back to silver to pay the taxes. Thank goodness that the emperor Nero (he had to learn to read and write and figure to take on this job) had produced the good new supply of copper coin which brought to an end all those copies which had sunk over a twenty year period to a disgusting standard - almost like the old British coins which are rarely seen nowadays. It would be rather fun to continue the story through the mead-man's family, but at the moment both you and I should get bored - well I certainly should - so we will leave the scenario based on virtually no material evidence at all - even for mead, and the next step is obviously for you to build your own.

The important point that this little fable has introduced is our uncertainty as to how the British brought and sold things, or exchanged things, in the early Romanizing period. By the first century AD it seems likely, though it is not certain, that the Mediterranean area worked on market stalls piled high with goods which were sold to anyone who had the coin to buy them; this is my descriptive shorthand for a free market economy, totally destructive of human ties and social life. But there are other ways of making goods change hands, and one which is often quoted is the economy which is embedded in social obligations, such as the mead-man. He was lucky in that he had enough mead to satisfy these social and economic obligations and have a bit left over to 'sell'; others might be trapped producing enough to satisfy demanding obligations. It is most unlikely that an embedded economy, if that is what was in Britain, would have changed quickly to nothing but a market economy, so the likely picture of Britain in the first two centuries AD is of a social exchange continuing side by side with a money exchange. This must have varied from place to place within Britain, and from time to time as the coinage produced did, or did not, seem suitable for buying lettuces.

At this point I suppose It would be sensible to look at the material evidence, and that will bring in train, what it might mean. The British coins are difficult to deal with mainly because they are on their own, and never interleave with the Roman system which has so many different supports and links by which to attempt to understand it. The coins which everyone seems to agree are the earliest to be struck in Britain are of gold and are closely related to the coinage of the tribes of north-eastern Gaul. One theory has it that they were payment for help when British tribes were sent over to Gaul to assist in the fight against Caesar. The gold was brought back, and the idea of coinage was endemic in that gold. Silver followed, copper appeared, latin letters spelled out the names of historical personages and others, and designs in some areas of Britain become remarkably Romanized. In other areas, such as Dorset, the centre of the Durotriges, designs remained firmly non-Roman and names did not appear.

A mildly interesting argument has been going on over the past fifteen years as to what these coins represent - we are back at interpretation, except that at least one side regarded the whole thing as clear certainty while the other tried to introduce the foreign concept of alternative interpretations. The certainty involved named people, known tribes, kingship, state finance, and thence territories of political power mapped out by the findspots of coins lost in antiquity. The second set of ideas questioned the basis on which the 'classical' ideas were based, pointed out the flimsy nature of the evidence, and proposed another set of ideas based perhaps, but not necessarily, on the issue of the coins by certain known people for their own ends, but then used in market areas which might or might not correspond with any royal, tribal, or political limits. As always, the argument got bogged down in which was right and which was wrong, on the mistaken assumption a.) that one was one or the other and b.) that we could know this. The argument ought to have considered the relative merits of the two insubstantial models in helping to understand the litter left from the British Iron Age. John Collis's new ideas did open the subject up for a little, but it is probably too soon to say whether they left a lasting dent on the old orthodoxy. All through such discussions the point is not that the old orthodoxy is wrong, but simply that since we can never know if it is right it is a good insurance policy to have at least two opposing or complementary models to chose from. There were probably never enough Iron Age coins minted for every person to have a good supply; it seems unlikely that they ever facilitated a free market economy of market stalls, and they therefore tend to be associated, as in my fable, with social and hierarchial beings and doings.

The Roman coins from Claudius I

onwards are clearly different. The gold is of a different weight standard, and the Roman gold usually maintained a high standard of purity throughout the empire, while the British gold had varied quite considerably in its gold content. The silver coins, denarii, were heavier, and of higher silver content than their British predecessors. The bronze coins were many times larger than the British bronze coins. Here we have to discuss the term 'small change', and to do that we have to make guesses, informed or random, about the value or purchasing power of Roman coins. We are helped by texts and graffiti, but these are in the Mediterranean region, which may have had a different price structure from that of a newly conquered non-monetised province. We also have to take into account not only the theoretical structure of the Roman coinage but what was actually produced and what, of the coins produced, came to Britain.

The system always had a gold piece. A soldier might have been given ten a year, in theory, instead of 250 denarii, which is near the wage around the year AD 100. If this represents a modern £5,000 then the gold piece is £500, the silver denarius £20, the brass sestertius £5, the copper as £1 (well £1.25), and the smallest coin of all the quadrans, 25p. This can be checked and cross checked with different prices and foods and subsistence diets and so on, but one example would be a good glass of wine in a Pompei tavern for an As. A good glass of wine in a London wine bar is going to cost about £1, so we may not be too far out. We may have to bring the whole thing down to half the values I have quoted, but even then when most of the cross checks

will be on the low side, the smallest theoretical coin will be well over 10p. The early Roman coinage system does not seem to envisage what we regard as very small change of 1p, 2p, 5p and perhaps 10p. The system envisages coins of about 10p, 20p, more likely 50p and £1, but the state produces few of the smaller coins up to the £1 size. That begins to correspond with the archaeological record in Britain where Asses are commonly found, but halfs and quarters are very rare indeed. This adds a further complication in what the coins found in Roman Britain might mean, because even if the British economy did want to become a free market economy the coins which arrived in the country were inappropriate.

The details of the system and the changes it underwent will have to be gleaned from one of the detailed books on the subject mentioned above. Suffice it to say here that during the second century there is a fairly smooth distribution of found coins over most of Lowland Britain, and parts of the Highland zone as well, such that the military establishments do not stand out qualitatively, only quantitatively. They have very much the same coins as anyone else, but more of them in smaller spaces. By the third century there has been a change from a carefully graded system of denominations to a state in which there is gold and commonly used and lost base coin, and that is all that is available. A reform around 294 tried to re-introduce a system of coins of different value levels, but it failed, and the same point is made several times in the fourth century. It is only around 356 that the system settles down to gold, good silver, and copper, and that lasts out the century. My present interpretation of the changes in the system are of an early system in which the state provided the gold and silver to pay its own debts and copper and bronze to oil the wheels of commerce in order to get the precious metals circulating and back into the treasury. Silver, though, seems to be fairly happily lent to the population at large. There seem to have been problems over silver in the early third century; the state debased the coinage and brought the silver standard down to 48% and then onward down to 1% in around 270. This seems to me to be muddled, if any, thinking on the part of the state who were trying to keep a duel purpose system, state and market, going at a time of rising prices and declining amount of silver (???). By accident it brought the only common coin down to a face value below that of the very scarce quadrans of the first century. For instance the silver denarius which was mostly silver had the purchasing power of 4 Sestertii, 16 Asses and therefore 64 quadrantes. The radiate coin of 270 with a 1% silver was lighter then the denarius therefore its intrinsic value is less than 1/100th of the old denarius, so perhaps half the value of the old quadrans. All this I see as happening by a process of continual debasement in an attempt to by the state to pay its way. The effect on coin loss in Britain, to stay in material terms for the moment, was dramatic, and every site shows a sharp rise, sometimes by 10 or even 100 times the moment that these small coins became common (c.260 onwards). It may be, to interpret, that the processes of exchange which were commonly going on suddenly joined up with newly low value coins. In other words, the coins became, by accident, relevant to everyday exchanges in Britain.

To the state, reform was necessary to bring the coinage back up to a 'decent' level. Even today we use these concepts and there is still this dichotomy between what is highly usable and current and convenient, and what is 'proper'. It happens in money, where we want our coins and our notes to look decent rather than be usable, though the two points are in balance, and it happens in the realm of ideas and aspirations when through 'institutional sin' any group of people legislate and try to enforce a more rigid code of ethics than any one of them would propose on his own, and certainly more then any one of them would try to live by himself. What happens naturally is one pole, and what ought to be is another pole, and we keep a state of civilization by steering between these two poles. What rubbish; but it seems to be engrained and, with a slight change of letters make sense of an erroneous Christian doctrine.

So the state wants a 'decent' level of coins both for display and the practical reason that unless the coins really are decent they will be no use to pay state debts. The gold must be of a high purity and known weight, the silver must be bullion and standardized, and the state will be content. It would be good if the lower coinage could also be decent, but state is less interested in this. The people in the market place are interested in this and there is a contrast between what the state would like to see produced, and what is relevant to the market. Eventually the system of the late empire evolved in which the gold and silver kept its high standard, but became more and more a very temporary loan from the state to the public; and the copper coins ran down to a minimal size, which we find fiddly, scrappy, worthless, deplorable, almost indecent as money, yet which the market stalls may have found very useful. The contrast between the poles in the period after the radiate is weighted heavily in favour of the people simply because when they were not provided with scrubby coinage they seem to have produced it for themselves by the well established British technique of copying. From 260 onwards there are ample finds of small value copper coinage, with or without an admixture of silver, on most sites in Britain, though with a tendency towards the countryside, and this may mean the existence of a fairly widespread money using market. On the other hand most of these coins were lost, or given to temples on the 'foreign coin in the collection' principle, so the fact that they are commonly found may mean no more than that administrators used them, and even copied them, in order to correspond financially with the men-in-the-fields, but, when they got home the the men-in the-fields lost interest in the coins and they entered the archaeological record without great efforts being made to regain them.

Nonsense, you don't throw money away.

Well there is not much that you can do with French aluminium francs except, give them to the children to play shops with; and worn halfpennies of George VI are little in demand even by coin collectors who will accumulate almost anything.If these coins are what the state gives out, but will not receive back, for example in taxes, the unless you and your neighbour band together to say we will give our own value to these things whatever the state thinks, there is little else to do with them. The end of the administration will bring the almost inevitable and immediate end to their use.

So the examination of coin finds scattered over an ancient site and recovered by excavation and field walking, and their interpretation is not a simple clear cut matter, but methods are developing and some agreement is being reached. But surely hoards of Roman coins, so far not mentioned lead to clear cut stories? Indeed, but what price the stories? Here we reach the dilemma of Hearts and Hedgehogs which is the real genesis of this book, its format, style and episodic acidity. This dilemma was all set to become a part of common parlance on hoards in general when it was a vital part of a chapter on hoards which I wrote for my book on Coinage in Roman Britain. The first draft, which I regarded as the text-to-be-printed-with-a-little-tidying-up, did not, in general please, and a lot needed doing to make it acceptable. One major sticking point which I gathered through my intermediary no amount of tidying up would have made suitable for the G.B.P. was the lovely piece 'On Hearts and Hedgehogs'. I was under contract to deliver, but I did not wish to change what I had written, so I spent a rather sad Christmas holidays writing a completely different book on the same subject with the same line drawings and a total ban on Hearts and Hedgehogs. This was pronounced acceptable and all has so far gone well, and the book is out, but it left the firm conviction that no editor or publisher was ever again going to be in a

position to change what I had written if it
mattered to me. What is this phrase that I
am determined to bring into being as a part
of the English language?

The problem is the interpretation of
coin hoards. Coin hoards are groups of
coins found together in a concentration
distinguishable from that in the surrounding area of casual coin loss. This definition includes coin deposits in wells and
fountains and other sacred places, so, as a
recent commentator has pointed out we
ought to keep these deposits in mind
whenever we interpret coin hoards. Usually however their archaeological context
is unknown, sometimes when they are
found under controlled conditions there
seems to be no surrounding information of
the same date as the hoard of any sort. So
we have a pot of coins, never, well once in
a thousand, of gold, sometimes of silver
and sometimes of brass, copper, bronze or
whatever. Once the hoard has been published it becomes a statistic, and once
several hoards have been published people
cannot resist trying to wring information
from them.

They are so romantic aren't they?
No.

**But think of the person who bur-
ied it, and why he never came back.
Think of those invading armies,
times of unrest, raiding pirates, and
civil war; the blood, the guts, the
smell of charred houses drifting
gently down the valley as the un-
milked cows moo urgently and the
pig which got away limps past on
three legs.**

Alright, lets give two interpretations of
a coin hoard, and you agree that the one

wins which fits most carefully with the
material record.

**Of course I am an archaeologist
after all.**

The hoard was there because its owner
lay breathless at the crossroads, his heart
torn from his twitching body to provide a
warm snack for raiding pirates. No, it was
there because Covdob the Briton buried
his coins between the Beech tree and the
Hawthorn and tried to memorize which
ones, as there were several of each around,
and then got muddled in the number of
paces because his wife's cousin came that
evening with a jar of potent mead and
filled his reeling head on the number of
paces his pet hedgehog had crawled for a
bet.

**Really, I thought you were going
to make a sensible point.**

I have.

**You have not, you have put for-
ward two rather silly ideas which
bear no relationship to Roman Britain or the intelligent interpretation
of coin hoards.**

Ah. Could you show me the points at
which you can disprove either of my two
interpretations as to why that hoard was
buried and never recovered?

**There is no point in trying to dis-
cuss a load of fanciful nonsense.**

But could you just explain to me why
it is fanciful nonsense compared with so
and so's published interpretation which
talks about coastal raids by the Saxons in
the third century and the trouble and disturbance they caused, as shown for instance by coin hoards.

**Well, his interpretation is seri-
ous.**

So why does it make it more likely than Hearts and Hedgehogs?

Well archaeology is serious, and at least we have heard of Saxon raids when we have no information at all on your nonsense.

So any interpretation is to be preferred if it is serious rather than light hearted? And any interpretation is to be preferred if it works within historically mentioned categories?

Well both of those are so clearly true they hardly need stating; of course a serious interpretation is better than a frivolous one; and of course it is better to work with something we know about.

I thought that new novel by Slodge rather good didn't you?

We have got to have some standards in our interpretation.

Especially the second chapter in which he showed how degraded life in the Victorian Workhouse had become by 1870.

It wasn't 1870, it was 1868, and it is almost certainly wrong. For instance......

What about the material and its interpretation though? The virtue of both Hearts and Hedgehogs is that it is immediately clear that the hoard consisting of 264 coins in a pot of perfectly normal, if superior, late third century type, buried in a squarish hole cut in natural clay protected by a stone placed on top of it, otherwise with no ancient affiliations or information, contains no information whatever that can possibly decide between the one explanation or the other. The trouble, or beauty, depending on how you look at it, is that this incapacity then spreads to every other possible explanation so that it is a general rule, to which of course there may one day be the occasional exception, that a coin hoard as such, buried in antiquity with no discernible material context bears no information on why it was buried or the reason for its survival as a hoard, or therefore its non-recovery by its burier. There are two important points here; first we can only deal with those hoards which were not recovered; second we may develop methods to discuss how hoards were put together, but on reflection, the reason why the burier never came back is in most cases nothing to do with the hoard, so not only can we not detect the reason from the hoard, but the reason is nothing to do with the hoard and therefore will never be deducible.

The non-recovery of coin hoards leads us further down the path of unknowingness. There are presumably two groups of coin deposits; one such as the contents of the shrine and spring at Bath, or Coventina's Well on Hadrian's Wall, are deposits that everyone at the time knew about, many contributed to, but few, if any, decided to recover. They were contributed to the goddess and, once hers, remained both physically and psychically immovable. Neil Aitchinson has rightly made the point that since we know of these obvious votive deposits we ought to watch out for other less obvious votive deposits in contexts which will communicate to us less clearly. So some coins were deposited or buried with no intention to recover. My feeling is that this is the minority of our documented coin hoards, but I cannot prove it, and it could be the majority. But it is likely that a number of groups of coins were put together in a pot or a bag or a holder and buried as a temporary measure for safe keeping with an intent and wish to go back and recover them in due course. When the mother-in-law had gone home, or the Saxon raiders were cleared out of the region. Mothers-in-law get 10/10 for likely existence; Saxon raiders get a grudging 5/10. There are also the bags and purses and boxes which were lost. They fell into the straw of the mead-hall, and no one noticed them when the straw was forked out on to the manure heap, or they were put down for a moment in the quarry and fell behind a pile of rubble and were buried. Where there was intention to recover we are dealing with a very odd sample which is 100% made up of failure. And in addition to that, the failure has probably no connection with the contents of the hoard.

The putting together of the hoard is a more interesting matter because really detailed work can make some headway here. The best example so far is the hoard of gold and silver and precious objects found at Beaurains near Arras in France. Dr. Bastien in his very detailed study has been able to work out an enormous amount about the hoard and the hoarder, but this is exceptional.

But if non-recovered hoards are dated and provenanced then surely we can use them to tell us about conditions at that time and in that place?

Maybe. But, again, there are very stringent rules which must be obeyed to get firm information out of the hoards, and few people have followed those rules to date. If you want to point to a burst of non-recovery of coin hoards in X at time Y then the the minimum you have to do is show

that the pattern of hoarding changed both before and after, and that the pattern of hoarding is particular to that area and does not occur either side. So you must do a good geographical study to show what area is afflicted by non-recovery, where the limits are, and what the wider pattern of non-recovery is at that time. Ideally this will result in a map of coin hoards of date Y, with a detectable clustering in place X. Then you must study the coin hoards of place X for the time Y-50 to Y+50, perhaps in 20 year periods, and show that Y-10 to Y+10 is a peak among a fairly uniform distribution. This is really no more than a specialized example of 'Dealing with material' in which you have to show that there is something unusual which demands explanation before you start explaining it.

The other problem about coin hoards and the diagrams to which they give rise is also a general one, that of the uselessness of nearly all distribution maps. I am not worrying at the moment about the fact that distribution maps usually reflect the distribution of workers in the fields, intelligent 19th C. local doctors with an eye for archaeology, or whatever. I am worried by the fact that no map that I have seen to date gives me any idea of what to expect. If I have no idea what to expect then I cannot estimate the importance of what is presented - nor, be it noted, can anyone else, they just pretend. This is another detailed example of 'Material': material can only be judged against a background. On a distribution map I first want to know which of the areas of the map are unlikely find spots. Maps of coin hoards have a strange hole in North Wales; strange that is to anyone who does not know the topography of Snowdonia, for even if you toil up a mountain there is rarely enough soil to bury a 12 inch high pot well out of sight. If there is a hoard half way up Snowdon then it deserves special mention because it is flying in the face of likelihood. The Snowdon area, for coin hoards at least ought to be shaded to show that it is an unlikely find-spot. The other problem is clustering. Of course this is a whole subject in its own right, but as a start I find any distribution map useless which does not give me the overall density of finds and use symbols to show higher then average and lower than average, and make some attempt to tell me how likely it is that these variations from the average occurred by chance. In other words, is that really a cluster, or simply a perfectly acceptable higher density given the overall distribution. Till this is done I refuse to discuss most maps of coin hoards because I do not know if there is anything worth discussing. The one exception is Prof. Anne Robertson's map of coin hoards which end with coins of Honorius in BAR 4 which show a clear cut-off across the centre of the country. Here is something to explain which needs no mathematical demonstration.

Coin

Countryside, settlement and TCT's

When we were in the countryside proper we fastened on the farmstead as the basic unit of existence. We allowed the possibility of links between farmsteads, socially or administratively, and saw that this might, or might not, mean that the farms clustered together or stayed dispersed. Villages have cropped up from time to time, though, again, a village is not necessarily all in the same place at the same time, or nucleated. There may be centres of dispersed villages, but these will presumably have a purpose and since different purposes will be different, the different reasons for centres will lead to different centres. Thus the temple or shrine may be the religious centre, but it may be on a hill top, or on the edge of the 'village' territory; the mead-hall may be the social centre for drinkers, but this will be where the mead-man lives; he might have good reason to be equidistant between his customers, but since he does not know who his customers will be till he sets up his vats and barrels, there is a circular problem here. The man who collects the census tax may be at the house near the Blasted Oak on the fourth Jovesday in each alternate month.

Stop hedging. Are villages in Britain between AD 1 and AD 450 nucleated or not?

Well you tell me how to recognize a dispersed village from archaeology, and I will tell you the answer. At least some settlements were very like nucleated villages in the Roman influenced times in Britain. Interesting that you should introduce hedges because that is one of my specialties.

No, another time, get on with the settlement pattern.

Why did some settlements grow beyond the expected aggregation of farmhouses? What is 'expected'? Well there is a limit to the number of people who live in a village in one place at a given time, a nucleated village, who also farm land, without giving themselves an unacceptably long walk to their fields. If we stick to our generous minimum 50 acres for a basic free household then the 640 acres of a circular mile will allow say 12 households with 40 acres for the living part of the village, without anyone having to walk much more than a mile to any of his fields. If we take four circular miles and deform them slightly to meet at the village point, then provided households have their land on one side of the village only we could have a 48 household village without major commuting problems. This might give a population of 200 to 250 people, which is a good modern village size, provided it is demographically normal and not like a modern Cotswold village, a geriatric ghetto.

Why get larger? From my own inclinations and understanding I am totally unable to explain this. True, the population may grow naturally, but the surplus should be sent away. I suppose it is a direct result of greed, laziness and lust for power. When large numbers of people congregate in one place a hierarchy develops which gives those at the top a wider range of selfishnesses in which to indulge than in smaller communities. When others see these they sometimes want to attempt the same things and they gravitate to the nuclei in hope. The fact that they end up at the bottom of the heap in worse state than they started seldom acts as a deterrent to others and they therefore act as fuel to the machinations of the greedy. The people at the top always become lazy, the exceptions simply act to point up the rule, and they enjoy telling other people what to do, and having the implicit power to make people do what they are told. Trouble comes, as always with power when it is challenged and has to be made explicit, for this makes it far less enjoyable. This is why all power should be challenged on every possible occasion, to bring it out, wherever possible into the open, to get it documented, and hence defined, and to decrease the enjoyment of it. Some archaeologists actually believe that social stratification is essential for the production of anything above the artistic rank of a kitchen table, and at least one has written a book to prove it. The fact that he is a very pleasant person, extremely helpful and unselfish, does nothing to mitigate the loathsomeness of the views. Hence the relevance of this outburst to this point in the narrative, for I will not accept under any circumstances that the beginning of TCT's in Britain marks the origins of British civilization, and their premature death in the 5th C. makes a Dark Age when culture went underground. This is to fall into the incredibly simple, but stupid trap, of insisting that whatever happened **had** to happen; that because things DID happen in this way that is the only way they ever **could** happen. And anyway in this instance it is just not true, for the 'culture of Roman Britain is, artistically at least, inferior to the culture of the Lindisfarne Gospels and the enamelled hanging bowls

which grew after the tension between Roman and British art had relaxed. Since I value the Lindisfarne Gospels I will recognize that they could not have been produced without a division of labour so that some brothers with five thumbs on each hand milked the cows and fed the calves to the right size to be good folios, and other brothers prepared the skins, others cooked the food, and others illuminated the codices. If the brothers were true to their calling then this was not a hierarchy, but a division of labour, and I find nothing objectionable in it. Since the town can probably not be created without subjugation I always find it objectionable.

But however objectionable larger concentrations of people or power are they did exist, and therefore they have to be looked at. There are villages, which are clusters of people rather than concentrations, and these people are at a density which still allows them to be basically a collection of farmers. The things at the top of the scale are then nucleated walled settlements which I have called TCT's. Here the density may be too high to allow everyone to be a farmer and, if so, this suggests the existence of service industries, administrators and other social parasites. In between come other settlements, walled or unwalled, densely packed or almost dispersed. The only other blots on the landscape are the TCV's, farmsteads, perhaps, which outgrew their simple form and opted for a Romanized veneer of architecture. All these types grow into one another and there is no point in trying to insert artificial divisions between them. We can add for good measure similar settlements with basic religious or military affiliations; that is, temples with associated settlements,

Set

and what from their architecture and bricks and mortar are called forts. One main reason for not insisting on dividing these into firm categories is the simple point that we do not always know which is which.

There is not too much doubt about farmsteads. But there is extreme doubt about this nonsensical category villa. Some farmsteads grow into TCV's so the dedicated type cruncher is forced into the impossible position of deciding that phases 1 to 5 of this site represent a farmstead, but phases 6 to 8 represent a villa, while phase 9 is only just a farmstead and certainly not a villa. This is pointless nonsense for the classification leads nowhere, and the vital test of all classification is whether it helps or hinders. But some TCV's have been described as Healing Shrines - Graham Webster on Chedworth - while others take the same villa to be a prototypical villa - Roger Goodburn on Chedworth. And some villas like Gatcombe (according to Branigan) are really small towns (according to Cunliffe). And even worse some obvious villas such as Barnsley Park (Webster, this time **for** villas) are really hamlets (my phrasing of J T Smith). Nettleton (Wedlake) is a village with a temple, or a temple with an associated settlement. Yes it does matter whether the raison d'être is as service for the temple or as a self-sufficient village in which a temple happens to have roosted. For instance, what happens to the life of the village when the temple declines? And Portchester is a fort, well (Cunliffe) at times. Some phases are military and others appear to be civilian. But if the fourth century fort is garrisoned by men living in a demographically normal community, also inside the fort, how do you sort out which is which and when.

The Deductive wing of archaeology who want our understanding to grow outwards from the texts (they would say, what is already known, I would not agree) point to the TCT's as a better state of things. We **know** the tribal centres of Roman Britain because they are written down. This works quite well in that these TCT's correspond with some of the largest walled blots on the landscape. But there are some small tribal capitals which seem to cover less ground than some large blots which no one has ever called a tribal capital. But because the Roman administration declared that these were to be second class towns when it set out the province they must be dealt with as second class towns by modern archaeologists. Nonsense. This is to let the administrative tail wag the material dog. I see why it happens today, because that is what all except dedicated anti-administrators want, but I still object strongly to both the backward looking and modern approach. Administration, like classification, is there to facilitate, not to impede, and we are letting Roman administration impede the development of real Roman archaeology (Comment 2: John Mann doubts this. I would remove it if most students of Roman Britain were not such bad archaeologists and were not prone to prostrate themselves in adoration of any historical fact or snippet. As things stand it only needs one Latin author to say that one "town" is different from another in some legal way for Roman Britonists to enshrine this as a basic unalterable fact in their dealings with the material; when the material, looked at without this accretion, might turn out to be totally similar on both sites. In a way then

I accept that it is not the knowledge of Roman administration which perverts real archaeology, but the practitioners of unreal archaeology.) We would probably all agree that once we have left the comfortable categories of Colonia, Municipium and Civitas Capital the lower end of the town spectrum is a continuum which grades through the small town into the large village and so on down (or up, as the case may be).

One interesting point is what we think the difference between a village and whatever is next up the list, town or TCT, is. As I have explained I refuse to use the word town as applied to Roman Britain because it brings in so much lumber with it. People are, or seem to be, incapable of defining a town in Roman Britain as whatever a larger nucleated settlement in Roman Britain was, that is, empirically and by inspection, and insist on bringing in their own childhood hangups about what towns ought to be or ought not to be, just as I would if I did not make my dislike of the things explicit. So I insist on working with TCT's which may, or may not have certain qualities and habits, but these have to be defined and attributed by inspection, not by individual psychology. I have already hinted that a village loses its innocence the moment that it collects social parasites in the form of people not gainfully employed by the production of food, clothing, shelter, or other human material necessities (Comment 3: John Mann again saying, I think, that such overt Golden Ageism prevents the attainment of a real view of the past. Yes, the Golden Ageism is so overt that it is clearly put on and I do know that I am doing it, and that the Iron Age was not a Garden of Eden. But there has to be some mental set; this is mine, which I know, and any reader knows, IS only a mental set, so I think it can do little harm). The existence of a working blacksmith or a parasitic priest does not stop a village being a village; we can allow the addition of those people necessary to the life of a human farming community. The trouble comes when instead of one farmer doubling as Blacksmith and another as part time priest the professional sets up to minister to the iron needs of several villages, and so creates a centre. The priest of course may already have done this, or had it done for him by having a temple on a hilltop between several villages. These foci grow. In the odd moments between making ploughs and hoes to order the blacksmith may make ornamental gates or door furniture and these will then be for sale at the focus but not elsewhere. If a teacher of Latin decides to move into a locality he might decide that the Blacksmith's shop is enough of a drawing power to settle beside him, and the attraction to the focus increases. Once Latin is ensconced the fringe parasites of the administration, those who have contracts to squeeze taxes out of the rural population, and those who are doing groundwork for Census or dabbling in law, may take root. What was once a respectable village becomes the haunt of numbers of highly undesirable, and respectable - the two often go remarkably together - inhabitants. They are undesirable, just as other foreigners in communities are undesirable, because they have their own collective good at heart, rather than the good of the fundamental community. The village has taken on another tier which is partly supported by the people in that one village, and partly by the inhabitants of the other villages around. Somewhere along the line, as this cancer grows, a balance tips, and it may be when one can no longer talk about the 'majority' of the workers being directly involved in farming in its wider sense; when service industries make up more than 50% of the adult male population, or when service industries are in a majority over the workers. At this point we have what I would call an administrative village, or a potential town. But the town has not been created, and this is the mistake that both the Roman administration, and their modern followers make. A town cannot be made overnight, neither need a potential town always develop into a real town, because the fundamental requirement of urban life, or town-wanting may be absent.

Starting the other way round, from the most tangled densely populated end, the Roman administration arrived in Britain with towns firmly in mind. They could not help it because they had been brought up on it, or at least converted to such unnatural practices at a tender age. The towns of the Mediterranean seem to have worked - judging both by the deficient real archaeology, as opposed to the ruin-stripping practiced by all expatriate teams masquerading as archaeologists, and the written sources which emanate from them. The Collingwood on Aristotle quote is so well known that it does not need quoting again. Those who do not know it must read Collingwood anyway, so they will find out. Classical Greeks and Romans advertised the fact that they grew out of cities and worked the surrounding countryside, re-

treating to their city for rest, relaxation and civilization. The fact, if it is one, that they believed they needed towns in order to live the good life presumably goes a long way to support the towns in times of economic or political adversity. The conviction, harnessed to the continuing life of towns even when under difficulties, gives a perfectly good reason for the Mediterranean man to assume that towns are a fact of life. Faced with an under-organized Britain the administrator who has spent time in the Mediterranean area and administered through Mediterranean towns would naturally try to support any move towards towns in Britain. With only a flicker of British interest to help the process along, the administrative centre, which the Mediterranean man would expect to be a town, was inevitable. To what extent this foreign transplant ever took root ant grew in Britain is highly problematic because we are always dealing with stones and mortar, while the real town is rooted in the need and belief of its inhabitants. The town cannot have taken root in Britain until the Briton came to think that towns were natural, and without them life would be unlivable. Such ideas and concepts simply cannot be judged from archaeology direct; I doubt whether even indirect interpretations are of the slightest validity. Since I judge much about the problem of town life in Britain from what happened after the third century I will leave this subject for the moment with the statement of a firm belief that while administrative units, in classicizing facades certainly existed in Britain these never became real towns and hence can only be called Things Called Towns.

It seems to be only these TCT's, which are, collectively, the high status towns such as Municipia, if any, Coloniae; Gloucester, Colchester, Lincoln and York, and Civitas or Tribal capitals such as Wroxeter, Cirencester, Verulamium, Silchester or Leicester to mention only a token few, which are planned from the beginning with a rectangular street grid on the Roman model. All other settlements were allowed to grow up in ribbon or straggly development however large they were finally to become. This suggests to me that the former are the settlements which the administration pushed for, and perhaps were even willing to lend expertise for planning and setting out, and anything else was left to local enterprise. It says absolutely nothing about the inhabitants two hundred years later, their social status, command of Latin, relationship to the administration and the army, participation in the world of the empire, and so on. There is no reason at all why people in AD 350 who lived in or near a grid-plan town should be any different, better, or worse than those who lived in or near a straggly town. The only point I am making at the present is that the Roman administration seems to have taken an interest in the setting out of some settlements, perhaps one per tribe, but not others. It is therefore reasonable to assume that theses centres, at least at first offered some attractions or necessities or compulsions to the man-in-the-field. And this was one of their major problems for they were very widely spaced as foci for the fairly densely populated British lowlands. The centre of Southern Britain was spread between Cirencester to the West, Verulamium to the East, Silch-

ester or Winchester to the South and Leicester or Wroxeter to the North. We do not know **whether** the man-in-the-field ever had to go to one of these centres, or whether, in the absence of compulsion, he ever wanted to go to such places, but, if he did it could have been a substantial upheaval. This means that since it seems likely that from at least the Iron Age man had ceased to be truly independent and become interdependent there had to be other centres between the Administrative centres, for more down to earth meetings and exchange.

This is the point at which our two approaches, from the tangled end simpler, and from the farmstead more complicated, meet. The different levels of compulsion, need and want, three very different things, must have given rise to different networks, and these different strands of movement and meeting might or might not have used the same places. It makes sense to us for the County Court to be in the same place as a large shopping centre, the place from which you get your car-tax, and the place to which you pay one set of monetary demands. On the other hand it would be rather pointless to get your bread and potatoes there, for there is so much else to get and do, and bread and potatoes are far more widely available. The trouble is that from Britain in the Roman period we have no information on County Courts, carttax, where the markets were with pepper and silks from the East, or where tax was collected; we only know the material which tells us where building materials come from, where pottery was made and marketed, and which animals were eaten. Given this major problem the approach which Ian Hodder brought in from Geog-

Set

raphy should have been welcomed with
open arms as a possible way forward. True
to form Prof. Frere has looked at it, sometimes hard, and accepted some parts and
dislikes others; but at least has discussed it
and argued with it, even if it does not in the
end contribute a great amount to his way of
looking at things. The general view is one
of total apathy which expresses so well the
horribly deductive and perscriptive world
from which I want to escape. The Hodder
approach is neither obviously right or
wrong; but it is obviously a different approach to the problem of how our bits and
pieces left over from Roman Britain might
fit together which, through its empirical
and analytical approach offers a way out of
the textual stew and solid dumpling of
heaped up fact.

If we do put things on a map, and look
for a pattern then there certainly seems to
be a non-random spacing in the grid-plan
towns. Between these there are usually
middle sized settlements, and the pattern
goes down to stopping places and route
stages. Below the level of smaller settlement it may well be that local conditions
have much more effect than any economic
or social forces. Two Ale Houses may be
better spaced out to catch different customers, but there is no reason against, and
may be some reason for, two farms being
side by side instead of in the geometric
centre of their respective fields. A hill or
a valley or a marsh may well throw the
local pattern way out of line, by a matter of
one or two miles, but this same deflection
will scarcely be apparent at the scale of
tribal centres and seventy mile separa-
tions.

I am not sure that much more can be
said, in positive fashion about towns and
the larger settlements. Most of what is
usually said is simple piling up of facts
which gets no one anywhere and is a waste
of time compiling and reading. TCT's
have streets, some have drains, some have
sewers, some have piped water supplies.
Some have amphitheatres but we have no
idea whatsoever a) why they were built,
though the army may be involved in several early cases, b) how they were used, or
even if they were used much, and c) what,
if anything went on in them. It may be no
accident that one of the only records of the
use of the amphitheatre, or Bull Ring, at
Cirencester, apart from tobogganing in the
snow, is a visit from one of the Wesley
brothers in the religious enthusiasm of the
18th C. It was in an amphitheatre somewhere in North Africa that Lucius snatched
some roses off a girl in a procession in
honour of Isis, chewed them with enjoyment, and became human again. Some
have theatres, but only that at Verulamium
has been fully excavated, and few if any
seem to be still performing twice nightly in
the fourth century, at least towards the
later part. Did anyone ever perform Roman
plays there, or was it a much more interesting diet of music-hall type mime with the
ladies in the front row tutting loudly and
enjoying every moment? This is a nonsense question which has nothing to do
with archaeology. It is fun to ask, but it
should probably not be allowed because it
suggests, with the contrast of Plautus and
mime, that they were theatres in our sense,
when they might just as well have been for
rituals even more boring than Church of
England Matins. No, I take that back, it is

Set

a nasty slur on the life of Romano-British religion.

Formal buildings included halls, meeting places, open spaces and temples. Again there comes the problem of interpretation for there is little more that can be said at the moment about a temple other than an account of its shape and a guess at its date of construction and date of last use. This brings the archaeology of towns back to the level of stamp collecting: We have a temple of Nodens; Oh, I have two, swap you one for a temple of Isis. Baths are a little more hopeful in that they show an initial substantial amount of money and effort to build them, and a continued interest in bathing to keep them going, for water supply and drainage pose problems which need to be continuously overcome. One problem with baths is the proof that they were still in use as Baths, rather than as convenient large heated buildings which could be sub-let for a multitude of uses. The emphasis ought to be on the water supply and drainage because here at least there is the chance of seeing flowing water, or not, at different dates and phases.

All big towns, and some smaller towns, and some little towns, have walls. We cannot know why; we can only know when, within the usual fuzzy limits of archaeological dating, say half a century if we are lucky. We cannot know why because that is a concept, it is not recorded, and material cannot tell us about concepts. So it is absolutely pointless for anyone to pretend that he or she has proved why town walls were built. Each person may give a current preferred hypothesis, and students may read the various hypotheses and judge between them, but it all boils down to opinion based on prejudice. Some military minded people say the walls are for defence; other military minded people say they could never have been properly manned without large numbers of troops and a lot of equipment, and it is most unlikely to have been worth the outlay. Others say that they are status symbols by which Britain had to keep up with other provinces; certainly there is virtually no evidence to date that any town wall in Britain was attacked and damaged. Most of the evidence relates either to faulty building in the first place or old age.

The dating of town walls is a very good example, or extremely bad example, of the unreasonable mature of much of archaeology in Britain to date. Richard Goodchild, years ago, in one sentence, undermined the whole idea of showing that town walls were built in datable plans of campaign for various political motives. Mike Jarrett, more recently in a very moderate article pointed out that archaeological reasoning is such that we can never gain the precision necessary to talk realistically about walls built at the same time and for the same reason. But this has had virtually no effect on what people want to do, and, despite clear demonstration that what they are doing is an exercise in fantasy they have persisted in pretending that it is high scholarship. Although the proof against any possibility of showing from archaeology, either the reason for building town walls, or showing the contemporaneity of the building of several town walls, people still talk about power struggles at the end of the second century as leading to the building of walls, and the fact that their dates at present span the second century and more show that really they all belong to the year XYZ. As always through these notes some people may feel that I am making a vicious attack on them, because they once wrote an article or a chapter on the dating of town walls. In fact that leaves few senior archaeologists not to feel hurt. But the fact that I have not quoted an exact date, when there are so many to chose from shows that I am not getting at any individual person, but at the whole atmosphere; if you have ever given in to this illogical atmosphere, then I judge you to have been at fault, but I have no person in mind when I write this, I have before me a nebulous idea which I would like to think is gone for ever.

A further addition to town walls are towers. This adds just one more grouse to my list before I turn to more congenial topics. Towers demonstrate most clearly the time-lag in archaeology, and its insulation from the outside world. Someone at some stage called theses towers which are about 20-30 feet square, outside, bastions, and in many circles this name has persisted. Someone else said that bastions were added to town walls as platforms for heavy stone or bolt-throwing equipment - ballistae. Several writers and thinkers have pointed out first that the towers are not large enough to get the large machines into, and, once in, give no room for manoeuvre or aim, and, second, that if you mean the hand held ballistae, then you do not need towers built onto the wall to accommodate them. They may be there to give a good cross fire along the face of the wall so that attackers, for whom there is no material evidence whatsoever, can be hit if they get close to the wall. The most likely

ammunition seems to be stones of various sizes. Once published, for example in the CBA London Conference volume, this ought to clear the air; but even in the conference volume people are still wittering on about machines and ballistae. They are also devoted to bastions. The point here is that those who talk about defences at all dates have a fairly clear idea of what a bastion is, and it is a projection forward from a defensive wall of considerable size - a fighting platform for many men and, by then (I think) guns. I think if it in terms of a bastion I noted in Rhodes which contained a tennis court and ornamental garden; that gives the scale easily. Now there is no reason why people devoted to discussing Roman Britain should not use such terms as they wish, and I often do this sort of thing myself, but when talking to a general public about the development of fortifications in general, it is unhelpful not to point out that the word bastion in Roman Britain is being used in an anachronistic and highly idiomatic way. This is usually taken to be nit-picking.

We have always had bastions, we know they were for artillery, get lost.

Certainly, but you now know why I shall continue to savage the words and their perpetrators wherever I find them.

Let us leave the noise and bustle of the non-existent towns in Roman Britain for the countryside. Ought we to cast a glance, on the way, to the villas and farmsteads which have been found inside TCT's? Simon Esmonde Cleary, in his work on suburbs, casts doubt on the interpretation of these buildings, such as the Beeches House at Cirencester, as farms, so we

Set

ought to open the record up, if we cannot set it straight. He pretends to be eminently open-minded and anxious and worried about the fact that excavators and commentators have jumped too precipitously to conclusions, for there really is no direct evidence that theses buildings, inside town walls, were farms. He does not say that they could not be farms, or even that they are not farms, just that there is not enough evidence to call them farms. On exactly the same evidence I think they were clearly farms. Which points out that we are both arguing from our basic philosophies of towns. Since I know that towns never really existed it is clear to me that large flourishing buildings, with plans just like farms in the countryside, sited perfectly to exploit the surrounding countryside, were farms because there is virtually nothing else in my way of thinking for them to be. Simon still believes in towns, so he does not want to see the countryside encroaching on the town, so he undermines suggestions that these are farms. Both my bold assertion and his scholarly caution are fair weapons in the war, so long as everyone realizes that what is happening is not examination of the evidence and careful debate about facts, but broadsides from overall positions of thought which extend beyond the bricks, or rather stones, and mortar of the actual material. To have two sides on any question in Roman archaeology is a luxury which must be a good thing and must be tended carefully so that neither side is ever allowed to win. But it is not a question of **who is right**, but **why does he think like this**?

With relief we can do the Roman thing, shake the town from our minds and return to the tranquility of the countryside, to our farm, our villa, our estate, where the bailiff has kept all working in our absence, and where we can be kind to orphan children, buy the odd piece of land, though this will lead later on to contradictions, and go out to our equal friends and receive their visits. We know that the buildings of the countryside are farms, and since they are farms they must be surrounded by the land that they farm, and the extent of the land will fairly obviously be dictated by the size of the central building. In most of what you read about the countryside of Roman Britain this synopsis holds good. Yet some of the people who have written along these lines, knowing that there is trouble in store, would begin to hedge some of theses statements. I am afraid that the countryside will prove just as peevish and acrimonious a battlefield as the town; no, I am delighted.

We start off, if we are deductive and want to be told by the Ancients what to think, with Pliny and his letters which form a main plank in any discussion of how the Roman viewed the countryside. While Pliny **was** in Bithynia, though we do not here much of his villa there, he was **not** in Britain. He is talking first in literary terms, and that might even act to the detriment of truth in the sense of what an independent observer would have seen. It is even possible that Pliny as a writer would have shaped a letter with a higher truth in mind than 'what actually happened'. What ought to have happened, what form dictated should have happened, were to him, as to the modern novelist or even the producer of television 'documentaries', an equally important form of truth.

Set

If the letter started out with an upward swing and a walk round the estate it might need to end with a downward swing to balance the literary form, and the fact that the route home, plotted out on a contour map was uphill, just did not matter. Secondly Pliny was right at the top of the career structure, a point which very few Britons, so far as our evidence goes, either achieved, or, just possibly, wanted to achieve. He was the correspondent of a sometimes exasperated Emperor, governor of an Asian province, of course he needed a farm manager or bailiff to see to things while he was away. But that does not mean that the owner of a villa, whatever that was, in Britain, was a man in a similar position, and if you give the Briton a bailiff you have to explain why. Reference to Pliny is no good for he is not of use for Britain. There is no evidence at all in Britain for widespread Bailiffs. But if, as Jeremy Evans has pointed out, we did not have one or two texts on Gaul in the fourth century, would we know from any other means that there were bailiffs in Gaul? I suspect that there are inscriptions in Gaul which mention bailiffs, but I am not wasting my time trying to find out. The fact that there are no inscriptions about bailiffs in Britain is, of course not evidence against them because inscriptions in Britain are so few and far between, and uninformative. But until someone shows that they did exist in Britain I refuse to have them in my scheme of things. For one thing, since there is no evidence of farm owners continually going to TCT's, there is no need of them.

What about absentee landlords or landladies? Malcolm Todd and I once had an exchange of two or three sentences in which he came off definitely best by a piece of brilliance. He had given a lecture in which owners of British villas figured. Inevitably the lady Melania, who owned land in many provinces and even in Britain, came into the story. I objected that this was to use one solitary piece of evidence hopelessly to unbalance the picture. Malcolm pointed out that it was not unbalanced since 100% of the evidence mentioned absentee owners. I obviously gave in. But absentee owners, and we do know that there was one at least, do not in any way predicate absentee farmers. The person in Italy who owns land in Britain presumably has a tenant, and the likelihood is that the tenant will be on the spot, or that his sub-tenant will be. In other words, I prefer to think that the person who is paying the basic rent for the land, if he does not own it, is there getting a return on his money. How far up a chain of sub-tenants this goes before it gets to the tenant-in-chief, or person who actually pays money to the owner we need not and cannot know. Enough for us, that in the majority of cases the person living in the farm had control over it to the extent of managing it in such a way as to pay either the rent, or the appropriate taxes, so he, or she, is a farmer.

But not everyone who lived in a house in the countryside needs to have been a farmer. And not every house in the countryside need be surrounded by the land off which the money for building and maintaining the house came. In the TCT called Cirencester, or Corinium, there might well have been building firms, just as there are today. And someone who made a killing on the new fashion for stone houses in the second half of the second century AD probably wanted to leave the firm on his 50th birthday, and his son could well take over. He would do his last job, before becoming a sleeping partner or consultant, by building himself a rather nice house with good appointments on a small piece of land, say 20 acres, which his brother-in-law willingly sold him for a rather inflated price. At a distance of five miles outside the town he was free from any disturbance, but near enough to ride in for a meeting or a dinner if anything important or attractive offered. He planted a few fruit trees, had a patch of woodland for fuel, some grazing for his horses, a cow or two for milk, butter and cheese, and let one or two fields to the small farmer next door for grazing his sheep. My point of this eminently reasonable scenario is that such a well appointed country house would play absolute havoc with any simplistic spatial analysis, with any attempt to tie houses to land by size and prosperity, with dividing up the landscape to provide money for the houses. A similar case could be made without any special pleading, for a well-appointed house in the countryside which was built and maintained by the yield of farming, but not farming of the land around that point. Thus, someone who had a small farm house which no modern archaeologists would term a villa, though the lawyer who drew up their title deeds did, inherited some land in East Anglia. Having been born and brought up in the Cotswolds the thought of living on a wind swept billiard-table, if uneven in places, filled them with horror, and they found a local tenant for their corn-lands who would pay well for

the opportunity to enter the corn trade while they could carry on their small-holding on the hillside. Naturally they used their rents coming from wheat growing in East Anglia to update their farm-house, so that the modern archaeologist joined the Roman lawyer in calling it a villa, yet such a house could never have been built on the proceeds of the land around it. Absentee owners therefore cut both ways, and just as we might have to reckon with their absence from a farm of high rank, so we might have to reckon with their presence elsewhere.

All this trouble comes, of course, when people have more money than they need. The basic smallholder, to whom we gave the luxurious free farm of 50 acres, could, if he worked hard and to good effect, feed and cloth his family, keep a good basic house in good repair, pay his taxes, perhaps have his children taught some language and ideas and literature, and buy the occasional luxury such as soft shoes, a silk scarf, or a thick wool cloak. But he would probably never join the league who worried about whether they could afford a mosaic this year, to keep up with the Lucii, or those who saved madly so that their son could be led astray and get into debt at the University of Lyon, or who took out a loan to send their daughter to distant relations at Arles, where she might with equal likelihood be ruined or married by an upstart oafish Gaul. We ought probably to be aware that our 50 acre landholder may be one of the first obvious people, going upwards, in the archaeological record, but that there will be a whole number of people below him who were not so fortunate in material things. All theses people may

Set

well have had a good and proper life. The trouble I referred to can afflict the most innocent family by the simplest of means, and it results form the concentration of goods above the level of need.

Thus our happy householder may have had a brother who died, whose children were weakly and died, and whose wife, in desperation, suggested that they throw the two 50 acre farms together and hire some extra workers with the surplus money of her share. The answer ought to have been No. She ought to have moved in with her brother-in-law and given her farm to that very pleasant and able farm-hand down the road with five children, as an incentive to him for the future, and as a reward for the way that he helped her husband when he was failing. Failing individual good sense there ought to have been a social pressure which every so often made sure that all the inhabitants of the village came back to a position of rough equality. Let us assume that this was a sick community who let people accumulate more than they needed. After two generations the descendents of our Happy Householder had changed into grasping climbers, and they had got control of four of the original units. We know how this happened because we have followed the original land division, the joining up of units, that attempts at rationalization of holdings which failed because another grasper was involved and he was not going to let someone else steal a march on him, and so on. We would not attempt to draw out the farm, now of 200 acres, as a simple block of land, because we know how it was formed. But an archaeologist many years later might simply look at one period of the main residence and estimate the land needed to maintain it, and draw a line round it on the map to give it that land. He might also give the main house two of the subsidiary residences because they came into his block, but not the third. He would be in a mess.

First of all how, would he know that one of the houses in the area under study was the main house of a particular block of land? How would he know whether the other houses around were less main, actually subsidiary, or nothing whatsoever to do with the 'main' house? Why does he assume that something that has virtually never been demonstrated in a living and changing society, that is, blocks of land around farm houses in single ownership, should be unique to Roman Britain? Whenever in a period with written records, land holding of a living and changing landscape is examined, landholding is disjointed and often a muddle. The only times that blocks of land do seem to be known is when land is carved up afresh by a new system of government, and this seems to be the case in the early English kingdoms. It is as if the ruler has decided that he owns all land, and so, in the process of passing it out gradually to others, he is able to divide things up as he wants. But this, of course only applies to land ownership at the highest level; whether the tax or rent or tithe went to one owner or another: it says nothing about the land attached to different farming units or how they articulated together. So movement of a large block of land from the hands of the king into the hands of an Abbey or Monastery **could** take place without having any effect on the countryside whatever. If the lady

Set

Melania in the fourth century had owned large tracts of land in Britain, put together by an unscrupulous agent who was willing to do anything to get a single large unit of land, then it might be possible to draw an almost perfect circle somewhere on the map of Roman Britain and colour it in for Melania. But the whole point is that will mean nothing in terms of what happened on the land, except that the farms, the separate working units which made up her British Estates, her British Landowning, were being screwed that bit more drastically that their neighbours whose land belonged to someone else. One point we might keep in mind when we get to The End is how an Anglo-Saxon king or his scribe, sorted the whole land which he owned, his titular kingdom, into tracts of land for grabbing and giving away. I suspect it was by the aggregation of smaller units, whether working units or administrative units, but that will have to be argued out later.

We seem to be working through the problems from the top downwards. All the evidence from periods where there are written records seem to say that colouring in neat blocks of land on the map for single landholdings is wrong. Very tempting, but wrong. If that is the case then 'subsidiary' villas or farms can no longer fall within the coloured block of the 'main' villa. The main and subsidiary are presumably judged by size and appointments. Even if the impossible did happen, and a series of buildings in an area of countryside were excavated, and the largest house had a cemetery near it, and the best tombstone was to Marcus Lucius Covdob, and all the farms, large and small, had tiles in

them stamped 'Ma L Cov' we are still not down to a single explanation of how the countryside fits together. One idea would be that 'Ma L Cov' was the landowner and that the farms and tiles with 'Ma L Cov' tiles were part of his property, and drawing lines on maps would go on from there. But even that is only one of the credible explanations which is consistent with the evidence. For if a landowner makes his own tiles it is perfectly natural that he should make a bit on the side by selling off those surplus to requirements. And the fact that surrounding farmers bought them simply means that they preferred to cart the 'Ma L Cov' tiles two miles rather than 'PLG' tiles fifteen miles from the nearest alternative kiln. But let us suppose that things could be clinched by some mystical means: it would have to be mystical because there is practically no other hope. Then we would have a series of one major building, with granaries, and a series of smaller dependent farms. How do they fit together? Well in fact as John Percival has pointed out several times we are no better off because there is no single obvious articulation. Do the dependents, or tenants pay rent in kind or cash? Is the granary in the middle of the main complex just to store what is grown directly by the main farm, or does it have to have room for a 5% levy from all tenants, or is it a 5% levy from some tenants, 10% from others, and pigs from the rest? None of these is in any way special pleading or odd or simply to cause trouble, they are all perfectly possible states. If this is allowed then there is absolutely no point in going through careful calculations about the land attached to any house or houses. Better to say that

Set

from the skeletons found no one suffered from malnutrition; from the mosaics found that a surplus of income over necessary expenditure is apparent, and leave it at that.

So :-

1) The tenurial relationships between two physically separate houses cannot be determined by material means, that is, through archaeology.

2) Landholding is a concept which is not susceptible to archaeological study.

3) Farming units might be susceptible to archaeological study, but the whole unit would need to be excavated.

4) There is no necessary connection between farming units and landholding.

5) The appointments of a house in the countryside do not lead to logical deductions concerning farming in the neighbourhood.

Which leaves us with the house itself. And this is the right way to approach it, from the land to the building, and not, as in archaeology to date, from the building to the next building. What is a villa? I do not mean 'How is a villa to be defined?' because initial definitions are pointless. Definitions in archaeology must come empirically and analytically from the material. That is a satisfactory definition which produces interesting or useful results in the study. In other words if we put together all the buildings of the Roman countryside and find that one group with certain attributes always march together it would be fair to call those villas. There might be a rumble from the classically minded in that they KNOW what villas are and our group do not fit. Simply ignore them, for deductive definitions have no

place in a proper archaeology which must be totally free and empirical. It may be that when the total analysis of country buildings is complete a talk with a classicist would show a congruence between our class 4 and what he deduces about literary texts and villas. Then that congruence would be worth pointing out, but that is the only possible order of work. For the moment I ban the word because it causes more trouble than it is worth.

The buildings of the Roman countryside in Britain range from squalid up to palatial. There is probably a continuum which can be broken up arbitrarily at many different points. Thus you could separate buildings with wood and clay, from buildings with stone. It may not be advisable unless you are simply studying building materials, but it is possible. If you are studying life inside these buildings it would be highly inadvisable because there is no necessary correlation between what goes on inside a wooden frame and what goes on inside a stone box, and vice versa.

Discussion of the buildings to date has been very down to earth, not to say simple in the wrong sense. Houses are owned by individuals, the better the appointments the better off the owner, the more rooms, the better off the owner, and all owners of houses in Britain had the same aims, which, translated into modern terms, would no doubt come out as a double garage and a dish-washer. Finally, and perhaps at the root of the whole lot is the equation building = house. This means the people inside a building form a household, instead of a houseful, which it probably ought to be. Depending on the size of the building, a building-full may consist of any number of households. This moves forward to a point where we can ask whether we ought to interpret the largest buildings such as Woodchester in Gloucestershire, or Bignor in Sussex as Chatsworth in the 19th C. or, perhaps even better, as the Duke of Omnium's place at Matching Priory, or Hampton Court Palace in 1987, split up into Grace and Favour residences for deserving state servants, or something on the Hampton Court lines, but on a much lower social level. In general British archaeology is still running on 19th C. Imperial lines, so the obvious interpretation, so obvious that it is not an interpretation but the truth, is that of Matching Priory. This in turn involves a great family, great enough to justify the number of rooms, and then a great number of dependents and servants equally proportioned to the size of the building and therefore to the grandeur of the owners. There might be agreement about the total numbers of people who might be found in and around the Great House at any one time, whatever the interpretation, but everything else in the discussion is likely to be different. What is an alternative picture? Well the best way into it would be to let it grow from the plans of the houses through the mind of someone who has immersed himself in houses and how people lived in them in Britain from the 14th C. to the present day. This is a dangerous route to follow. First, we are leaving the safety of deduction for analysis and empirical observation; or, only slightly less worrying, leaving the deduction from Roman sources to go to deduction from British sources. This is an interesting choice.

If you want to interpret how a large Roman building in the British countryside worked, who lived there, and how, what do you use for your inspiration? Whatever path is chosen those who work deductively want to stay in the safety of Latin texts while musing on the plans of theses houses. They cannot have total freedom because the texts constrain them and make certain things possible and certain things likely and other essential. This is why I cannot work, in this case, deductively, because I will not be bounded by irrelevant and predetermined categories. These ideas may well be interesting to consider as one of the many possible sources of inspiration, but they hold no special place. Another source of inspiration, and again I would refuse to accept it as a source from which to work deductively, is how people lived in buildings in Britain during the period when there are written records. In the first case the written records are of the right chronological bracket, but have no necessary connection with either the climate, the society or the way of life; in the second case the written records take account of the land, and how it has been worked, but are in a different time bracket. Neither source is suitable for laying down any law; both sources are interesting to think about. Unless, of course, I take the advice of one teacher, as reported to me, in that the person who knows about medieval and later houses knows nothing about Roman villas and so must be wrong. Since no one knows anything about Roman villas in Britain except for their material details I do not think this criticism has any weight at all.

Since we have heard from Pliny, we need to hear from J T Smith. He makes a number of points about buildings in Eng-

land. Upper floors need to be demonstrated rather than taken for granted. From
ordinary buildings in England the idea of
an upper floor does not come in till after
the 13th C. It may be that the Roman
period in Britain is not a part of the continuous tradition of building which is otherwise obvious from , say, the 9th C.
onwards; or it might be that upper stories
are one of the things that got forgotten
between 400 and 800. But unless there is
good evidence there is no reason at all to
assume that a farmstead in Roman Britain
would build or even want an upper story.
Yes, there are Pompeian pictures of two
story buildings; yes, houses in Rome went
up to seven or eight stories; so, yes, the
ideas were there in the empire and the
building technology could do it. But, until
someone actually decides that it is a good
idea, an upper story is not a fact of nature
and needs to be argued out, from structural
principles other than the width of foundations which otherwise seem hopelessly
variable, and unrelated to what is built on
them. Another Smith point is that until a
small number of people needed to build
parade rooms - rooms mainly for public, or
even Court show - living rooms for a
family might have been normally limited
to four or five, and that is at the upper end
of society. If a parallel is needed for a
Roman building then a modest gentle-
man's farmhouse of the 16th or 17thC.
would suggest a limited number of rooms
for everyday life. A farmhouse in Roman
Britain with five rooms is therefore high
on the social scale judged in this way. Ten
rooms needs special research to fill them,
for one family, or needs to take some of the
rooms for state functions, or administra-

tive functions, and more than ten rooms
for one family is inexplicable. Here at last
is a method which, to me, promises a way
forward.

If we follow John Smith on his disruptive trail through Roman villas we find few
large buildings that can be split up into
living accomodation and display rooms,
but we find a difficult number of very
unremarkable rooms which villa planners
are usually reduced to labelling 'reception
rooms'. Duplication of Bath Houses is
another point which causes problems.
Suites of rooms, interconnecting with one
another, but isolated from the general circulation, give food for thought. More than
one doorway in a facade is interesting.
And things get more interesting when a
doorway seems to connect with one suite
of rooms while another doorway connects
with another suite. And the doorways may
not be symmetrically placed in the facade,
so one is more central, and therefore important (?), than the other. But plans never
stay immutable for long, and the two doorways and their suites may be thrown into
one range of rooms with one new doorway
slap in the middle of the facade. This must
suggest a different use of the rooms inside,
a different emphasis on whoever lives inside, and a different organization in the
house. Or the whole thing may go the
other way round with a symmetrical facade and a set of rooms being split up
unequally. Again, surely this must say
something about what went on inside,
before and after. We have fallen under the
spell; once these things are pointed out
they seem so sensible that words like surely,
and must, spring inevitably to mind. It all
makes sense - which of course does not

Set

mean that it is the RIGHT explanation or interpretation, in terms of what PC Plod would have seen had he inspected the house and households, but it makes human sense.

Up to this point we have remained firmly inside the one obvious stone and mortar, rectangular building, which must be 'The Farm'. We have ignored the Aisled building to one side, the wooden building rather like a modern barn with a line of pillars down each side like the pillars of a church with aisles; we have left out of account the smaller wooden building in the next door fenced yard, and we have certainly removed from any account save animal shelters, those round stone-built features, even though they may have good floors and evidence of doorposts and therefore doors. We have left those out of account because once there is a good stone, rectangular house it is obvious that people, well perhaps not slaves, but proper people, will live in them, and them alone. Square houses are obviously further up the social scale because they are romanized and round houses are not. Stone buildings are better than timber buildings because, because, well they just are.

Look, we are dealing with a time when everyone had mosaics and wall paintings, so what is so odd about an animal pen having a stone floor, the Roman period in Britain was a civilized one.

So, according to you the population of Roman Britain was about 600 times 2 times five or ten, say 12,000 in the countryside and a few more in the towns?

How do you work that out?

The number of known villas, doubled to give the rest unknown, with 5 to 10 people in each villa.

Well, no.

No indeed: the mosaic owner is the tiny tip of the population.

Well at least he is the most successful.

Prove it.

The people who have houses with the best appointments are obviously the most successful people in the country because they have managed to gain what everyone wants. Leaving aside for the moment the question of whether these buildings that we are discussing are single houses for ordinary people, or nasty communes for groups of undesirables, why do you think that Romanization was so successful, and so all embracing, and for so long, that it became the only way of thinking.

Well, what other way was there?

How about the British way, which most people in Britain followed before Romanization began, kept to while Romanization was in full flood, and which came back into fashion, or rather became the general way, when Romanization was no more than a symmetrical memory. The problem here is that, while Romanization had clear cultural markers and a discernible material assemblage, Britishness did not. Buildings were simple, either wooden, sometimes earth fast, sometimes post built, sometimes on sleeper beams, or dry-stone walling, round, rectangular or what you will. Utensils seem to have been made out of wood and leather to a great extent for, from the fifth century at least, very few survive. Metalwork was minimal and fashion as such, as seen by material remains, scarcely existed. This was the way

Set

of life of the majority of people in the Iron Age before say 50 BC; this was the way of life of virtually everyone in the West of Britain in the 5th and 6th and 7th C.'s. It is very likely that it was the way of life of a number of people at the time when Romanization ran riot in Britain between these two more obvious periods.

Now what I am objecting to is the idea that while Britain was subject to Roman influence there was a single scale of values which left the culturally unmarked, the unrepentant British, at the bottom of the heap as clearers out of cowsheds and choppers down of wood because they were rustic idiots, up to the highly successful business farmer, who probably rooted out old hedges with abandon to make bigger and better fields, and naturally demonstrated his superiority, taste, and arrivedness in the Roman fashion. There were at least two ways in Roman Britain, in tension, and one was Roman and one was not. So the clearer out of cow-sheds could demonstrate his affinities in the Roman way by the use of pottery and other knick-knacks which were cheap and easily available; and the sensible farmer, who made a good profit on his land without ruining the land in the process, chose to live out his life in his mainly wooden house without wall-paintings, without under floor heating, without mosaics, and with only little use of pottery, and no affection for brass trinkets. This was a choice. Once a surplus was produced from farmland the person to whom the surplus went could chose what to do with it. He might decide to go in for the villa fashion, but he might not. His choice of what to do about housing will not say anything necessarily about the state of his farm, the way he runs it, or how profitable its is. His house, without going the Roman way, is not necessarily dependent on that fashionable monstrosity over the valley, put up by those get-rich-quick cowboys who moved in from Sussex. They bought a piece of land and have built their house, but that, in turn says, or need say, nothing about how the countryside is articulated. I realize that this is not the right decade to talk about a choice of fashion, or to suggest the inessentialness of the status symbol. There are people who cannot believe in freedom, the sort of freedom that I am putting forward. One person was horrified to hear that I, as a university lecturer lived in a loft with no running water, no drains and a very leaky roof. She cheered up however when she realized that I had several rungs, senior lecturer, reader, professor, to go, and assured me that I would move out into something proper as soon as I was promoted. I have proved her wrong, though local authorities have forced running water and drains on me, but the tragedy is that she was incapable of believing me when I said that I would not change my status symbols as, or if, I moved up. This was not a matter of someone difficult to persuade who thought I was joking, but someone whose mental set did not allow anything other than the rise up the status symbol scale. If I could do nothing when present, arguing strongly, and trying to convince her, what hope would a dead Briton have who never liked the Roman way of things.

Don't be silly, of course he would have a Roman villa if he could afford one; it just shows he should have had those hedges out and enlarged

the fields, then he would have been efficient and he could have had what he wanted.

So the form that the Roman Villa takes is a matter of choice? Well, choice which is available to those who have money to make it, but that modification is always applicable in our society and apparently does not need to be voiced. If your daily work leaves you at the end of the year with a surplus of income over expenditure, in goods, in kind, or even in coin, then one of the ways in which you might chose to release that surplus is by Romanizing your dwelling. One way forward, which involves the total disruption of the room and surrounding accommodation for some time would be the insertion of a hypocaust; this would inevitably mean a mortar floor at least, rather than the earlier earth or stone and might as well involve a mosaic or tessellation since all the mess will only occur once. It depends on how big your disposable surplus is. Another way forward would be mosaic or tessellation without a hypocaust and just carry on with the braziers. Or some painting on the walls, or a new long room on the front to unify a rather scrappy facade, or a new bath block. And so on, and so on. Some people will take to this way of living, other will not. Some will have the disposable income to enable them to do this, other will not.

Outside such a form, living may well go on mainly in single households, judging by the size of wooden buildings and round stone buildings which are at least as commodious as a cottage, and therefore deserve the name, and ought not to be called huts. Inside the Romanized form John Smith's work strongly suggests that several households occupied a building which, from the outside, looks architecturally unified. To look only at the single facade and imagine a Roman Chatsworth or Matching is to make a tremendous leap of interpretation which does not square with many of the facts. It is not wrong to do it, because such a leap, if held in mind flexibly, may be a help in understanding some points of structure and organization. But such a leap is an experiment, and a fantasy, and must always be though of as such. Experiments and fantasies are highly useful, perhaps essential in any interpretation, and I propose having far more rather than far less. But we must be aware of their status. John Smith's work is rather more basic, in that it actually comes to grips with details, and it is of a rather different order from the Chatsworth leap. Once put forward it is very difficult to shake off in detail, which is presumably why so many commentators do not want to give it a chance to get established and dismiss it in a general way which allows of no argument. A little living and let live might be appropriate here, but this verges dangerously on The Basis of Belief, a subject yet to be dealt with.

If the interpretation of the stones and mortar of the buildings always known as villas requires care and flexibility, we have seen that the interpretation of the land around such buildings requires even more care, and can only be done in a very general way. Since it is impossible to point to a modern wood, which was probably a 15th C. creation and say 'I think that wood belonged to that villa', and then to add upland, and valley, hill slopes and quarries to create the estate that you would want if you lived in that villa, with any chance of knowing whether you are right or wrong the exercise seems to me rather divorced from the study of the past. Much better, but less satisfying, is to say that so many baths and so many hypocausts would consume so much wood, which, if coppiced would suggest so many acres of woodland. And a population of 15 people would need the following supplies of wheat, barley, wool, milk, cheese, leather, vegetables and fruit, which demands a basic territory of so many acres. And the house and its upkeep suggest the sale of surplus from a further x acres. So for that villa to exist, however the people inside were organized, on the assumption that they were more or less self supporting, a minimum of so many acres somewhere around is likely. This can be cumulative, and, if several buildings are dealt with in the same way, and the landscape seems to be getting heavily oversubscribed we have some further ideas on rents coming in from farms further away, and extensions such as that which can be explored. At present we KNOW so little about Roman buildings in the countryside that they are a fascinating subject for further study.

Set

Cemeteries and Demography

People at last. Dead is better than nothing, but if we have them dead then we might be able to say something about them when they were alive. And not just individual stiffs but cemeteries. If the old cry of 'Archaeology is the study of People' were true then cemetery archaeology would be far better understood today than it is. Since cemetery archaeology has been so neglected in the past, and still needs continual support in committees, it is clear for this, and many other reasons that the catch-phrases about people are not true now, and never have been true in any full sense. The only time that you can come in contact with people from the past is when you find their bodies, and in one sense this ought to be the point from which all archaeology grows. If you are obsessed with people that is. Personally I prefer my people with flesh on their bones because they are more fun that way - but far be it from me to cast aspersions... If what you want is people, then live with them now; if you are interested in the litter from the past, and sorting out probable and improbable fantasies about what the past was like, than an interesting part of that litter consists of human bodies. And statements about what is found in cemeteries are to me highly interesting statements of what is.

There is not a lot to object to in the past study of cemeteries or demography because there is so little of this study. This section is therefore not an attempt to shift a badly entrenched and erroneous view of the past, but an appeal to take an interest in an under-studied part of the past. Bodies have always caused interest, and have often been noted in the literature when pots,

coins and walls were hardly noticed. But there is little that can be done to study an individual body left over from Roman Britain. It just is, and its relationship to anything else is missing. When the body forms part of a sequence, part of the continuing activity and life of a cemetery, then it begins to have a greater potential for interpretation. It is somewhat the same as a hoard of coins found with no knowable context, compared with a sequence of coins through the gradual build-up of layers on a site. The fantasies which can be woven round a disembodied coin hoard are unlimited, and, since there is nothing against which to judge them, and nothing by which to moderate them, the whole exercise, after a moment of fun, becomes virtually meaningless. The same for a single body in a hole in the ground with no associations from the ancient world. You can weave any fantasy about it that you like, and no one is better then another. This is true even if it was known to be part of a cemetery, but is the only body to be recovered or properly recorded; there is just not enough limiting information to make it worth having fantasies about. When the body is one of a row, which is part of a cemetery of known limits and dimensions, where certain rites of burial were more commonly practised than others, and certain fashions predominated, then fantasies begin to be limited and interpretations begin to be falsifiable - which is the first step towards knowing what actually happened.

There are at present two types of information which come from cemeteries and they still form an uneasy alliance because we do not know how properly to unify them. There is the cemetery report and the bone report.. This is most obvious in a cemetery publication such as Trentholme Drive, York. This report was a triumph and a milestone, and , for that reason some people would prefer not to criticize it. Yet is is clearly not perfect, and, to help other writers in the future it is essential to make its imperfections clear. First the site was not a good one. The burials had all taken place, as at Cirencester, which suffers the same deficiencies, in topsoil, black garden earth, so only very rarely could the cut made for the grave be recognized, only occasionally could a grave be sorted out and opened up as a unit, and therefore pots, coins, or other finds could seldom be reliably associated with individual skeletons. There were also cremations which of course are easier to keep separate, but, again, the difficulty of seeing the pit into which the pot was put robbed the excavators of much potential information. It was not only the excavators in the 20th C. who were unable to find individual graves, for the people of the 3rd and 4th C. who wanted to bury relations clearly did not know where previous burials had been. Graves cut one another in a haphazard way, and so many skeletons were incomplete and damaged. When the excavator started there was really no blue-print for digging a cemetery, or what to do with the results, and the final report is in these circumstances quite remarkable. If the excavator were to say that it was only following common sense I would agree with him, but I would still find it remarkable because so few people allow themselves to do this.

As published, which, untypically it was, in reasonable time, it consists physically

of two parts; the first part is the archaeological report of the digging and the second is an anatomical statement of the bones found. The anatomist was probably not competent to dig the site, and certainly had no wish to. The archaeologist was not trained to report on the bones. So two reports were produced in the same covers, and the same problem continues today. The next great cemetery report to be published was that of the Lankhills cemetery outside Winchester, and here the division between the two reports is complete, for the cemetery report is just that with a few notes on the bones, and the bone report is due to go in another volume which will include all the human bone finds from Winchester. I am glad to be able to set the record straight here because I had been given to understand that there was a danger that no bone report was in sight. Martin Biddle quite rightly took me to task for publishing this fear when, if I had asked him as the general editor of the whole works, he could have assured me that I was wrong. Once more I am delighted to have been wrong; but I am still waiting for that report, and I shall have to tie it in to the rest of the information from the cemetery by annotating the digging report by hand. I know that Giles Clarke, the excavator, wishes that I would be content with one statement of this grouse, and not keep on about it. This makes it more and more difficult to keep up the pressure, but in an exposition such as this where I want to influence what people do in the future I am sorry, but I have to keep on saying what I think is wrong with the past.

The cemetery report from Lankhills is a triumph by which English cemetery digging and reporting caught up with fifty years of experience on the continent - Germany, France, Austria, Hungary - and passed it, all in one go. Again, as at Trentholm Drive there is no bare-breasted soul-searching development of a new and wonderful methodology, based on years of explicit study of what has gone before, and numberless papers on how they got it wrong, it is simply a very able person digging a site with the knowledge of modern archaeology, living with it to the extent that he had recall of all the graves and what was in them, and putting down on paper what he though he could do with the material. He could and he did, and the result is brilliant. Admittedly Giles started off with certain advantages: all the graves, or a high percentage were dug into solid chalk and therefore there was seldom any doubt as to what constituted a grave or what belonged where. When graves intersected they could usually be sorted out with care. The buriers seem to have known where the previous graves were, and cutting, one by another, is not the rule. So most of the graves were intact, and the bodies were mainly complete, though in a bad state of preservation in many cases. Those people survived best who were tipped into a grave wrapped in a sheet; those on whom time, energy, materials and money were expended with wrappings and clothes and coffins and goods rotted so slowly that the products seem to have caused dissolution of the bones. The Lankhills people in general were more generous to their dead than the Trentholme Drive people or the Cirencester people, and this made the whole process of providing dates and sequences much easier. It

also gave many other attributes which could be listed and examined in relation to one another. The limits of the site were within the area available for excavation and, again, this meant that the cemetery could be looked at as a whole organism rather than as a sample of unknown value, or a bit of some unknown whole. And, finally, the excavator thought cemeteries, and burials, and regarded the people there almost as acquaintances, and had in his mind what was normal in the cemetery and what was abnormal.

Normal and abnormal bring in a lot of extra factors and sometimes heaps of criticism. To decide what is normal is presumably normative, and, I am told, that is a bad thing. No one has ever been able to explain to me why deciding what is normal, or being normative, if they are the same thing is a bad thing apart from the fact that it involves taking decisions which may turn out to be arbitrary or even worse, wrong. So what? Most of what we are doing now will be seen as wrong in the future, and, just like the bones and their survival, it may well be those who take the most trouble to be eternally right that will be the first to be proved wrong. Or is it the arbitrariness which grates? Again I see nothing wrong in arbitrariness, in taking decisions, in deciding what is, for the moment normal, so long as the arbitrariness is expressly set out, and the methods of taking the decision are included with the decision. The whole process is then explicit and temporary and is seen to be done just so that things can move along, and until a better arbitrary decision can be made. Giles's method of deciding what was normal for his cemetery - normal as regards methods of burial and accompanying rites - was to look at the majority and to look around the rest of the country to see whether his majority were seen elsewhere or not. Near parallels were obviously more comforting than far parallels, because we might be trying to join up two different normalities, and parallels from large numbers, such as there were, were more comforting than parallels from small numbers, mainly because small numbers could be the odd wing of something much larger. From this a picture was constructed of what might reasonably have been expected in a cemetery in Britain in the third and fourth C.s. From the general expected spread some points stuck out and they needed explanation- he had followed the general rule of trying to say what might generally be expected and then holding out the rest for explanation. He had decided on the norm and wanted to discuss the deviations from that norm. Yes, he had created the norm himself. Yes, that norm could well have been created from his own consciousness and world view and life and so on.

Why did he not get a computer to do the dirty work for him, to create the norm? Because in my terms, the computer could only do what it was told. At present a computer cannot think creatively, but it can do a lot of hard work if you know what you want done. So if you fed into a computer the Lankhills graves and asked what was the most commonly occurring feature, you would probably get the answer skeleton, and then grave, and then you might get on to what you wanted, certain grave goods in certain positions. And then at the other end you might ask what

were the rarest finds, and that would give you even more nonsense because it would start off with the one fragment of flower pot in the bottom of a grave, and a frog skull and so on. Then it would get down to the types of object which occurred together several times, but only rarely. The computer has done wonderful work and correlated everything with everything else, because to ask it only to correlate certain things would be to intrude your own modern world view on the process, and, once you have the full lists you can go through and decide which correlations and occurrences are deeply meaningful. Or would that be a subjective imposition of your own world view and feelings on the ancient information? If you do not impose your view of what matters either at the beginning or the end, say what you are doing and why, so that everyone knows the process is yours and how it got out of your brain, then you will never get anywhere, objectively or subjectively. So the Lankhills cemetery was analyzed by a mind, subjectively, and inspection then agreed that this was probably the same conclusion that as objective as possible an analysis would have come to anyway.

Grave-goods are there, but are not particularly common or particularly rich compared with some continental cemeteries. Hob-nailed sandals or boots commonly occur in graves by the feet, but probably not worn in many cases. There is little evidence of clothing worn in the grave, though this depends on the survival mainly of metal dress accessories and purely organic clothes would have left no visible trace, just like sewn leather shoes. Heads can occur between the knees, or even on the shoulders, but only balanced there, since from time to time there is clear evidence of decapitation. All these are points which seem to occur fairly generally through the cemetery and which can be paralleled in other British burials. Then there is a little group of graves which suggest worn personal ornaments such as brooches and bracelets and belts, with pots in certain positions, seldom any sign of hob-nails or decapitation, but a rather showy spread of grave-goods. A small number of these burials stand out, if you have focussed in on the great majority and taken their attributes as normative, and a few more seem to be a cross between the classic oddities and the norm. Giles Clarke interpreted these classic oddities as strangers, because they stood out so far from the basic norm, and the half and half's as second generation cross breeds between oddities and normals. He thought he saw a new burial practice suddenly coming into the cemetery, fully developed, about 350, and a second generation dispersing the new ideas, and then the ripples died away and all went back to normal. Except for a further group of oddities who are rather more difficult to deal with; the main thing they have in common is oddity. He went one step further and pointed out that most of the odd characteristics of the first group can be easily matched in the cemeteries of Roman Hungary, and one explanation could be that the strangers came from there. I regard this as such a good clear and sensible piece of work that I have little patience with people who do not want to accept it and try to find all sorts of theoretical reasons why it should be wrong. The basic point which is quite clear is that

certain burials in the Lankhills cemetery are difficult to parallel inside the cemetery, difficult to parallel in Britain at large, but easy to parallel in Hungary. A burial rite seems to occur in Lankhills and in Hungary, but has not been noted so far elsewhere, so the suggestion of a link is fairly obvious. How the link happened, apart from independent invention in the two places, is a matter of interpretation, but, in the common market of the Roman Empire the suggestion that a family or two from Hungary moved to Winchester need cause no worries, and solves the whole set of observations without doing any violence to the observations or using any special pleading. Of course one of the problems with this interpretation, is the number of wide open spaces on the Imperial map in which we do not know anything about the burial rites because few cemeteries have been dug, even fewer published, and none of those has been anaylsed. Most of the older foreign cemetery reports just state what was found in each grave, and leave it at that. Some of the newer ones are doing the same thing as Lankhills and sorting out different types of burial rite from the combinations of grave goods and grave features, but there are very large areas where we have virtually no knowledge of different possible rites at all. So then, again, of course, the Lankhills strangers, if they really are strangers, might come from any of those gaps in our knowledge. Well, yes, that is in sheer logic true, but it is so unhelpful, when you do have a good straight parallel to hand, that you cannot expect me to take it to heart. Every explanation in archaeology is subject to the caveat 'but better examples, or other examples may one day be found elsewhere' but this caveat seems only to be used when the reader has a built in reason for not wanting to accept what he or she is reading. First of all get these objections out into the open so that they can be looked at and then weigh them against the pros and cons of waiting till the whole Roman Empire has been dug up. Our ideas of what happened in the past are interpretation; the knowledge on which they are based is partial, and always must be partial since so much no longer exists: not to be willing to argue on the basis of evidence as it exists is to run away from something that you do not like. By all means stand up and say you do not like it and so you refuse to believe it, but don't take refuge in pseudo-scholarship.

We seem to have got stuck in a hole somewhere in the suburbs of Winchester. Not surprising when we are dealing with cemeteries because, at the moment that is where cemetery studies have got stuck. There are other reports, but they are much smaller than Lankhills, or, like Cirencester and Trentholme Drive are Black Earth cemeteries where graves could not be defined. That means in those cases that the main information to come from the site is the bone report. Perhaps we ought just to give a quick sketch of burial in Britain before going on to bones and people.

It used to be said that Iron Age burials did not exist. It is true that in some areas they are not at all obvious, and in others seem to be very casual, and scarcely burials, more disposal of bodies, but there are definite traditions of burial running through certain areas of Iron Age Britain. The most obvious tradition is fairly simple and straightforward inhumation. Then, in the South East cremation creeps in, at the same time as wheel thrown pottery of new designs. The two often go together simply because ashes are often buried in containers, and pots make suitable vessels. The two new traits together certainly suggest outside influence, but whether this is the spread of fashion or the movement of people is not known. I favour a spread of fashion because the movement is from a contiguous area, the nearby coast of Gaul and can be effected by the travel rather than immigration of a small number of important people. The Hungarians at Winchester are from a totally separate area with no intermediate purveyors of tradition. Both points are interpretation, both are basically unknown, and the ideas are therefore nothing more than figments of the imagination. This spread of cremation can be seen as an early sign of creeping Romanization. Whatever the motive which brought the idea of burning the dead back to South East Britain and however it was effected, it does bring the conquerors nearer in habit to the to-be-conquered, and this previous growing together must have had an effect on the adoption of Britain as a province of the Empire. But that bland and eminently reasonable phrase - brought the idea of burning the dead back to Britain - goes beyond the evidence and is just as dangerous and tendentious as some of my more inflammatory statements. Since we do not know what method of burial, or disposal of the dead the majority of inhabitants of the South East used in the last years BC we cannot talk as if burning the dead was absent in those years. All we know is that the remains do not get detectably buried. The bodies may be exposed, or they may be burned and than scattered into the sacred waters, and the only change which happened was the growth of the idea that Mother Earth wanted to guard the dead rather than The Sacred River. So what was previously scattered is now gathered together and buried detectably in the new fangled pots.

Many provinces, just about the time that they are incorporated into the imperial administration show a sudden burst of highly demonstrative burials. Graves are loaded with tens of vessels, provisions, metal objects and other grave goods. This is a short burst and then sanity, in our terms returns and the ashes are placed in a pot with one or two subsidiary vessels, and all is simple and decent again. Judging an English country church-yard against a French cemetery it is obvious that we do not like to make a fuss about these things. Then the idea of not burning the body, but simply burying it, takes strength again, and cremation dies out, or almost dies out during the years 150 to 250. There is a period of perhaps 100 years or more of overlap, even in the same cemetery, and then by the end of the third century inhumation rules. The occasional cremation proves the rule. This is not a sudden change; it takes three generations or more to become complete. It is not a sharp division of society because cremators and buriers go on using the same cemeteries without apparently feeling enraged. It is a gentle change in fashion which takes a long time to happen. In many cases it does not even seem to be an important point for many aspects of ritual continue without particular reference to whether the corpse

was burned or not. So the way the corpse was laid, the direction of the grave or pyre, the inclusion of the hob-nailed shoes, the supply of extra vessels in the grave - all these points can be seen in some conditions to continue unchanged, or to go on side by side, whatever was happening to the body. This is important because we can so easily assume that something which comes through the archaeology as a great change must have been a vitally important point in the life of families or even the whole community. Putting all the evidence together it seems as if it is our obsession with something that is easy to recognize rather than their obsession about disposing of the dead. The change is a good one, from our point of view, because an unburned body is so much easier to study than an efficient cremation which can lead, in over efficient circumstances, to a bowl of dust.

Suppose we start with age. We have a cemetery containing - like Poundbury in Dorset, 1400 bodies. We therefore have a section of the population and can sort out life expectancy, average age at death, and What Life in Roman Britain was Really Like. What a waste of time, says a Deductor (someone who works deductively).

If you must use such words then Deducer would be better, but still rather silly.

You have, as usual missed the point, for a Deductor is someone who works deductively who deducts so much from the final result by so doing), for we have a range of tombstones which tell us the age at death of a sample of the population; study those and save your money. I admit that in this case my deductor is a mythical character because no one who has read much in the last few decades would be unaware of the problem. Keith Hopkins set out to do this study of tombstones for different areas of the empire. His results are rather odd for they give populations who lived as children, and then died off like flies in the maximum breeding time of 15 to 25, and then, those that were left calmed down and died more reasonably. Hopkins was worried by these results since it is difficult to see how a population can be stable if a majority of people born do not have a chance to marry and reproduce. He was even more worried when he compared the Roman results with modern statistics from a whole range of countries from the most sophisticated to the most squalid. All showed the same picture of high infant mortality, good prospects if you reach the age of five, and declining prospects of staying alive after 40; in other words a trough of death where the Roman gravestones found a peak.

The procedure from here on is particularly important for archaeologists. I say that Keith made a uniformitarian assumption and acted accordingly. He does not like this, but as we only argued it out going down in a lift I have not reached the end of the discussion, and if he finds it objectionable I withdraw the charge. Whatever he did in High Theory, in simple practice he said - the gravestone results are nonsense because the pattern of death that they show is irreconcilable with a stable population; the modern statistics **are** so reconcilable, therefore the gravestones do not represent a true sample of age at death of the Roman population. The further results were interesting in that the answer lies not so much

in the body in the grave, but in the people left behind, and it becomes reasonable when it is pointed out, that some age groups, such as young teen-agers and young husbands and wives will be over-represented in the sample simply because their deaths were the more tragic by being less expected, and there was at least some one left to mourn them. Infants died so often that the fact has to be taken for granted, and a family cannot tear itself apart with grief every time that happens. It is a commonplace of Victorian novels that this picture of high infant mortality is taken as a fact of life; if one Edward died at the age of two we try again and hope that the next Edward does better. In the same way failing aunts are expected to die off in the end, after surviving their husbands by some years, so there is really no one to commemorate them. And why should those few people in Britain who took this highly suspect foreign fashion of writing on stone - an extremely small portion of the population - and those who could afford such things, be typical of the whole, even if their gravestones were an accurate reflection of their ages at death? So we have to get our hands dirty if we want to know things like this.

It is not worth spending too much time on the subject of uniformitarian assumptions but it is an important subject in archaeology. Put basically, the Roman epitaphs can only be wrong if we KNOW what the pattern of death in Roman Britain was. At the moment we do not know this, but we do know what all modern populations are like. Either we say that man has not changed that much in 1600 years, so modern death patterns are representative of the human population over the past

30,000 years. Or we say that from our evidence the Romans were physically quite distinct from us in their patterns of life and death. I follow the first course without any doubts at all because the evidence is totally against any such observable and absolute changes in the human machine over the past 30,000 years. The suggestions from the epitaphs run directly counter to all bone information gathered to date and the bone information, for me, takes precedence over a series of epitaphs. Whether I would take such a bold view if Keith Hopkins had not pointed out the things wrong with the epitaphs as a sample of death ages I do not know. But I still think there is an element of 'Knowing because some things are obviously constant', and this must remain a theoretical worry. If we take it too far then we can never find out anything about earlier populations because 'They were just like us really'. So it is very uncertain what, if anything, in archaeology is worth getting your hands dirty over. First we decide, apparently a priori, from some inbuilt first principles, that certain aspects of past behaviour were allowably different, and then we are allowed to spend money investigating them. But if the subject is one where we KNOW that man has always been like that, no expenditure is justified. If we never make this assumption, that some aspects of life are constant within the post-palaeolithic time scale, then every nutty result on biased evidence reached by faulty reasoning is equally valid until the faults of the method are pointed out. So, a cemetery which is the only one known for the Ante-Penultimate Bronze Age of Cornwall (invented) which contained only women shows that there were no men in Ante-Penultimate Bronze Age Cornwall, so, in the absence of artificial insemination, virgin birth is proved. **But that is silly.**

Yes, I know that it is silly, it was invented specially to be obviously silly, but there will be many cases where the silliness is not so obvious, or, more worrying, people have a vested interest in supporting it. It is silly because we know that children are produced by the conjunction of men and women, and if there are only females buried it means something else was happening to the men - exposure or cremation and scattering - and that explanation is greatly to be preferred to any wild ideas on the prevalence of virgin birth. This is obvious because we KNOW how men and women work, and if we don't make some assumptions about uniformity we cannot sift the wheat from the chaff. The problem is, which assumptions should be made before we start. And having decided on this, will people abide by it and accept that their research project is a waste of time? Let us leave this for a later chapter.

Look at the problems which have been thrown up: age, sex, health, number of offspring, cause of death. And the moment you have worked on these points, through bones from cemeteries you have so much more information to feed back into the cemetery study because you can see to what extent men and women are scattered through the cemetery or segregated, young people are kept apart, infants are or are not buried in the cemetery - and what does this say about the attitude of society to them? - groups have family composition, or even family bone characteristics, physical nonconformists, which is my way of labelling those, whatever their abilities whose bodies, rather than minds, are detectably different from the norm, are they among their peers, or separated? But first, seductive though these points are, you have to work on the bones.

I am glad to report that sex is settling down. Different workers have now reached some sort of agreement such that a cemetery full of bodies can be sexed by two or more different workers, or methods and still come out with general agreement. Of course (watch it) sexing skeletons is rather a waste of time because grave goods, when they exist, are so much more reliable. Spears and shields for men and bracelets and beads for women. Usually that is (nudge, leer). Be careful where you nudge and leer because a rather tough, beringed man, with gold bracelet and chain round his neck may take exception to the smear, and he and his undecorated girlfriend may beat you up. And you would thoroughly deserve it for trying to impose your view of interpretation according to 'What always has been' in defiance of a possible alternative which would allow more freedom. The alternative would not necessarily be right and the spear and bracelets wrong, but when there are two methods, they ought both to have a say. Where they agree a greater degree of certainty prevails, where they disagree something interesting may result. The skeletal method of sexing is on my terms unashamedly uniformitarian. Today the bones of men and women form a continuum with peaks at either end of the distribution. In other words there is a definite male area of any distribution, such as the dimension of a particular bone, and

a definite female area, mutually exclusive, and in between there is an overlap including both males and females. As this can be seen be inspection today, and there is no evidence for overall skeletal modifications since the Roman period, I assume that this bimodal distribution applies to Roman skeletons too. There is a bit more, in that one of the characteristics, the notch in the pelvis through which the sciatic nerve passes has a practical application. Women tend to have wider notches, men, narrower. As the pelvis moves in giving birth a larger notch gives less chance of the sciatic nerve being nipped, and therefore less chance of later problems. I would find if difficult to believe that in an earlier population it was the narrower notched people who bore the children, and I would suspect that such a characteristic might count fairly heavily against their continued prosperous existence. That or rampant sciatica which might make further mating unlikely.

Age on the other hand is a problem. There is something approaching agreement on putting skeletons in order according to their age at death; the older ones can be distinguished from the younger ones to some extent. But it now seems certain, and studies in progress will probably document this, that you cannot suggest an absolute age for a skeleton from any presently known characteristics. This will be documented by the study of a large sample of skeletons of known age at death. So the 30 year old cannot at present be separated out from the 40 year old, though a 20 year old would be classed as younger than a fifty year old. It may be that up to about 18 to 20 the changes in the body which are hormonally directed happen to most people at roughly the same time, plus or minus two years or so, and internal hormonal direction overcomes nearly all other influences. After this the hormone balances are less obvious, and more variable from individual to individual, and are nearer in power to external forces which will obviously vary considerably from individual to individual. Whatever the cause, aging at present is rocky, and that means that all previous aging is almost certainly wrong.

This knocks out for the moment any idea of sorting out an age structure and profile for the Romano-British population, which is probably just as well, as it should probably never be attempted on cemetery evidence anyway. To discuss a population you need a section through that population, preferably in the form of a census. A cemetery is simply the burial record of a population spread over an unknown time with no records of completeness. The population bears no knowable relationship to any nearby town, villa, village or whatever, and, usually, many of the graves in it are neither dated, nor can they be put in sequence. A cemetery is very interesting in its own right, but it is one more of these examples in which you must take the rules and subject of study from the material and not try to twist the material into giving information for which it was never intended. If you want census type information you must use census type facts; cemeteries bear no relationship to censuses and cannot be used for that purpose. If you doubt this fact, think back to the outbreak of parthenogenesis in Cornwall. When all is going well, and the results from the cemetery seem to be fitting to what you expect from census data you will bask in a glow of well-being. That is totally illusory because if things were not going well, and parthenogenesis seemed likely to spread to your settlement at Wandlewick, you would willingly rubbish the whole thing and wonder where the men were because you KNOW that communities are not like that. If you are willing to admit that cemetery evidence is dangerous when it gives you poor results, you must admit that it is dangerous when it gives you the results you expect and you have to admit that they have no more validity than the most stupid results ever produced. It is no good asking an Art Historian whether this particular anti-inflammatory drug will aggravate your kidney trouble. You must ask sensible questions of appropriate sources and temper your enquiries to the ability of the source to respond. Far better, ask the art historian about the chances of Cimabue painting true likenesses, and the medical man about the kidneys. In other words let the questions be suggested to you by the source; the answers will be far more interesting and authoritative.

So, the body was male, or another was probably male; particular traits such as suppression of wisdom teeth were shared with two of the four other people buried within that little enclosure, and that allows talk of family groups, especially if that anomaly is rare in the rest of the cemetery; and he was decapitated. Ah! now this is something special in cemetery studies or even in Roman Britain. One cemetery expert has very recently called this evidence of barbarity which just goes to show how prejudiced some people can be. I hate to think what he would write about the customs of unconventional neighbours. Decapitation is apparently particular to Britain, and,with so many candidates at hand one wonders why it was ever allowed to die out. Perhaps the technique was lost, for it is a very delicate operation. It has been suggested as evidence of execution, as human sacrifice and so on, but close attention to detail shows that these will not work. Some cases are obvious, as when the head and top few cervical vertebrae are found between the knees. Other cases are less obvious, and many must have gone unnoticed, as when the head is in the correct position, just a little astray, as is so often the case, but there is a gap between the third and fourth cervical vertebrae, and there are cut marks between them. Typically the cut marks run between these two vertebrae, they are delicate cut marks such as would be made with a sharp knife, they enter form the front with the occasional miss so that the knife hits the dense centrum and leaves a mark, then goes between the articulating surfaces where the disk would be, and trouble then comes at the back of the neck where there is no simple straight way out since the different bones interlock. This is where even the most skilled operative would leave marks because the muscle-linked, interlocking bones have to be separated out. The point is that several bodies show faultless entry from the front , neatly between the two vertebrae, and only leave traces at the exit. This means a very high degree of skill, and a dead subject. If you do enter from the front there is a lot of tissue in the way, and if the subject is alive cutting that tissue will produce actual fountains of blood. This is

not conducive to delicate dissection. If you have cut the windpipe and the blood vessels it is somewhat superfluous to sever the spinal cord as well, so this cannot be the means of either execution, or human sacrifice. Commentators have suggested that for sacrifice the victim would be drugged. They may keep the body still and give the operative better aim, but it will not help the blood problem. Even a drugged victim could not be so delicately dispatched in this way when he was alive. To get the observable results you need someone who knows his job and can take his time about it on a dead subject. Pity, because that does downgrade the whole thing to the level of an element of undertaking rather than a ritual spectacle. Until all cervical vertebrae are examined with this in mind we shall not know how common this practice is; it remains a good example of how to come in contact with cultures different from our own at little personal risk.

There is still a tendency, in bone reports, to go to the anthropological side, or the medical and anecdotal. My perfect and preferred bone report will never be written until the practising doctor and the anthropologist both produce reports on the same material. For the anthropologist the bones grow together to form a population and the individual is most important as he fits into the group or as she stands out. For the medical man, as one might hope, the bones represent an individual who is worth a biography. For me, the master of this art was Calvin Wells, and I think he reached his peak in the report on bodies from North Elmham, post-Roman, but the ideas are still the same. It is difficult to explain how his work was regarded; damned with faint praise, perhaps, or agreed to be a jolly good read, but not quite sound - no jolly good read can be, or just too speculative. His ideas were always based on observations, that much seems agreed. The problem came when he opted for one explanation of the observed characteristics rather than another. We run up against the idea that to write something down is to stake your life on its truth; if you do not do the second you ought not to do the first. Calvin said what he thought, what seemed to him a good idea at the time, and what made an interesting report and brought the bodies back to life. If someone came along and said, look this characteristic does not mean this he would have listened (a few people excepted), and if convinced would have changed his story. This seldom happened because things were rarely so cut and dried. When people said that they disagreed that this was the **likely** explanation of that observation there was little to do but say, well I think it is. We return to this process of interpretation which to so many people is the writing of the truth instead of the giving of an opinion. Which must be the sign for my favourite quotation from an original thinker who suffered more than most - Sufficit mihi in omnibus que scribo opinionem meam magis exponere quam difinicionem veritatis promittere - Peter Abelard, Ethics. It is enough for me, in anything that I write, to say what I think, rather than attempting a total definition of Truth.

The good cemetery report is therefore still to be written. At the moment the great cemetery from Poundbury near Dorchester in Dorset is being written up and this should take things a bit further along the way. We need to know accurately what was found where, whether it is the graves and their position and their alignment in the cemetery, or the bodies and the goods within the grave, and the relationships of graves to other structures. We need tables of what was found in each grave and it would be nice if, as at Lankhills, something were done with this, though at Poundbury many graves were totally unfurnished. We would like to know the details of each skeleton as a minimum, and I would like to see each one integrated back into a brief biography even if it means a lot of repetition. I can then use the graves and the people to make up my own fantasies. I think these requirement will be met, though they are minimal. To ask for more in the actual circumstances of lack of money and time which obtain is probably unrealistic, but with this minimum more work can be done in the future.

A footnote here can take in alignment. A grave, by its very nature which is longer than it is wide, has an alignment, anything from NS round to EW and back to NNW-SSE. Some cemeteries seem to take the East as an important point, and if they are Christian this is explicitly directed so that the resurrected corpse can face East. A suggestion was made that East was determined by observing the rising sun on the day when the grave was dug, because graves which do have a tendency to face East vary round that exact point by a fair amount. If this were true the season of death could be deduced from the direction of sunrise, and the death rate through the year could be found. This was working well until a schoolboy in Winchester, Giles Kendall, got up early, sighted the sunrise, dug a grave, went to school and went back to the site to plan it. He found that he had no hope of getting nearer than about ±5 degrees to the theoretical sunrise, even on a good day, and this cast doubts on the idea. Later, in his undergraduate dissertation he plotted out the seasons of death of pre-industrial villages in the same area from records, and found a very much more even picture of spread round due East than any cemetery suggested. The sunrise theory of orientation therefore ceased to be a preferred explanation.

Deduction, analysis and thinking

I had been a Chemistry teacher for six years before I got so exasperated with some of my colleagues that I started to think about teaching in general, and schools, and why people came to such different conclusions. I wrote the results down and a friendly publisher found them interesting to read, but rather too interesting to publish. I had forgotten that further example of censorship until this moment. I then taught Archaeology for at least twelve years before I started thinking about thinking and what effect thinking, if any, had on what archaeologists do and say. I am still not sure that it is time yet to express things on paper, but I have sniped so often at Deduction and complimented analysis that I ought to try. As I do so the Church of England is thrashing about in a procedural muddle, and the same problems seem to apply. The state of politics is also at an all time low. We are worrying about thinking about archaeology here, and I promise not to make this an undercover sermon, but the general rules do apply to all branches of thinking.

For instance, if an archaeologist goes to church, and votes in elections and expresses a view about towns, a knowledge of two of these characteristics will give you a very good chance of accurately guessing his attitude to the third. Thus if he votes towards authority and thinks that towns go on to the end of the fourth century he is likely, if he has any connections with religion, to be against the ordination of women and to believe in the actual factualness of the Virgin Birth. If he questions what went on in towns in Roman Britain, and admires the Bishop of Durham, he may well vote away from authority. There will be exceptions who will be either very mixed up people, or people who think hard for themselves on each issue; but even these hard thinkers may have grouped conclusions. I am leaving on one side as not worth bothering about the few Classical Archaeologists left who KNOW what happened because it is written down; those who believe that nothing written by Karl the Great can possibly be wrong; and those who enquired of a friend who entered Keble College Oxford to do Theology what he was reading only to respond "Oh, I could not study Theology, it might conflict with my Faith". These people are all absolute deductionists, certain things are known, are taken for granted, or just are, and that is that. Do those who go in for analysis believe in anything, and do they accept anything as real, factual, or demonstrated?

I do believe in facts. What do I mean by facts, and why do I believe in them? To answer the second question first, I think it is because I was a chemistry teacher. When I was in the second or third forms my chemistry teacher made me mix up iron and sulphur and heat them in a test-tube to produce a totally different substance called iron sulphide. It worked for every member of the class. As a chemistry teacher I pushed very willing classes through the same experiment, or rather procedure from my point of view, and year by year there was 100% success. Some of these people I taught are even now ..... and they get 100% success. It is therefore for me something which I can rely on that if you take iron and sulphur and heat them up in a test tube they will glow and combine to form a different substance which, on the addition of dilute acid will fill the lab with the smell of rotten eggs - something neither the iron or the sulphur, or a mixture of the two will do. It is a convention to which I happily subscribe to summarize what happened as Fe+S=FeS where Fe is that grey powder which is attracted to a magnet, sulphur, or S is that yellow powder which melts at 96 degrees C, (from memory), and burns with a quiet blue flame, and FeS is the black, almost waxy looking solid which is produced by heating the two together.

I must be a very old fashioned scientist to be so sure of all this. Have I not heard of the uncertainty principle which is all the rage, and which tells us that you can never know the position of anything for certain. How do I know that when I put the sulphur in the test-tubes it will still be there when I come back - all the particles may be somewhere else. Perhaps it is because I am a scientist rather then old fashioned that I fail to misunderstand the Uncertainty Principle in this way. Yes, there is agreed to be uncertainty, a limit on what can be known, when we look at the atomic level, or at sub-atomic particles. No one at the moment can predict which atom in a radioactive isotope is going to split up in the next few minutes, But the uncertainty is limited to times and places and levels of knowledge. If these are all put together I suppose it is possible not that one electron in the sulphur will be found outside the test-tube rather than inside it, which would hardly be worrying, but that all the particles which went to make up the sulpher would have migrated at the vital moment.

There may be a calculable possibility of this happening, though any computer print out might take time if all the 0's after the decimal point were to be expressed. From theory, if this is possible, the probability can be shown to be very very small indeed, and from practice it has never happened to anyone once in the millions of Iron and Sulphur experiments that have been done. Unless the behaviour of sulphur changes drastically there is no need to worry about it. In the same way, it would not be profitable to lay odds on which 6 atoms of uranium in a lump will split in the next hour, but, from a week of counting, I am willing to put a fair amount of money on what I regard as a fact **that** between 5 and 7 atoms will split in the next hour, and the next and the next. The uncertainty is there and is vital to any understanding or prediction at a sub-atomic or atomic level, but in aggregate, events are predictable with a high degree of probability. So my facts are those matters which, by inspection and observation, I can predict with a high degree of probability.

How high?

I don't know, it varies.

So then there are no such things as facts.

Go back to the first year of university where such brittle brightness belongs. To know that there is a continuum from the highly predictable to the unpredictable does not either invalidate the highly predictable, nor does it force some arbitrary division into the scheme for the sake of sureness of things. Let us take things as they come and worry about the probability of each matter as it arises. Above all let us be willing to try things out. What if ....

Ded

Again, as a scientist I prize highly repeatable observations. Not most highly, necessarily. But if we are in the business of observations as such then repeatable ones seem to me to be better than unrepeatable ones. We need to separate out the observation itself, and the possible meaning, interpretation, implications, or whatever. A series of excavators might have seen things in the sections they dug, and an archaeological movement might start, fuelled by these sightings, which has validity and importance, but those sightings may eventually be untraceable when the trenches were re-opened to 'prove' them and they may even be found to be wrong observations. But the movement concerned with towns in the fourth century might go from strength to strength because those observations in the trenches had by that time become an insignificant part of the cannon. The meaning or interpretation of what was 'seen' was more important then, and eventually independent of the sightings. The point about repeatable observations is that, though they may not mean anything at all, they can either be taken for granted or checked up on once again. If you have an unrepeatable observation the best thing to do with it is to ask what it implies, and then try to check up on it another way.

So there are archaeological facts - of differing reliability, but those which are repeatedly verifiable, can be treated as bases for further work. It is just as well to say exactly what the 'fact' is, but most people would anyway. If you have an empty room with just a heap of pottery and tile on the floor and you send in 20 people, quite separately and independently armed with paper, pencil, plastic bags and spring balances, tell them simply to 'quantify the material' the results will be closely comparable. Some may count sherds, others may weigh them, some may do both, but there will be limits within which all the values produced will lie. It is as well to keep a note because some people reared on bad digs will only weigh the pottery because the tile was thrown away on their dig and they do not regard it as material. If noted this causes no problems. The heap can stay for years, and another twenty people quantify it, and the results will still be within the same range. The amount of material in that room will stay constant; the number of sherds might increase gradually as pieces get broken, and the weight may decline very slowly indeed as powder and dust rub off on the workers and drop on the floor, but on any general scale that pottery is a fact.

But how do you know the pottery was in the room when no one was looking at it?

Oh dear. I believe my senses when what they tell me is repeatable and when what I perceive is perceived and repeated by others.

But that may be a cultural mirage.

It may, I doubt it, but if it is I am happy to work within it. What I say about anything is provisional and relative, I recognize this, and it does not upset me. To say it, does upset others and they try to obtain truth. I know for the moment that truth is far beyond attainment. So ... ah, someone asked that question once before. Never mind, I am happy to give my answer. Truth is either the relationship which exists between everything, or the knowledge of that relationship. Note that this is a description, not a definition, so I still agree with Abelard. It does not consist of facts, or the stock-piling of facts, or finding of new facts. It consists in the relationship between these facts, new, old, or indifferent. It is the object of research and is the standard against which research should be judged. Good research points out the previously unperceived relationships between things. But then so does good thinking. All these increase our knowledge of truth. So perhaps this justifies the practice of archaeology, as a part of the whole.

Up to now you have sniped at Deduction, the acceptance of certain points in order to proceed in the search, and called analysis the great and good unfettered search. Are your facts not just as limiting as your Deductionist premises?

Good question. They would be if I were tied by them in the same way that a Deductionist is tied by his scriptures. The Deductionist finds the religious scriptures, or the Marxist scriptures, or the classical scriptures necessary - without them his thinking could not exist and could not be right or Right. I find my facts, and sometimes even his scriptures, merely convenient. This is a vital distinction between what is necessary and what is convenient, what people need and what people want, and that which cannot not exist and that which we could do without. The fact that there is virtually no material in the Cotswolds for the period 400 to 800 AD will not hinder me from fantasizing about the past, there and then. I am mildly constrained at either end by the appearance of material evidence, and the material evidence is such that it cannot be argued away. But its existence does not constrain me in my interpretation to one possible result for the simple reason that there is no one simple explanation or interpretation of material. I must take account of it, simply because it exists, but how I fit it into my fantasy is completely my own choice. If I do it hamhandedly this may adversely affect the reception of my fantasy; rather worse is to do it brilliantly because that never goes down well - it is distrusted. But however you construct your fantasy it will only be accepted by those whose fantasies it fits, or those whose have a fantasy shaped hole at that point, and will never be accepted by those with whose fantasies it conflicts. A bit depressing really, you can only preach to the converted because they are the only ones who will listen enough to hear what you actually say. Everyone else will react to what they thought you said, or what you must have said to remain unbelievable. Depressing until you realize that this is the case and work for yourself, and the occasional reader who is willing to listen.

I have said that I must take account of the material because it exists. Why will I not accord the same rights to written evidence? When that written evidence is direct and contemporary I will take it into account as something which might come in useful. For Roman Britain such evidence is virtually non-existent - the few writing tablets, the occasional inscription, so long as it is a personal statement and not a political one, and the few lines in St. Patrick's Confessio. That is about all we have which is direct and tied to the times.

Ded

Anything political is out as direct evidence because it has a purpose, usually untruthful and probably nasty, which simply is not there in the broken pot. So the biography of a politician is out, the foundation stone type of inscription is out - such a shame, Mr Bloggs spent all that time and energy getting the money for that building, and he's never even mentioned - unless we happen to be studying political biographies through the ages, or foundation stone type inscriptions, which, as archaeologists we are not.

I therefore will not accept any study as valid which starts out from fixed points. Unless of course it has the aim of rubbishing them, or, less interesting supporting them. Note the difference. While it is possible to disprove some accepted idea by showing that either it itself leads to contradictions, or that it just cannot be reconciled with the material evidence, it is not possible to prove an accepted idea. The fact that it does not lead to contradictions proves no more than that it does not lead to contradictions. The fact that it is consistent with the material evidence proves no more than that, and that is an absolute minimum to give it the status of 'possible explanation'. Any study, to be valid, must be free of fixed constraints, fixed points which MUST be true, set texts and fundamentalism, and tradition. Perhaps I now see why some people dislike the idea of being normative, of finding a norm and noting deviation. They assume that the norm, once found, has some sort of value and validity,and that to be normative implies deductionism and coercion. Obviously that only applies to the deductionist, for, to me the norm is simply the norm.

The mean height of English people in 1987 is so much, plus or minus so much, to take in a good chunk, perhaps the majority. This is the norm and any clothing manufacturer who was not in this sense, normative, would soon go out of business unless he were in the special markets. In exactly the same way, the majority of the burials in the cemetery are like this, and this is therefore the norm, the rest are, to some extent different. They may be qualitatively different in that they seem to form a different population, or they may be quantitatively different in that they are the extremes of the one distribution, but I like to know that they are outside the norm.

Those who have texts, sacred or profane, generally wish to limit analysis. Now it should be obvious that I do not mean that any one who studies texts is against analysis; I mean that those who value their texts above all other evidence or means of argument are generally against free analysis. Texts is in fact the wrong word, for just as much trouble is caused by appeals to tradition as texts. Thus in the church there are those who are attached to the direct word written in scripture, though they are remarkably unclear about which words, which language, and in which text. These will only deduce from what is given, strangely, in the King James version. But equally obscurantist are those for whom tradition is an immutable guide. This is how it was; that has a special, revealed, sacred, value; this is how it must be. The good tradition of course, not the Inquisition or the Crusades - well the Crusades might get some supporters in the present unpleasant atmpshpere, to rid the Holy Places of the Infidel. I apologize for this excursus into Religious affairs, but I have the feeling that if I can sort some general ideas out away from archaeology it will be all the easier to see how they fit to the study of the past. There also seems to be a greater chance of working on a more general plane and avoiding the chances of getting bogged down in specifics.

Political deductionists also exist in at least two main flavours, and, again it is a matter of texts and tradition. The text for the left wing seems to be built up from a series of written works and ideas which have gradually formed into orthodoxy. The right wing is not based, so far as I can see on a text, but on tradition, and hence the general label Conservative. We might well therefore expect two deductionist wings in archaeology, one perhaps based on written sources and the other one devoted to tradition.

In the middle of politics comes a group who are labelled pragmatist, liberal, radical, or whatever, whose main characteristic seems to be to try to think thinks out - liberally or radically, as they occur. When all is going well the centre tends to grow with allegiance from the moderate parts of either wing; when the going gets rough the wings re-group and pragmatism is ridiculed. In the middle of the church are people who try to work things out as they come along and have little patience with the flappings of either wing. In both church and politics the people in the centre are not a party and do not have a philosophy because they just are, and have rather higher goals than the achievement of some theoretical set purpose, carefully defined from time immemorial. The centre people are not particularly articulate because they are

neither 'political' or 'religious', and to be articulate you need to have a platform. The policy of the centre in both church and politics is difficult to set out, and dull when it is set out; fair game for those with ideas and ideals. We can push a little further before we return to archaeology.

The wings, church or politics, right or left, are not given either to reason or free range analysis. In politics there is no point in joining a Communist party in order to think things out in opposition to Marx and Engels; in the church it is clearly a sign of pride to set up feeble human intelligence against either the revealed word of God or the tradition of God handed down in the church; a Conservative is basically devoted to keeping what he has rather than discussing it. Thinkers cause trouble unless they start off from the right points which should make sure that they reach other right points in the end. The reason for all this must presumably be that none of the fundamentals can stand up to critical reasoning or uncontrolled analysis. The fundamentalist Christian finds difficulty in coping with the enquiries of the New Testament scholar. When he says 'saved' does he mean this that or the other, and is he aware that this is a minority reading of 'better' manuscripts and what is his criterion for choosing between more, poor, and less, good, manuscripts? The traditionalist wing of the church have recently been shown yet again by the Bishop of Durham that a simple appeal to tradition solves nothing, for in tradition there is good, bad, very bad, and indifferent. There is no reasonable way why the future should already have been revealed in the past, so tradition may offer no help at all. Ah, but there is a point beyond which reason is powerless; I have gone there so you cannot follow me unless you also go on to higher forms of argument than reason. The Marxist and the Conservative follow strangely similar lines, with difficulties over texts, and what they ought to mean, especially when it is clear that they are wrong if they do mean that, and a flight into the British People if all else fails. I have no doubts about the rightness and wrongness of these arguments, but my purpose is not to worry about this, simply to sort out some possible scenarios for archaeological thought.

We might expect two wings, neither fond of reason or analysis, preferring deduction, one perhaps based on written sources, the other on what has always been, or more cosmetically, the body of opinion. We might expect a populous centre who, if they think about these things at all, as they get on with the job, say, a plague on both your houses, for goodness sake take it as it comes and argue each case on its merits. We might expect the wings to be vociferous and with manifestos; the center might not even have a written constitution, and, if it had, it might not be very exciting. All we have to do is to identify the wings and cheer up the centre before sorting out how interpretation should happen. It would also be good to try to understand how the different positions come about, and why.

The first group to be identified are those who KNOW what happened in Roman Britain because we are told in the texts - they equate directly with the Biblical Fundamentalists and the Political Textbashers. It is not so much that any of these are actively or explicitly against reasoning

things out inductively or analytically, simply that there is no point in wasting time thinking out things that are written down. It is not always, or at least on the surface, an anti-intellectualism, but a pained concern for time lost on a pointless pursuit. There is the inbuilt reverence for the Word so that if we are concerned with things Roman, the Roman word prevails. Anyone who cannot see this is rather odd, and, if not dim must have motives for this deviance. In the church the motives for deviance are satanic, in politics, disruptive, in archaeology -?-. We might get further on this if we look at reasons for opinions.

The second group are the conservatives, those to whom tradition is a determining factor, if not the final adjudicator. Again it is possible to state their case, or my version of their case, with some sympathy. It is not that what is left over from the past - that is everything published up to yesterday - is determinant for the future, that would be a failure in understanding and simply setting up an Aunt Sally that can too easily be knocked down. It is a matter of wanting evidence that the replacement will be better than the original before any change happens. What is the point in destroying X when the new version will not be so good. In prayer books, in schools, in views of Roman Britain. If there is nothing particularly wrong with what we have now, and if I cannot prove that what I want to put in its place is better, why do I not get on with something useful instead of wasting my time, and other people's, stirring things up? My answer, which I think depends on arguments yet to be drawn out, is that this is a misunderstanding of how archaeological argument works, for the new case cannot be shown, from the material, to be better than the old case, because archaeological explanations do not grow independently out of the material, they need people to put explanations on to the material. So a new case can only be made out by a person putting his ideas on to the material in a full dress way. You probably cannot have a trailer, it is the whole film or nothing. An archaeological case will then have to be judged by how well it fits in with the material, and all the other likely ideas, and, again, that cannot happen until it is in working order. The past and the future can only be compared when they are both running side by side in working order, and, for that to be possible, the future has at least to be admitted.

In the middle are the silent majority who wonder what all the fuss is about, are not particularly devoted to the ideas they learned in their course on Roman Britain, quite like the ocassional new idea, especially when it fits in with what they are digging, are not particularly interested in written sources, unless they illuminate some aspects of the rubbish pit on which they are currently employed, and would certainly never accord some text priority over their own experience. They will take note of an argument drawn either deductively from a text, or analytically from a heap of pottery; they may well prefer the Roman pottery to the text, but do not have very strong feelings on deduction verses analysis. I suspect that what upsets them most is any claim, either from textual deductors, or people who deduce things from theories brought in from other disciplines, or those who see the possible future as worse than the present, that they have the answer and must have supremacy. If some political archaeological struggle, or perhaps one could equally well say religious archaeological struggle, took place and everyone had to take sides, the deductive wing and the conservative wing would lose simply because either would threaten uniform domination. Analysis would not win positively as a lovely thing, and the Right Way, but simply as not monolithic in its philosophy, and without any one claim to dominate. It would be the lesser evil. Assuming of course that archaeologists and those concerned with Roman Britain are a somewhat more intelligent section of the population than the average.

Which leads to the why of archaeological positions. And, as always, I find it useful to sort out ideas on politics and the church at the same time. This dig at the average in the last paragraph is vital to the argument, for, if archaeologists are a typical cross section of the GBPublic, the victory would at present go to the wing who want to rely on standards and values, which must mean the past, rather than try any future. This means that at present the GBP are afraid and selfish; afraid of anything new and untried, and determined at least to keep what they have if not able to get anymore. When things are going well you can experiment, have forward looking ideas, and the centre gets a major group backing it from both wings, leaving the rumps on either side mumbling disconsolately and predicting gloom. When the going gets rough the centre splits up again and diverges back to its appropriate wings, and the medicine becomes the mixture as before.

Ded

The majority in the church do not yet believe that a crisis is upon them so the majority are still congregating in the centre. The vicar of the London church with a congregation of eight knows that neither Hell-Fire and tub-thumping, nor a weekly dose of incense will fill his church again, so he goes on in the way set out for him. He may well shut up shop, and the church may become Redundant, before there is any suggestion of analysis being allowed, so that the church might provide what people need, rather than what elements in the church KNOW they want. This seems to suggest several points of thought. The majority in the middle are not there because they are analytical, simply because they dislike the activities of either wing. They are not individually deductive but they have only once or twice been encouraged to be analytical - I am thinking of occasions such as the Honest to God debate, and later outbreaks, or threatened outbreaks of thought in the church. Happily for the wings, who will unite on such occasions to suppress such horrors, the hatches have been battened back down. And all this brings in another aspect which has escaped notice till now, that of hierarchy. I suppose that the word itself - rule by priests? - should have alerted us to a danger of church-type problems in any area where it is used. Of the three institutions or areas that I have compared, the church is incomparably more hieratic and hierarchical than politics or archaeology. Yet this creeps in everywhere. I said somewhere earlier that only politicians ranted about politics, because if you are a humble voter somewhere in the middle of the political mess you do not want to take sides

in this self-guying way, neither, you are quickly told, do you have the knowledge or understanding. This I fear comes from the church in which there is no hint of one man one vote, but Those Who Know legislate on our behalf. We must keep this in mind when we get back to archaeology. We also have to add in, fear of being wrong and personal ambition.

Analysis will presumably be inversely proportional to rigid rule. At one end, the church knows what is best, so analysis is unnecessary; in the middle politics is sometimes less rigid and analysis can sometimes be allowed, but not in crises or emergencies; is archaeology at the liberal end of the scale? Fear of being wrong perhaps is tied up in this. In the church the penalties could be eternal. In politics, long-lasting. In archaeology - does it even matter? Personal ambition follows a different path, but then it will be complicated by group ambition - perhaps it always is. Here the top must be politics for the only reason for the subject to collect together so many unpleasant nonentities must be that they aim for the top. And a job most of whose members have nothing in common but ambition, must be distinctly unpleasant. A great majority of people still enter the church without ambition, in this world at least. A bishopric is not the goal for most, and even a full church can be seen as a worldly snare to be avoided, in some cases most successfully. Group ambition has recently reared its ugly head, so that we want so and so in that position because the other candidate is on the side of Women. And I suppose that some people really do think that it is their job to be in that office because everyone else will do it badly. It is so much easier to sort out these ideas away from archaeology, because inside, they would inevitably reek of personalities, whereas here I have genuinely thought all the time along political and church lines. If the caps are ones that fit, then that just happens.

So, a hierarchy, fear of being wrong, and personal ambition as determinants of archaeological attitudes? There is definite stratification within the archaeological ranks, but I think this only affects people as much as they allow it to. I think my position is aside from all this, and is the personal perch of the jester, so my comments are likely to be more faulty here than almost anywhere else. Having been given the licence of the jester I can move up, or down, or sideways at will, and say roughly what I want. Whether my licence will be taken away now I have started having delusions of grandeur in telling people what is right and wrong remains to be seen. The point then arises as to who would take away my licence? The fact that I can think of no-one who could do it says something about the loose structure of archaeology; the fact that nothing would do these views so much good as to be banned says that fundamentalism does not rule; and the fact that by now there are many of my ex-students who will no doubt continue to support me when they think I am right, and say so bluntly when I am wrong, in a varied and dispersed number of places suggests that confession of orthodoxy is not the only way to a job. It is possible to say that archaeology is so unorganized, not disorganized, just unorganized, that there is nothing to be democratic about.

Fear of being wrong is more serious. It is serious simply because it is usually totally mistaken. Not mistaken in that the person is going to be right, but mistaken in that everyone for most of the time will be found to have been wrong. It is Abelard again; say what you think, and take every effort to make it as good as you can, but there is no point in hoping that it will stand for ever as a bastion of truth. It will not; we know from past experience it will not; it will be out of fashion, if not irrelevant, if not proved wrong or mistaken, in fifty years at most, so get it down quickly, warts and all, and let it go into the melting pot for others to play with. It is not even as if the results would be long-lasting, as in politics, or eternal, as in religion. Even in the latter there is the decidedly worrying possibility that as I go to Heaven I shall be greeted with a cordial handshake and told to take a place in the probationers section of the harpists, only to settle down to see following me someone who I KNOW had got it all wrong in life, welcomed with compassion for the fact that he **had** got it all wrong for so long, and given a big hug to make up for it. Don't worry. The worst that can happen to you is that someone can show what you have said is inconsistent with the material; this removes your idea from the front rank of preferred ideas, but it may always have a chance to come back when new material is discovered or the old material is newly understood.

We now need to tack back to look at the business of replacing archaeological interpretations, and this might lead us back to deduction and analysis, and even to the way of interpretation itself. The main problem standing in the way of discussing the replacement of archaeological inter-

Ded

pretations is that at present the majority of participants do not regard such things as interpretations, but facts. This view is totally inconsistent with the one I expressed a little time ago whereby facts are material or observations of material that can be reasonably be taken for granted, and preferably allow repeatable observations. If these are facts, then interpretations of these facts, or deductions from these facts, or pictures built up from these facts are not themselves facts, but something different. Thus in a perfect world in which all excavations were consolidated and put on display it would be a matter of fact that of the five stone buildings in this part of the countryside, two had mosaics and tesellated floors and three only had mortar floors. It would be a matter of interpretation that there were two properties involved, with two owners, one of whom had two tenants and one of whom had one; the owners had the mosaics, the tenants had the mortar floors. It would be a different interpretation that we had five farmers, two of whom chose to spend their surplus in the Romanized way, and three who did not. There is no need for one interpretation to replace the other, both are equally consistent with the evidence, as presented, and they should continue side by side, with others wherever possible, till the accumulating evidence begins to whittle down the possible explanations by making some of them seem much less likely than others.

This seems to me eminently reasonable and sensible, and I suspect that any one within range of either my hand or tongue would find it equally so. Yet, left to their own devices many people would apostasize as soon as the pressure was off. They would probably not do it explicitly, because that might lead to refutation which would be inconvenient, they would do it implicitly in cosy serpentine phrases such as 'and although some purists would want to show that nothing is believable (chuckles) it really is obvious that people with mosaics in their houses are higher up the social scale of success than people without (applause)'. Which means that they are the owners, and the other people are the tenants. And this can be taken as a building block, a factual building block, for higher stories. Because we KNOW. So the difference is the point at which we say we know, or at which we stop saying we know. I stop saying I know the moment I move off the repeatable observation of material, the moment I move off what I think are facts. Other people regard much interpretation as at least as secure as the observable material and proceed accordingly; others regard other given information, from past enquiry, or written texts as much more secure than observable material. I wish nothing to be taken for granted beyond personal experience, supported by the experience of others, always in both cases repeatable if at all possible. From that point onwards I want to explore, with no constraints, the relationships which can be demonstrated between my observable material; I want to analyse. And then I find it fun, jolly fun - and I hope that sets your teeth on edge as it is intended to - to make up fantasies about How the Roman Villa got its Mosaic Pavements or any other Archaeological Just So stories. Jolly fun, and setting your teeth on edge because it is an activity that must never be allowed to be thought of as serious or scholarly or worthy. It is not because it cannot be. It has no eternal validity that we can be sure of, but it sells books, it keeps the GBPublic happy, it gets the subject on television, and it stops the Archaeological Society members from going to sleep till halfway through the lecture. It is the compromising archaeologist's link with the real world of other people. The one valid use of Just So Stories is to upset people enough to make them look critically and analytically at the material; which is what teaching is basically about.

So the two approaches which I have labelled analysis and deduction seem to boil down to two poles, between which, I hope, most archaeological thinking takes place. First there is the very hard line concentration on what is a repeatably fixed observable fact, the quest for relationships between facts, untramelled by any fixed points, the noting of these relationships, and then a launch into fantasy. Second is the gathering of facts, the statement of a framework necessary for deduction, and the making sense of the facts within this framework to produce a true picture of what actually happened. And the remarkable thing is that even to me, who knows that the first method is the only one which anyone should ever be allowed to follow, and that the second method is false and stupid, the first sounds an odd mixture of coldness and insanity, and the second - sweet reasonableness. Which means that I can understand when people give in and follow the old line, and the promising student, having looked over the edge, draws back and produces something safe. For the cosiness beckons, just as it beckons the atheist, in his last gasp, to rat on his

mind and don the warm slippers of KNOW-ING.

It is worrying that this cosy part of archaeology, no, of the interpretation of archaeology, is the main point of contact between the specialist and his audience whether reading his book, or watching on the screen. It is worrying for two reasons, probably more, but two for the moment. The point of contact is at a particularly soft point on the body, and the attempt to communicate through interpretation is inevertably untruthful. The point at which contact happens is soft, yielding, and constantly changing, even in a conservative subject like archaeology. The professional and the amateur digger are aware of the change which goes on, and, even more important, the reasons why the change goes on. The consumer may be uncomfortably aware that something is changing , but knows neither the reason for it, not the process behind it. It is as if some two machines have been set in motion, dependent on a connection between them which needs to be fairly finely tuned, yet the point of contact is made of marsh mallow or Turkish delight.

Communication through interpretation is bound to lead to trouble. On my scale of things interpretation is something which everyone should do for himself. If I communicate my interpretation to someone else it is in the hopes of setting him off on his own track, and I emphasize how unsure all interpretations are. This is the relationship of teaching and this is not a relationship which is common, or even accepted, in journalism or television or radio. The idea of teaching, in a deductive world, is that the professor professes what must be

Ded

believed, the reader reads out what others have believed and the demonstrator, the lowest form of animal life, demonstrates what can be seen. In an analytical world the teacher is the one who feels the need to encourage other to explore. I will not allow myself a full excursion on the value of newspapers, radio and television, but communication there does seem to be at one extreme, the expert, and at the other total equality where the teacher is an elitist and authoritarian idea to be repressed, with little in between. The expert can give his interpretation to an audience who have not the equipment of the facts to make their own alternative; the equals can play in the sand-pit, but cannot climb out of it until someone points out that direction of some sort is needed. The fault seems to me to lie in the telly view of the public. I think a few tougher programmes with unashamed teaching would meet a good response because they could begin to be honest.

Interpretation

Interpretation got lost somewhere a long time back. It was fobbed off with the advice go and look at examples and then describe what you see, and follow what you think to be the better courses. The usual side-step of define by description which is fought bitterly by every science teacher from the first forms upwards. Jones, define refraction. Please sir, refraction is when - at this point either all Hell will break loose as the teacher tries to make the point that you cannot say, or rather must not say, something is when, you must just define what it is. Jones would have gone on to say that refraction is when you see a stick half in and out of water, and it looks bent or broken at the surface of the water, but you know it isn't because it wasn't when you put it in, and it won't be if you pull it out , and you can see it isn't if you push it all the way in. Jones should have said that it was the change in direction of a wave motion as it passed from one medium to another medium of different refractive index.

Since it got lost, interpretation has always been referred to as related to fantasy. I think I define fantasy as the arrangement of thoughts and ideas without limiting rules. The psychologist would no doubt tell us that, since we all need some rules and regulations to see us round our daily life, it is most unlikely that fantasies produced within the human mind will be free from rules. This introduces the eternal worry of the fantasy as to whether it is worth having if it is not believable, and whether it is worth the name of fantasy if it is believable. If you create giant slugs, tens of feet across, and forget to set your

fantasy on a small planet with low gravity, or cancel out part of the earth's gravity, there is little point in waiting for them to move because they could not. Yet if you do take gravity, and conservation of energy, and Newton's Laws of Motion into account, can this really be called fantasy? I think there is no answer. To some people fantasy must not only be beyond their actual experience, but impossibly so, to be worth while. To others the impossibly so ruins the whole thing.

So the fantasy I keep referring to is one in which facts are taken down and woven into a set of ideas, the original of which, if it ever existed, you can never contact directly, so that the construct is consonant with general individual experience. To some people this is not fantasy, but at least the misunderstanding is now cleared up. This subject has already come up under cemeteries and uniformitarian assumptions. I should not build an idea of Roman Britain which demands that the majority of the inhabitants had 36 teeth instead of the usual permitted maximum of 32 for two reasons. First, the number of bodies dug up from Roman Britain with more than 32 permanent teeth is negligible; second, there is no evidence whatsoever for any suggestion that human evolution has moved so quickly in the past 1600 years as to suppress 4 human teeth. In other words they were just like us. The second objection is more important than the first because it takes much more getting round. The first one is absolute child's play to avoid. The 'normal' population of Roman Britain did in fact all have 36 teeth, but unfortunately they followed the 'normal' burial rite, which had developed in the Iron Age of cremate and scatter, so no 'normal' people from Roman Britain survive to be gaped at by researchers. There were deviants who had from 28 to 32 teeth, according to the suppression of wisdom teeth, but they were shunned and not allowed to take part in the proper burial rite, they therefore survive, just like coin-hoards, a totally abnormal selection from the general population. Well the material limits are not too difficult to explore, either in the build and function of British bodies, or their material surroundings, and I must fit my fantasies within these limits if they are to be believed, but the limits of thought and attitude are at least equally important.

What I seem to be doing...

What you seem to be doing? Don't you know?

Of course not; if I knew what I thought there would be no incentive at all to go on writing. The whole purpose of writing and talking is to find out what I think and why, and perhaps change it in the process. I cannot know what I am going to write in a book or an article until I have written it; I am proud to say that I never planned an essay when I was at school, in spite of continued pressure from limited minds who could only work within rails. I have never planned anything since, and I have no intention whatsoever of starting now. What I seem to be doing is fixing limits for interpretation in the hopes that once these are described it will be easier to look at the process inside.

So the plan is to start off with some material, to organize it and analyse it and point out the relationships and implications for relationships that have never been

expressed before, and then, taking note of necessary and agreed limits, to build a picture, a fantasy, an interpretation of that part of Roman Britain which will help towards a coherent whole if you ever have time to think that out. The limits established so far are the human body, with virtually no leeway for change between AD 300 and today in terms of structure and function. This seems draconian, but in fact the variation available today is so wide that I will not accept that it is a hardship to keep within it. Thus the number of teeth does vary between about 28 and 34, height varies within the 'normal' part of the population by a large amount, and there are plenty of individuals outside those limits, sensitivity or even allergy to foods or other factors varies astonishingly from cows milk to adrenaline to cats hair.

The second limit is the material surrounding the Romano-Briton. Here I give a warning. It is far more use to know the material, than to know what people have said about it, but that leads to punch-ups and tears. I am afraid that they are necessary, but they are seldom enjoyable and rarely productive. There is a division here about ways of working which I find interesting and I hope may be useful in putting together our final picture of how to interpret. Although I refer happily to this at the moment I am fairly sure that it is a mirage which will never be actually reached. The older British style of working is one that I find objectionable. It came to me in two particular encounters with classicists and ancient historians which I think are worth relating. They both occurred in Oxford which may be symptomatic of something.

The first was during my course for the Diploma in Education when set texts arrived on the scene; I chose Aristotle and Plato because I knew little about them, had never read any, but had an interest in the past even though my main subject was Chemistry followed by Biology. All the others who chose thus were classicists and ancient historians. I had a chunk of Aristotle's Poetics, I think, in which he found flute music indecent and not to be allowed for infants - I paraphrase. I went through the passage, it was fairly simple and straightforward, Aristotle seemed a remarkably straight laced and joyless teacher, and I was able to summarize quite clearly and quickly the what he actually said, and than sat back assuming we would discuss the ideas from our experience. I was disillusioned. I had not considered the possible meanings of xyzos - true, I had worked from a rather battered Bohn classic translation over 80 years old, but cheap in Thorntons - and I had not taken account of what Fraenkl, was it? had said about the flute, and we never got round to what we thought because it was so important to know what everyone else from time immemorial had said. I wonder what Aristotle would have thought of it?

Eight years later, back in Oxford I was a Biochemist doing a thesis on the distribution of Roman coins, and therefore belonged to the faculty of Literae Humaniores, division one (or two), history and texts. We had a graduate students group, and we met to keep our culture up from time to time, but the event which had me worried was the projected discussion of Aeschylus 'Agamemnon'. I brought my Penguin translation and absorbed it back at my lodgings in eccentric splendor in Wheatly. Each day I travelled in to Oxford

with Dr. Hassall, and one day I voiced my misgivings. "Don't worry", he said, "I'll fill you in on Greek tragedy tomorrow morning, and you will be perfectly alright". The next morning gave twenty minutes for him to tell me what every good prep-school boy knows, at the age of ten, about Greek tragedy - that everyone knows the story, and the art is to get them on the edge of their seats waiting for the inevitable but horrible moment which must come. Duly elated I attended my culture grope, and a flash-back occurred to that room in the Dept. of Education, but this time I had not opened my mouth. We got bogged down in the long speech where Agamemnon dithers over whether he will walk up the purple carpet, and where in the play it was supposed to be and had it got transposed? Eventually, since no one had enunciated the Hassall doctrine, I got fed up and burst out "If we are looking at it as a play where we know what is going to happen, then that is exactly the right place because I could hardly read it for thinking 'Oh, for heavens sake stop dithering and get on with it - you have no choice'". There was silence, faces turned towards me, and what sounded like an enthusiastic babble, of "Of course" and "Well if you want to look at it that way...". Either they were trying to be kind to someone so obviously out of place, or they were so sophisticated that prep-school ideas came as inspiration. I never chanced my luck again, so I never found out.

This attitude, of making a soufflé out of the ideas which (almost) everyone to date has expressed weighs down most of the foreign students that I have ever taught or met. It seems particularly worrying in

Germany, France and America though it is of course much more worrying in other parts of the world because the attitude never lifts. At least in Germany, France and America, once you have shown that you can do as required, but often up to the level of a doctorate, you are allowed to go on and think for yourself. Elsewhere thinking, in archaeology at least, is just not a part of the academic scene. I am not pretending that all is well in Britain, but at least thinking is alive and well among the better teachers and the better students; and when it happens there it is like a disease and can quickly spread. Which is why firm measures are sometimes needed. I fear that absence of thought is now more endemic among some types of scientist, certainly at first year levels, where there is virtually no contact with basic material and all that is possible is the regurgitation of received ideas. Certainly, teaching two refugees from the Natural Sciences to Archaeology at Cambridge, it became apparent that one thing they most valued was being asked to get down to the material and produce their own ideas about it, for the first time. And, of course, they did have the equipment with which to think, which artists do not in general have. This is a puzzling paradox at the moment; the 'A' level scientist has been taught to think well, but never allowed to do it, and never given the material on which to do it, unless he does a biology project; the artist has continually been encouraged to think great and beautiful thoughts without ever being brought anywhere near a thinking discipline. Which may be the reason why so few 'A' level scientists, of any ability, go on to do science degrees, and migrate in

numbers to areas of Beautiful Thought. And judging by the Institute of Archaeology over the past 18 years, do so much better than arts sixth formers per capita.

Know the material for yourself and do not believe anyone else, especially if it is written down. Try to base everything on what you yourself know, or what you have squeezed by interrogation from friends, colleagues, visitors and teachers. The result will be attack, either dismissive, pained, or virulent. Almost hardest to take is the pained, and it is usually administered by the older practitioners. All three attacks usually start off from an assumption of your either ignorance or wrongheadedness, but I will come back to that.

The pained attack looks at you sadly and says that he supposes that Blatenbulger's wonderful analysis of belt stiffeners was stolen from your library years ago, but you still ought to have known about it.

You might, or you might not have known about it, but you decided to do your own work on belt stiffeners, and you think that what you have done stands up in its own right. It totally disagrees with Blattenbulger does it? Well then, we have two analyses and that is far better than just one.

But everything since B. was based on his work, and no one up to now has seen fit to question it - he was a remarkable and very able man (warming up now) and for a first year research student, to question such a great mans achievements is most unwise.

I didn't question B. I just did not bother with him: my work was straightforward listing and analysis, and if it comes to different conclusions, may the best man win. I do not disagree with him, I have not attacked him, I am not saying everyone who has used his work is an idiot, I have just done a piece of work. In fact, now you point it out, they were rather silly to accept his conclusions, especially if mine turn out to be right. Of course such a conversation never actually happens because I cannot bear to cause further suffering to nice people. It ought to have happened, and I shall try much harder in future.

The dismissive attack is more difficult to deal with. and is therefore the attack more favoured in this work, because it often consists of complete silence. You look a bit of a fool writing later that you cannot understand Blooges complete silence on your great work a) because it makes it even more obvious and b) this is just what Blooges wants. You have to gather a certain amount of steam before anyone can take a writer to task for dismissing you. After a certain point it perhaps reflects more on the dismissor than the dismissed. The virulent attack is often the most puzzling if all you have done is to look as objectively as possible at a group of material and, as a result, simply say what you think. The examples are most easily seen when someone strays across the border line into someone elses territory, the Saxonist saying something fairly obvious about things Roman, the pottery person saying something fairly simple about coins, the Kent archaeologist commenting on Hadrian's Wall. As one person was heard to say of John Smith's work on villas, "He is wrong, and the reason he is wrong is that he is a medievalist and does not know about Roman villas". The

alternative is, in a weary voice "But we don't deal with coins in that way". In part it is the old 'what have people said' syndrome, for you have not immersed yourself in the conventions of the subject before commenting, you just studied that heap of brooches. Good for you, go on doing it, and giving your unbiased, or ill-informed comments, because some of them will be useful to open-minded workers, and the ones that are wrong will just drop out.

Limits again: the human body and its workings; the material surrounding that body when alive, taken from first principles and if possible disregarding what has been said about it before, SO LONG AS WHAT YOU SAY STANDS UP factually; and being human. Here is the great snag. Either most interpreters do not know what being human means, or, more likely they do know, but think that such knowledge is irrelevant in scholarship. I feel that I am actually approaching Ian Hodder here, and that makes me feel happy and confident - probably wrong on all counts. I think this matters so I will explore it further.

The academic, and all archaeologists, whether paid by Universities or not, tend to be academics, is supposed to be in the business of separating the gold of scholarship from the dross of humanity. He is supposed to avoid the dispute over the garden wall on the actual cost of sprouts in the market, and concentrate on the cost of tanned sealskin in a new copy of Diocletian's Price Edict; or skirt the cost and trouble of building a new house, which he must leave at home, for the delights of talking about the building of towns in

Roman Britain which he does in his study. He must regard people, in his academic work, as living by rules, maximizing information, following precepts, and accepting the changes of fashion, when each one of these things is flatly contradicted in individual cases by his neighbours at home. John Percival makes this point about his strawberry bed: he knows in his mind what he ought to do to get the best crop, but he has never yet got around to doing it, and an estimate of his yield would always be too high because the estimator would insist that such a well informed person would of course go for maximum yield. Interpretations are inevitably made on the assumption that people are rational and disciplined, when every possible observation made on live specimens tend to show that they are not, self-observation included. It is the severe problem of the committee view, which I think is related to institutional sin. A committee has quite different standards from those of its constituents. This happens because people act in committees in groups, or as scholars and academics, as they are expected to act. A problem comes up in a meeting, the problem is expressed in terms of shock-horror, it is clear that shock-horror is expected, most of the participants obligingly express shock-horror and the rest keep quite and allow it to be thought that they share the prevailing view. It takes considerable courage to say gently - as a person I do not find any shock-horror about it - neither, if you act as the individuals I know, do many of you.

The academics' committee is the world of scholarship which will dissect out their works to see if they conform to some mirage of scholarly standards in which omission is just as important as commission. Humour, unless extremely heavy footed and referential, is out; accurate references in the approved manner, are in; humanity is out; a complete account of all that has gone before is in. A personal view, from a person, who has done his best to set out carefully collected material and say what he think it means, from his own experience, is not scholarship, just as admission of personal feelings in a committee is not discipline. And this is what is missing in any discussion of the material from Roman Britain, and its interpretation.

In summary interpretation must abide by the workings of the human body, the material which you understand to have surrounded that body when alive, and a guiding principle of being human in your interpretation. These are the rules, all that is left is to find if it is possible to see how they work in practice, in order to flesh them out, and then, if possible to suggest some ways in which we may judge whether a given interpretation is a good one.

Few interpreters deviate from human physical specifications though they do throw considerable burdens on the inhabitants of the past. There is a commendable tendency to try out limits of what people can and cannot do, ranging from David Sellwood's experiments in striking silver coins, to the experimental earthwork of the 1960's, but this has not spread so enthusiastically to the reconstruction of huts and houses and actually living in them, with a few heavily publicized exceptions. Material studies are rarely well done beyond the point of gathering material together and describing it. This is simply because most students and teachers do not have the scientific training to deal with material, but think that gathering and description is all there is to be done. I am not leaving out the interpretation, I am objecting to the failure to prepare the factual information in a way that is susceptible to testing, either as a gathering of material, or as the basis for ideas. I have always insisted that the interpretation of material is a different activity from the collecting and describing of material, but this inevitable and inescapable methodological gap is aggravated, made wider, when the material is not organized for interpretation. I found these coins in these museums: I think Commodus reorganized the coin supply to Gaul. Once the basic facts, the repeatable observations, have been quoted, the job is to organize them explicitly to point the way to an interpretation. If the organization is good, and the reader has an open mind, the interpretation will seem to grow out of the organized material. It does not, and cannot; this is the construct of an able mind on manageable material. This last jump, from the repeatable observation to the assertion about meaning, has to come from a human mind, and will be the better the more open the mind and the more aggressively human.

This must mean that in details most interpretations will differ. It is far more unlikely that two very different people will come to the same interpretation than different ones, yet disagreement is generally thought to be a sign of trouble, error, or downright bloody-mindedness. It is not, it is a sign of open-ness and healthy thinking. Why should someone brought up a strict Lutheran in Sweden, influenced by a time as a postgraduate student among the flesh-pots of Copenhagen, later getting an administrative job involving politics in Norway, think the same about the end of the Roman Empire as the third of a family of five reared in a liberal farming family in Cheshire?

Because they would both be working from the same facts of course.

Oh dear, is there no hope? I carefully said "think" about the end of the Roman Empire - think about a concept, not list a load of material. There would be something wrong if they could not agree on the material finds on which they both wanted to base their analyses. There are either five or six sherds of that category of pottery unless they have been so foolish as to start their discussion without standardizing the categories of pottery. Given goodwill, a decent scientific training, and an openness to fact on both sides, they can standardize their categories, and their disagreements will be less than 2% or 3% of any totals. The can then agree only to work with differences of more than 5% in any figure's. The trouble is likely to come when each tries to turn his or their material, into ideas because this has to go through each individual mind. Even if rules are set out - which would be extremely silly, but possible- such as compare the ratio of red to black wares with your attitude to capital punishment, or whatever process you like to invent, two different people would get in the way of a single interpretation, and this is highly desirable and to be encouraged. Interpretation IS an individual act so it must be recognized as such.

You have been brought to study some

material, you have been put on the brink of interpreting, armed with some fairly general rules of conduct, you take the dive, rather nervous because there have only been general rules rather than specific instructions, and you have produced something. How can it be judged? You want to know if you have done well so that next time you can hope for the same, or do something different and produce something better. It is no good waiting for opinions, or reviews. Opinions will be either, yes, I like it, it fits well with my ideas; or no, I don't like, it does not fit with my ideas so it must be wrong; or worst of all, I find it repugnant to my basic beliefs, unstated, two of your references are wrong and the percentages on page 5 do not add up to 100% so it is wrong. Reviews will not appear, if they ever do, for years after actually typing the article and will be of two sorts. Non-specialists will welcome the positive aspects of your work and, as a new-boy, encourage you; people in the same field will see you as a rival and will concentrate on the negative aspects to see you off on to another field as soon as possible. Neither of these have any bearing on your ideas; reviewers seldom recognize these. This is not just personal pique; in book form although I have been criticized, this has usually been fair and justified, and in article form the comments have been even-handed: my complaints come from a more general view of the world of reviewing. So you have to do your own assessment, which of course is central to the whole idea; you are alone, right from the start, so you may as well get used to it.

There are two lines here which may lead forward. I am taking for granted that what you have said is firmly based in material and in the demonstrated relationships between the different parts of that material. After that your latest production must fit in with the rest of your work in an effort to produce a whole without contradictions; and as that becomes more extensive and complete, and more internally consistent, so you can be sure that you are doing your bit towards the increasing description of truth. You do not set out to do that; you set out to produce a working model with no loose ends or jarring parts, and a consequence of that, if it is done properly, is that the total world around you, of material and of thought makes better sense. The reason that you are on your own is that whether you like it or not, and most people apparently do not, a fact I find continually amazing, you are an individual and it is therefore no good trying to make what you do consistent with someone elses world. You can add on what you have done, to your favorite extant world, but unless this is worked through it may set up a nasty imbalance later on, just like adding to a car a new wheel which experience later shows does not really fit. The course I advocate is the doing of pieces of work, and the publishing and storing of them, without comment, until you are ready to sew them together yourself. So on this level, your own estimate of what you have done might have to wait some time before it can be properly done. The chances are that all other estimates will be wrong simply because they are done by others who do not know what your world is going to be like. If commentators are honest they can only say - this does not fit in with my picture, I wait to see what X's picture is going to be.

The second line is really an aspect of this in that the people and the situations that you create, the builders of the villa and its successive alterations, the people who choose the mosaic design and the wall painting, must turn out to be acceptably real people. This cannot be assured by the application of sociological rules because, if they can ever be enumerated they must depend on the aggregation of individual peculiarities. In other words, general rules about what people do, or do not, do come from the observation of a large number of individuals and then the stripping of individuality to produce a mean or majority result. The discussion of a Roman villa must be exactly the opposite, for it was planned and built by an individual, or at least by a family, and not by a committee. This is why institutional sin, committee principles or however you describe mass thinking cannot properly be applied to individual actions in the past, and why the individual interpreter, replete with kinks and cussedness is the right commentator on the past. At this point we have reached Collingwood's doctrine by which the person who wishes to interpret the past must work his way through the processes of the

past, so far as they are known. If it is a matter of building a Roman villa, or enlarging a simple farmhouse to form a villa, then the interpreter, armed with all the material facts that he can command must follow directly the Collingwood method of working his way through the possible thought processes of the builder to the triumphal conclusion of the new house. This is not a scientific path, it is not a work of scholarship, it is an act of faith, guided by the material remains. It is not scientific because there is no conceivable way of testing the result either by experiment or repeatable observations. It is not scholarship because it has no relevance to everything that has been said on the subject before because that is overwhelmingly irrelevant. It is an act of faith simply because the only way of assessing it is by doing it and continuing to live with it. If it fits in with past and future experience it was a good act; if it does not fit, if it causes irritation to other parts of the system, if it grates and impedes, then it is probably wrong, and needs revision. If it facilitates it is probably right.

Now that we have reached this conclusion we can put everything together to form a picture of THE END.

Britannia to England: The Transition

All the sections up to this point form for me an introduction to the really interesting subject of how something which is studied as Roman Britain turns into a totally different thing, taught by different people to different students in different courses, with different text-books, materials and methods, namely, Early England. Immediately two strands separate out; the reality of what actually happened in Britain between say AD 200 and 800, and what people have said about it and how they have studied it. There is no hope of ever knowing actually what happened for sure. We can have ideas and manipulate the material information and the picture we create may be perfectly calm and hopeful, but even if we have judged it to be a good picture, and others have accepted it, this still does not mean that this is actually what happened; it remains our picture, or your picture, or my picture, and should not be confused with reality. Once this is said, and taken in and believed, then we could talk for shorthand about the evidence, the reflection of what actually happened, and what people have said about it.

I hope, by this time in these notes it will be accepted as commonplace that what people have said about any subject, talking here about archaeology, but it is a wider point, depends on them as persons, as voters, and church-goers or humanists, and disciplinarians, and money-makers or just ordinary pleasant people. This is because what I shall call from here onward, for brevity, the Transition is not a fact, or an assembly of facts, or a model, which is a way of looking at facts with reasonably simple parts which can be explicitly communicated from one person to another with good hope of success, but a myth. And a myth is either an inbuilt part of you, or is made up of such parts. In logic I gather that the tightest argument depends on the idea that you have premises and a conclusion and they may be described as formal logic if, given the premises you cannot avoid the conclusion without falling into contradiction. There is something parallel working in inbuilt equipment, fears, emotions, likes, hates and the resultant myths. It seems almost as if, given your equipment, there are only a certain number of myths that you can hold without getting into mental difficulties. It is not up to you to decide that you quite like a myth; you cannot hold it unless you are equipped to do so. If you are not equipped to do so, then you have to have a grand spring clean in order to take on this newly promoted myth without internal contradiction. You may have to desensitize yourself from spiders and give all that you have to the poor, or to cut your hair and stop smoking anything stronger then Earl Grey's tealeaves; it will be much simpler to take on board only those myths that you are fitted for. This does not mean that you have to disregard all others, such as the myth on the Transition which I am going to put forward. You can examine it without danger to your internal arrangements, you can flirt with it, but you may find that you have to keep it on one side as a second best, because of your present appurtenances. I ask no more;but I do demand that.

Why is the Transition a matter of myth, of deeply embedded reactions, rather than a simple matter of a model communicated from one to another? The trouble comes in the contents, for there is religion, politics, decline of towns, revulsion from fashion, turning the back on wholesome Roman society with its careful safeguards and limiting ordinances, for the wildness of the hairy Dark Age potentate, or perhaps leaving the effete Roman administration with its silks and perfumes, even for so-called men, for the homespun roughness and basic sense of the British cattle-raider. Moving out of light and organization, for a penumbra of cured hams, sheeps wool and only local knowledge. Personal reaction to any of these things will depend, not on reason, but on gut reaction; it may be dressed up as scholarly, but, in the end this is a blind. The way that you see Britannia turning into early England is going to say far more about you, or me, or the other person, than about Britain from AD 200 to 800; and if you simply take over some extant explanation that tells me so much about you that I wish to know no more. We are, of course, getting very near to each person's absolute presuppositions, and as Collingwood noted over 40 years ago, "people are apt to be ticklish in their absolute presuppositions".

This transition is perhaps the thing which started me off on archaeology - certainly it is the first thing that I can remember worrying about as an idea from the past. I grew up in Cirencester, and it was not the same as Corinium. Why not? Why had the street system changed? Why was there so much from the 1st to the 4thC's. and again so much from the 13th.C. onwards, and so little in between? I was already at that time on the track of the linking material, because it was obvious

that it simply had not been found. That, in turn, started me digging, and the reports the I wrote on small excavations had to account for the absence of layers between about AD 300 and AD 1200. I apparently did even worse than most other archaeologists because my sites did not even go on to the end of the fourth century, never mind beyond that. One site, at Ashcroft, had been gardens and the later layers had been dug away; another site at the Grammar School was on the outskirts of the town, not quite correct but still, so later layers might more reasonably be missing there. The first site I dug in Querns Lane seemed to stop by about 350 at the latest but that was just beginners bad luck. In each case the evidence was quite clear. At Ashcroft, whole late third century pots standing upright on the latest floors with no later disturbance, building or whatever, except for a Dark Age ditch. At the Grammar School the latest floor dated by pottery below and above to the early fourth century. At Querns Lane a fall of rooftiles from the building with both pots and coins below and above making a date of about 340 to 350 quite clear for the fall of the roof, the last thing apparently to happen on the site. Under the influence of a glass of warm champagne on a hot June day, sitting on a mosaic floor that we had just cleaned, a co-digger who had just been given a first class degree in history lent me a copy of Finberg's 'Withington' and perhaps attention moved from the non-existent material, or the material that I was not destined to find, to more conceptual explanations. Larger and longer digs in Cirencester had no more luck than I did, for bodies in roadside ditches which have been pressed into use to demonstrate fifth century plagues were known to be medieval from the moment they were dug up, late Roman refuges in the Bull Ring seem to be complete mirages supported only by a few bits of non-local Saxon pottery, and the one site that has a lot of pottery and coins of the last quarter of the fourth century, the Beeches Houses or villas, were clogging themselves up in foot deep mire somewhere between 380 and 410. It is not only that the material for the fifth century simply is not there, in the Cotswolds, just as for the 6th, 7th and 8thC., but that it is difficult to prolong the life of the town up to the end of the fourth century.

This realization grew, despite what I wanted to believe, so it is the opposite of wish-fulfillment. Other towns seems to be in the same plight. London seemed to be even worse off, for on many sites it was difficult to make any case for a full continuing occupation after the Antonine fire. The explanations there have obscured this for a long time. Victorian basements had clipped off all the late levels of London. In other words it was generally agreed that London archaeology lacked a fourth century, but this was a modern lack, caused by large scale modern interference, not an ancient lack caused by economic or social interference. The tide turned as sites were dug in which the debris of the Antonine fire was seen never to have been cleared away, and never to have been built over. A fire somewhere around AD 160 had ruined houses, and the mess was left there and the site was never reclaimed. In other sites the succeeding black earth, which in places directly overlay the Antonine fire, contained virtually no fourth century material.

In this case I mean no coins and perhaps twenty sherds of pottery from a site at least 40 meters square. So later rubbish pits, and rubbish burying could not be blamed for destroying those many 4thC. houses we KNEW were there. If rubbish had been buried the layers of the fourth century would have been disturbed, but not taken away, so that 4thC. material ought to be there. Now no theory ought to be based on London because it is all on its own. It is the trade centre, we are led to believe; at times it is the capital or metropolis of Britannia, or of one of the part provinces of Britannia. Anything which affects Roman life may well affect that isolated trade and administrative centre, which is at the centre of no tribe or living group, except its money making parasites, and London may well show signs of distress when all is well elsewhere. True, in part. But although London can be described as isolated money-grubbing personified, that disease would have spread out into the other towns and that aspect of the other towns may well have caught the draught at the same time as London. They may well have had enough other ploys to survive for longer, but the London blight could well have been a feather in the wind for them, and ought perhaps to be the same for us. It may be that London is the most marginal town in Britain because it had the least foundation in real life. It might be interesting to speculate on what the City would look like if my prayers were answered and finance collapsed overnight; it would almost be a square mile of desertion. Croydon and Muswell Hill would show a few rotten teeth in the High Streets as financiers crumbled, but the greengrocers would continue, by barter of they had to, and the carpet shops would probably survive. While not wanting to suggest London was in any way as depraved as the present money market there may well be a parallel.

These then are some of the pointers which set me off thinking about the failure of the densely nucleated settlement, or TCT, in Britain at the end of the Roman period. The material started in Cirencester with direct, hand-dug experience, and then took in London, and added other towns such as Exeter, Chichester, Winchester, Lincoln, Gloucester and so on, as the evidence came to hand. From these sites there was enough material to start my train of thought which led to the article in World Archaeology. One main argument against that article is that the material evidence does not compel that train of thought because there are sites in which occupation continued in towns through the fourth century, and in very rare instances beyond. The classic site which gets quoted again and again, though it is only one main site, and one extra site which helps, is the late house excavated by Prof. Frere at Verulamium. This can be shown to have continued in use, if not occupation, into the fifth century because of coins underneath the latest period of house alterations; then there are two phases of further change and use, and this must take us towards the middle of the fifth century. The accompanying example is simply a house renovated towards the end of the fourth century, but unfortunately this is not followed by later changes on the same site. Evidence such as this from Verulamium, or other evidence excavated by Phil Barker

from Wroxeter compel belief in the occupation in towns in the fifth century; once this has happened, my story of towns declining in the fourth century cannot compel belief. I think I have stated these points reasonably fairly: my case depends on more observations than have been quoted, the opposing case depends on more cases than have been quoted; the case rests.

The trouble here is that we are not talking about the same thing. First we must distinguish between life in towns and town life. It would be good to add the category of occupation on sites which happen to be in former towns. This gives a gradation from a building which is there because it is part of a thriving town organization, through a building which, with others, is grouped on a town site, down to almost isolated buildings which stand on sites which were once towns. I have no reason to think that certain sites in Britain, on which Romanized towns once stood, have ever been totally deserted. I have said this before, and it immediately is used as evidence that Reece thinks that town life continued from the Roman period to the present day. All that I meant and mean is that I see no reason at the moment to insist that certain spaces in Britain remained building free zones after they had ceased to be towns. Shepherds no doubt camped in the ruins. Enterprising farmers would salvage beams and stones for cattle pens and farmyards, if not for patching up their own farms, and cows and sheep, not to mention chickens and goats, would graze among the stoney heaps which showed former occupation. We all agree that this does not constitute town life. The middle category does not, to me, signify town life either, because a village on the ruins is not the same thing as the town of the same name and at the same place. So the occupation of a defined area at a density higher than that at which every person can support himself by direct labour on necessary subsistence, therefore involves unnecessary labour on services and worse. It also involves the people who are living communally having a wish to do so, and some reasons which keep the community together and functioning as a unit. In other words the inhabitants of a town have diverged from a natural and subsistence life and chosen an artificial life with the communal feeling that this will be better for them. If this group selfishness fails then the town will fail, for an awareness that they can do as well on their own will spell the dispersion of the townies. It may leave a hard core who have neither the skills, nor the initiative to survive naturally, but these can hardly be expected to keep up town life if they cannot keep up basic life. If the density of occupants falls to the level at which all the inhabitants can be concerned with basic living, food, clothing and shelter, then I have severe doubts about the continuance of the Town as an institution. There may be a name, there may be a council, and there may be buildings, but the superstructure of services cannot possibly survive on the basic foundation. Put at its absolute minimum my contention is that after the middle of the fourth century there is not a sufficient density of population in town sites in Britain to allow the idea of continuing flourishing urban life. This is stated so moderately and so modestly that I think it would command at least majority assent; it would not have been a majority opinion in the 1970's, so that opinion has swung in the last ten years. When I first put forward my ideas, reports on excavations followed the line that I myself took at first, that although this particular site showed no signs of great activity in the later fourth century this was no doubt the luck of the draw. Now it is more likely that reports will note the absence of later fourth century activity as something to be expected from general attitudes, though "the earlier activity on the site gives no support to the extreme theories of Reece".

Leaving aside moderation, if the last paragraph is accurate, and I think that it is, then I have won (Comment 4: This has caused more complaint than any other sentence. I am astonished. I suppose it is more normal to take pleasure in saying that other people are wrong rather than to take pleasure in saying that I was right, but I find that a negative and rather unpleasant way of going about things. And if it seems likely at the moment that I was right, and I am sure it will not stay like that for long, then why on earth should I not say so, and take pleasure in it. What a joyless existence at least three of the first readers want to wish on me. Or is it worse that I have said I have won? Is the fault that I am demoting the hard and highly meaningful business of research to the level of a game? If so, then codswallop; as far as I am concerned it is a very enjoyable occupation and only unlike a game in that it doesn't matter who does win. I react only because I was so surprised at the readers' reactions and to forestall any further deeply meaningful expressions of distaste). Together with other people thinking in the same way

I have forced the admission that the town does not constitute a healthy British organism to the end of the fourth century "and probably beyond". If not to the end of the century then certainly not beyond. This was the main objective of the original thrust, to separate the decline of towns from the physical and material transition from Roman to Saxon. Thus the decline of towns is now agreed to be something which happened within the time of Roman material, even Roman political and administrative domination, so that it is not the casualty of the change-over between the two types of material. In other words if you believe in Saxons, they, as defined by Saxon objects and gravegoods, did not kill Roman towns in Britain.

So much for the material. In fact I would say that it is not a matter of my imposing a new idea on the interpretation of Roman Britain, but at this level, and as far as we have gone so far, of liberating the material to be taken at face value. This is, I submit, what is now happening. I think it is a case of the material making one idea less acceptable and another more acceptable idea being suggested. So long as the matter is agreed I am quite happy to drop out of it altogether and agree to the lie that it is what everyone really thought all along. But my ideas went much further than this, though they had to stay very much on the level of ideas. It is at this point that I part company with the majority who still dally timidly on the brink of any far-reaching explanations. I said quite categorically that if towns were flourishing in Britain by about AD 200, they were decidedly seedy by the end of that century, and the cosmetic fillip of the early fourth century was

no more than an unsuccessful facelift. The wrinkles were showing by the middle of the third century and the town proper was a thing of the past by the end of the century.

At this point it must be noted that I have lifted off into the realms of explanation, and am no longer in the realm of material dictated observation. It is therefore no good telling me how many new buildings were erected in the early fourth century, firstly because they never fully replace the losses from the earlier period so that the towns of AD 320 are not the same as the towns of AD 200; and secondly I am talking about the concept of the town and its driving force and communal life, and not about a set of buildings. If the space occupied in 320 IS less than that occupied in 200 then something is happening. And if, as I suspect, the buildings are different, then this may confirm my suspicions. The later buildings, whether at Verulamium, or London, or Cirencester, are the large well appointed stone houses which, in the countryside would be called villas. Even Prof. Frere, a staunch champion of the town, admits that "the new Verulamium was rather different from the old. In the period before the Antonine fire we get the impression of bursting energy, and quickly increasing rewards for commercial activity; ...... It appears that the curial class had at last come to town, but its arrival had changed the cities character to that of a residential, perhaps slightly sleepy, country town." (1981). In 1975 I had said something similar about Corinuim, though I had got the century wrong "The one class of citizen who had no reason to move was the farmer who attended to his fields and animals around the town from a town house indistinguishable from a country farm, and it may be that the population of the fifth [this soon became fourth] century Corinium was no more than a collection of farming families." It is therefore no good complaining that the material available does not press every one to accept my ideas on the failure of the town in Britain after about 250 because material can never press people to certain ideas. They can unsettle some ideas, and make others more acceptable, but there must be a predisposition to change, for the material can probably never be marshalled in such a way as to prove only one necessary, logical and inescapable idea. The sitting tenant of an idea has the benefit of being part of your thought, but it is unlikely that the material evidence is more strongly in favour of that idea than any other. What we need, as I have insisted all through, is the awareness that these explanations are only ideas, and that the more of them there are, within reason, the better.

As an extra plea for keeping in mind at least two explanations at once I will quote the recently published example of suburbs in Roman Britain and what they mean. In his recently published study of suburbs Simon Esmonde Cleary mentions my odd notions about the decline of towns, but sees in the flourishing late suburbs a clear disagreement with my ideas. Since the suburbs are flourishing the towns must be flourishing - or else, we have no reason to think that the towns are not flourishing; the reverse, with just flourishing suburbs "would require a highly distinctive annular morphology for which there is no convincing reason or parallel". This publication appeared very much at the time when there was a newly published study of the extra-mural settlement at Silchester, and the two follow much the same line. My problem is that while I am very happy to accomodate the suburb observations in my theory or interpretation, the suburbians do not seem to want to use my ideas as one way of interpreting their material. In both cases it is made clear that these odd ideas exist, that the established ideas exist, and that the odd ideas have not ousted the established ideas, so these, for the moment are still right. If I were given to gloom this would probably fill me with gloom, but as I have never expected people to act reasonably I am not too upset. My main worry is the same here as it has been everywhere else, that the accepted interpretation is not regarded as a fashionable interpretation, but as fact, as things actually were, the true story of Roman Britain: if these are right, then everything else must be wrong.

The theories of the suburbians are rather like my view of the later Roman town; they have a hole in the middle. Simon Esmonde Cleary's study was of suburbs, so it obviously, sensibly, clearly and without any blame, is not a survey of contemporary settlement **inside** towns. That survey, simply going through excavation reports and drawing up areas occupied at different times has never been done, so we rely on feelings; the feelings of those who, if pushed into a corner by a demonstration that in certain towns there is a much smaller area occupied in the fourth century, and especially the later part, will say that the area excavated so far is such a small sample that things will balance up when we know more. And my feelings, that we ought to take our small, but remarkably random, sample of towns so far excavated as evidence. In the absence of this survey it is assumed that town life, like suburban life, is flourishing in the fourth century. The one complements the other; suburbs would be unlikely to flourish without a central town, and the town's flourishing is suggested by the suburbs. At Silchester the suburbs flourish in the fourth century and presumably, so does the town. Let us look first at the holes and than at the likely explanations.

Just as a survey of fourth century town occupation has not been done to compare with the fourth century extra-mural settlement, so, at Silchester, little is known about the later part of the town life because most of it was dug off the top of the site in the full-scale excavations around 1900. There is one site, right in the centre, which has been re-excavated, and which did give some dating evidence; this was the building referred to as the church. I put it like that, not because I disbelieve the idea that it is a church, but to underline the point that this is interpretation and no one may build on it as if it were fact. This building had mortar and mosaic floors and in and under these floors, in the mortar make-up, and in pockets of wear, there were coins and pottery. In Prof. Ian Richmond's first lecture to the Society of Antiquaries I am quite sure that he put his faith in the dating of the building in one particular coin which he described as Constantine I AD 307 to 337; I am so certain because John Kent who was sitting next to me whispered, "I think we could narrow that down a bit". Marion Wilson who acted as site supervisor was also quite convinced that this one

coin, found on edge in the mortar, and in fact of AD 313-320, was separate from the other coins, found in a muddy hollow in the mortar. This worry, that there were two separate lots of dating evidence, came through, as always in Prof. Feres's report where he allowed me a footnote to say that the coins as found made a very peculiar single group. Taken at face value they suggest a date of building in the 320's, and a date of desertion and ruin in the 360's, or 370's. Again, this possibility of a ruin in the town centre, next to the Forum and Basilica, worries Prof. Frere, and he admits as such. But since we know that a flourishing town would not have tolerated a ruined 'church' in the centre, the "pottery and coins are irrelevant to the date of the squatters occupation and merely represent residual material such as must exist in quantity throughout the latest levels of Silchester" (1975, p.297). If we did not know that Silchester flourished into the fifth century this evidence might make us think that the town centre was in decline in the middle of the fourth century; but then, the suburbs make it quite clear that all is well, for who would go outside the walls if the inside were not full up and flourishing?

My answer came some ten years before the question was asked, so it is not special pleading to try to fit in awkward new facts into my theory. Tim Tatton-Brown, after some years of excavation in the centre of Canterbury was beginning to get worried as to where the late Roman occupation was, for there seemed to be large open areas in the late City Centre, and several large buildings were looking in bad shape in the second half of the fourth century. Yet there are 'Saxon' settlements around the town, and foci of late burial, and Canterbury is one place where whatever the archaeology says, the sources insist that some sort of occupation must be continuous. This seems to me to be a reasonable question, and even the appeal to written sources does not put me off as much as usual because they happen to relate directly to the problem under examination. In a letter, of which I wish I had kept a copy, I obligingly made out a picture to account for his evidence that there was not much going on in the centre, and his suspicions that there was something at the edges. In the fourth century my theories already ran the town down, as an urban unit with a will and a promise of its own, down to almost nothing. I left in the centre a few owners of large houses who may well have bought up the land around them, and then where the countryside proper started, at the walls, whether just inside or outside, I put the living places of the groups who worked the nearby land, and if you want to call them villages you may do so. The centre becomes a High Preserve, suitable later on for a Royal and Church centre, but this does not in any way predicate a town or urban spirit, and the majority of the population lived in small communities towards the countryside. There the people still were when they adopted 'Saxon' fashions, there their graveyards are, and there units spring up and continue. The Gates may be particularly popular, just as the survey round Silchester showed, for this is the obvious point of connection between the walled area, only really good for living and grazing, and the farmland proper. The centre with its white elephant of a basilica, never completed as such, and its ruined church which should have been taken down years ago, but no one really likes to touch it, remains a particular place, perhaps legally as well as emotionally, and the local council might even meet there each Hogswatchnight, just for old times sake. So I am afraid that I take the excellent surveys of Esmonde Cleary and Silchester as clear evidence that the centripetal forces of the urban unit, those forces which concentrated all that was best in the centre of the town area, had broken down irremediably in the fourth century, and people were once more spreading out, and reversing the movements of some five or six generations before when it seemed possible that towns would catch on. I must emphasize that this model of urban distribution was made up to explain the lack of late activity in Canterbury city centre and not to explain the activity outside the walls of many other towns, of which Silchester is such a good example. But that new evidence does fit in remarkably well, and there is nothing better for a new theory than to account for new evidence before it is even discovered.

All this, in a way, is of the past, and I want to get to the future of our ideas about the end of Roman Britain. We have got bogged down in towns, even though they do not exist, and there are other strands to introduce before trying to sort my ideas out. My thoughts moved on by an important amount in October 1987 when I was invited to a conference in Toulouse, organized by the four southern *circonscriptions* of French archaeology on the subject of burial. After the main conference there was a day in which the four directors reported on archaeological activity in their regions during the past two years, and it was the framework within which they worked that gave me to think. They divided their accounts into the later Iron Age and the Haut Empire and the Bas Empire and the early Medieval period. This interested me particularly because it seems to be what I have advocated for British archaeology for some time, and here was a chance to see what the result of adopting it might be. In brief, the Late Iron Age and the Haut Empire made excellent sense as a coherent story of growing and increasing success and organization; or vice versa, while the later period was something of a rag-bag of odds and ends.

The earlier period was studied, dug and reported as a coherent trend towards the goal of all good communities, the town; it was the period of urbanization , of civilization, and of increasing organization, complexity and administration. While the Romans came in on the act explicitly and materially at a historical point they were further removed in the earlier stages. In other words, the movement in the Later Iron Age towards larger nucleated settlements with organized plans and defences may have been the result of Mediterranean influences creeping fungus-like through the South of France, but the classical world only reared its ugly head at the time of the Roman conquest and exploitation. There are two highly important points here: a general scheme of study underlies the whole of the work on this period, and a process is being studied which is visibly independent of the mass movement of Roman men and materials into the area under study. The period of urbanization has a unifying theme, and the Romans

came in on it half way through without great effect, except to bring in some cosmetic building fashions like grid-plans and stone gateways. All this builds up to a climax somewhere around the year AD 100, and then there is some stability, and then a change in the third century. From say 250, if not 200 all has changed to the Bas Empire, which grades imperceptibly, and in different places at different times into the Early Medieval period, and the whole structure of study changes.

The later period came through the surveys as a series of subjects in a very bitty way. There was virtually nothing about town occupation, though some sites did go on to the later period; a little about late defences, something about cemeteries, more about churches, and so on. While the great Process had welded together the earlier period and given a firm framework within which to work, well dated by widely spread material, nothing tied together the later observations except that they came above Roman levels and below medieval levels - both properly so called. I strongly suspect that this lack of an overall scheme of study, the lack of any ideas as to what is happening, means that an awful lot of information is being lost, and even more is not being looked for. When any trench strikes the earlier levels there are all sorts of idea to be checked, points to be looked for, tendencies to be noted, that it is likely that a great deal of the information available is gathered. Trenches which strike later deposits just have not the same questions to respond to, so the information is not gathered within a framework, and much must therefore drop through the observers net. The early ideas provide a framework

Trans

of questions by which to interrogate the sites and look for new sites and choose important sites, while the absence of later ideas means that all these points go almost by default. Unless a church specialist is chasing a church, or a cemetery fanatic chasing a cemetery, or a defence buff looking for defences. These are separate branches of archaeology, just as the Bronze Age has houses, and earthworks and barrows, and seldom the thrain shall meet. Whereas a sequence of deposits in the earlier period needs to be dated by decades, and if calendar decades are too hopeful a good material sequence equating to relative decades is perfectly possible, later sequences, such as thcy are, might be attributable to the 'sixth or seventh century' but no nearer. The later archaeology is back in the prehistoric mould where subjects rule, and, presumably, cultural labels have to be attached according to material changes.

This suggests two necessities. Firstly we need a general myth in which to study the archaeology of the period AD 200 to 800; and secondly we need a series of studies of different aspects of life and death, such as building techniques, cemeteries, churches and jewelley which accept a wide time scale, and recognize the convenience and temporary nature of labels, rather than exalting them into period divisions. In France there are signs that this is beginning, with different 'periodization' for different subjects. Thus churches are changing both site and shape quite fast in the Early Christian period, but settle down into comparative stability in the Early Medieval period. Jewellery has been labelled late Roman, or Merovingian or Caro-

lingian, but these labels will not work very well for churches. Burial rites change from cremation to inhumation, but that change does not fit at all well with the other divisions. The church archaeologist therefore works on a different timescale from the cemetery archaeologist, and both work independently of the study of jewellery, though jewellery and pottery are very useful in dating anything with which they are found. Similar things happen in Germany with the Cologne glass industry taking remarkably little notice of the end of the Roman Empire and the beginning of the Middle Ages, and the Mayen potteries changing their products at times which just do not correspond with history syllabuses. If only we can find an enveloping picture for this period, within which to work, or, better, two such pictures, then the way is sketched out on the continent as to how we should proceed.

Two people who give me hope are MM Pilet and Buchet. They believe in continuity and their work demonstrates it. Christian Pilet should be best known in Britain for his publication in BAR of the cemetery at Frénouville in Normandy. That cemetery appears to cut across the period boundaries by running smoothly, as far as layout and organization are concerned, from the 2ndC. to the 7thC.. The gravegoods are far more disciplined in that they change fashion as directed from late Romans, to Merovingian, but, if we take these labels to apply to real people, then there are severe problems of interpretation. There does not seem to be much admixture; most graves belong to one type, the other, or none. But we KNOW that the Franks came in droves to France, killing off the late Romans, and replacing them. Luckily a gravedigger survived the massacre, all of whose subjects were buried elsewhere, and he was able to instruct the newly arrived Franks on how and where to bury their dead in the strict continuation of the Late Roman manner. In fact we might never have known that there was a change over, especially since the massacre was so carefully concealed, if they had not insisted on being buried with their outlandish jewellery and belongings. If we believed this we would be further in difficulty when Luc Buchet puts forward his study of the bones, for he can see no change in the population to go with the change in jewellery. Not only can he see no change, but he says quite firmly that the people wearing jewellery thought typical of the Merovingian Franks have no Germanic or Nordic characteristics and are otherwise indistinguishable from the people that have been buried in the area for ages. Pilet thinks this is the cemetery of a continuing local population; Buchet thinks that the local population buried in the cemetery are unchanging. It seems that travelling tinkers and jewellery makers provided different fashions to the Frénouville population at different times.

First of all this is only one cemetery and it is just like you to build a whole castle on tiny foundations. Secondly, how widely spread are Buchet's uniform population, and by what means is he declaring them uniform?

If of course grieves me that though only one cemetery is published there is another in the pipeline which is even worse for it seems to go on in stable fashion for

even longer, and there are other smaller sites which seem to make the point quite clear for this region of Normandy. Yes, indeed, the limits of this uniform population are vital, for, if they stretch right up to the Rhine the evidence is undermined. If the population of North France and the Rhineland were found to be uniform between about 200 BC and AD 600 then no population movements could be documented from skeletal studies; it is important to draw some sort of limit around this stable population. M Buchet accepts this problem, but, from other studies on other cemeteries further East in France, he hopes that distinct populations, or at least distinguishable populations will soon be seen.

Ah, but is he is distinguishing on metric or non-metric characteristics, because it would be difficult to accept ....

Look, let him get on with it and meanwhile be honest and simply say that you will disbelieve his results unless they fit with your ideas.

Perhaps, provided that you agree that you are only likely to approve of his results if you can use them for your own hairbrained ideas.

No, you have gone and misunderstood the relationship of material and ideas again. You are still working on the bad, wrong, old idea whereby ideas spring from a heap of material. Material gives straws in the wind, from which ideas may be developed, or which may make some ideas more easy to hold than others.

Which really brings us to the end of the basic introduction to The End, and gives some of the straws in the wind, the ways things have been done and argued and the signs of where things might be going. The next stage is to get back to whatever is happening. What is going on at the time of The End, both as regards material and underlying events? We started off from towns and we ought to pursue that for the moment. Is The End of Roman Britain the fall of the Roman town in Britain? This would be supported by my interpretation of the French straws, in which I want to see the time from say 500 BC to AD 200 as the period of increasing urbanization and organization, and the period from AD 200 to 800 as the opposite. We have lots of words for the forward process - urbanization, nucleation, organization, but they all seem to be good; the reverse process has some words, dispersion, and disorganization, or failure of organization, or lack, but there is no concept of ruralization or de-urbanization. These are more than straws in the wind, they are great barriers and their outward signs. Words for the increase of organization are good and many, words for the decrease in organization are fewer and worse; this is how the general mind thinks, and it is the underlying reason why the period of AD 200 to 800 is badly understood.

To be lead astray for a moment by the material; if we see the process of nucleation, growth in size of settlements, addition of new population to old settlements, increasing specialization of building plans, and an increasing regularity of overall layout, then presumably we should be able to read any reversion in the material through a similar but reversed sequence. In fact it always seems to be far more difficult in a purely excavational way to see clearly the end of a structure then the beginning; it

comes at the top, stratigraphically, and is therefore more prone to damage, it is open, chronologically, unless the site is further used or developed, and a millennium of different uses may all take place within the rough walling left from the true purpose. If populations slowly begin to dwindle we will have to have complete plans to spot the gaps, whereas growth has to take place at the edges and is usually spotted; and the house next door from which the inhabitants moved last year is very useful as a stable and cart-shed, so it is well worth our while to keep the roof intact and the doors so that they can be closed. One thing which might give a clue is a standstill of alteration.

In a simple stone house, common in the town in Britain by the early third century there may well be a considerable lag between the last new building operation and any failure to re-build. It has been pointed out, quite rightly, that a well built stone house should need little major structural alteration for, say, 100 years after it is built. Yet where there is a history of continuous occupation from rubbish pits and garden refuse and the occasional deposit of pottery. we often see a remarkable sequence of changes sometimes small, sometimes not so small, as generation succeeds generation, ideas change, and newly-wed brides refuse to accept out-of-date furnishings. Some villas in the country show what often seem to us frenetic changes over time spans which material suggests may be fifty or seventy years; but in terms of occupants this is the lifetime of two or three married couples. It may be that failure to change is one of the things we should look at more closely in any scheme to gather the material evidence on The End. But whatever index we do collect is likely to be behind the times. The house and buildings next door that we have patched up and used as a cart-shed will go on for many years before enough rubbish accumulates on the floor and in corners, to give a firm date for its change of use or for its abandonment. It is therefore no good pointing to a well worn piece of fourth century pottery on the floor and saying that that dates the end of the useful life of the house. This is the background against which I am tempted to celebrate the triumph of seeing the beginnings of ruralization in the later fourth century: within the full 'Roman' period in Britain.

Which drives us even further back, from the collection of archaeological details, to consider the underlying processes. This again comes full circle because I suggested early in this work that beautiful ideas will not grow spontaneously from a heap of pottery, or a list of grave contents, or even from the detailed discussion of coin typology or distribution. We will not arrive at an idea after twenty years of making notes on archaeological reports because, as we can see at present the existence of a bad idea, the Saxon conquest of Britain and the Roman fall, or the non-existence of an idea, leads either to misdirected collection of facts, and their misunderstanding, or simply to a list of material. In the earlier period, where there is an idea and a framework, discoveries are made much more of and followed up much more enthusiastically, just because they appear to be making sense. In the later period they cannot be followed up either because no one knows where they are supposed to be

going, or they come up against inflexible period barriers. The process **is** the other way round: understanding of material will grow from the formulation of the right, or let us say for the moment, better overall ideas. I am not appealing for people to work in a different way, I am being much more conceited and pointing out to them that at present they are wrong and the only way that things have a chance of working IS the other way round. I therefore react very sharply against any moderate opinion which says "Yes, there may be something there, of course we have always known that things were not perfect, but our data base at present is far too inadequate to launch such great new ideas, we need a further ten years of work, and then we might be in a position to stand back and indulge in theoretical speculation". To repeat: the inbuilt ideas, models, myths, what you will, control implicitly the collection of information; if you continue to gather information for the next ten years on the old bad models you will be no further forward and a tremendous amount of potential information will have been lost simply because it does not fit into the current preconceptions. But then, as Collingwood said, "people are apt to be ticklish in their absolute presuppositions" (Collingwood 1940, 31).

So, where do we go? No one, however conceited, can provide a totally new set of models for the newly discovered period of de-urbanization. which lasts from about AD 200 to somewhere after AD 700. What is needed is discussion, and, arising from that at least two sets of models so that any collection of material may have two different ways of judgement, and the material will not be forced into the one accepted way, as at present, even when that interpretation is manifestly wrong. It would be good if the adherents of 'the old way' could become flexible, and see the need for an alternative alongside, so that the two sets of models were the 'old way' and some 'new way'. But I fear this is highly unlikely to happen. The example of suburbs gives little hope, for here was a study in late Roman Britain made during a time when two models of the late Roman town were available, one suggested that the town centres were thriving, the other that they were dying, yet the final product seems unable to take the second idea into account, and ends up with a study of the outside of the town without considering the possibilities of the health of the inside. If we bring post-Romanists into this I fear the worst. The moment we only consider ideas and leave out of account the people who are expected to have them and to manipulate them we might as well give up. Because of myths. People are not *tabulae rasae* on whom bright and attractive new ideas can be set at will, they are a horrible complicated mass of preconceptions, emotions, certainties and fears, just like the writer of this work, and they may have strongly built-in resistance to ideas, however reasonable they appear.

Discussion, then, of this process of ruralization or de-urbanization. Yet using this word several times makes me wonder why we should hang onto this great aim of the town. Why should this be the period of de-urbanization, of failure to make the grade, and incompetence in organization, instead of a period of normalization, back to proper natural groupings of farms and hamlets and villages, whether nucleated or not, in which a person has an equal importance to the milking of a cow. This is shorthand for describing a job which has to be done at least every day, involves a relationship between the milker and the milked, and gives an essential end-product, food. The majority of readers will not accept this tweedy account of normality and normalization because it makes them abnormal and puts them in an abnormal time. And this is just the sort of thing that could finish any hope of seeing this period of which I am speaking as a whole. People, being human individuals would be quite capable of reading through the whole chapter, agreeing with many of the major points, then forgetting them, and classifying the whole thing as the work of a health-food fanatic because he talks of the end of towns as a process of normalization. So let us work on de-urbanization, the Dark Ages, the time when people were not organized sufficiently for their own good, except of course by the Church, but that was for their Eternal Good.

My only way of understanding the whole process at the moment is to assume some relentless sequence by which increasing population first makes possible the specialization of some people in endeavors non-productive of food, and then reaches the stage where it is almost necessary to get them off the land and into enclaves so that the essential work of food production can go on unhindered. I am not talking here in strict terms of the carrying capacity of land; the number of people that a certain area could support given every possible assistance; I am talking about the number who can easily be fed from land, who will produce food, and who will not, who are efficient and who are inefficient. Once the idea of the town has surfaced it would seem that it acts as a haven for inefficiency. This process of population growth was happening in the last few centuries BC. We must then add to that, fashion. The appropriateness of towns had reached the Mediterranean littoral some time in the early first millennium BC so that the fashion of towns was available for spreading as the population of Iron Age France and Britain increased. If is difficult to know now the classical equivalents to jeans and transistor radios which made the idea of towns so apparently attractive, but it may simply have been the old mistake of assuming that what is, must be. So if towns were seen to produce wealth and splendid buildings it was assumed that wealth and splendid buildings could only come from the establishment of towns. Many people still hold this sort of view without realizing the hopeless non-logic of it.

This is one possible model, but another needs to be set beside it, and the two may well work together. We must allow for the possibility of urban mission; for the idea of traders and others who stood to benefit, reaching out, settlement by settlement, to bring the natives within reach of their profits. Thus the Iron Age societies can be seen as well populated, with some slack perhaps to be taken up from the duty simply of growing food; as susceptible to fashion; and as the victims, either willing or not, of growing Mediterranean profit-making. The apostles of profit-making reach out toward the natives, converting them to the Better Life, and the natives in turn get the idea of this nastiest of human habits. Commerce, and centres for commerce creep up through Gaul, even before the Roman politicians have accessioned it for their own nasty motives, and the blight affects even the British. The Mediterranean fashion spreads, the profit-motive spreads and so towns spread, and these aspects of growth continue fairly evenly over political change and conquest into the first and the second centuries of the empire. It seems fair to call this the Roman period, for if we are judging by the cultural markers distributed throughout North West Europe, for the period AD 1 to 200 must have been the time of the furthest spread of Roman objects. This period affects areas well outside the Imperial frontiers in Free Germany and Denmark. So far our model holds up well; but the test comes when the tide, astonishingly to many people, turns. Italian goods cease to travel so far; different areas of the once fairly homogeneous empire begin to diversify and produce their own exports, but these never seem to travel so far; and as the tide of trade turns, so the centres of trade, the towns, fall on hard times. We are in the crisis of the third century which at one stage I called the time of slack water, between the outward spreading tide of Italian profit-making and the return or reflux tide of provincial domination. The model that I have just outlined, and the earlier idea of slack tide are not in agreement; in fact I doubt if they can be held simultaneously. If trade really did turn round, and move from the periphery of the empire towards the centre, instead of the earlier idea by which Rome and Italy made a killing in the provinces, then there was no need for the towns to wither, and

Trans

later, say the last quarter of the fourth century, begin to die. The time of slack tide, of little net trade movement, might have been a difficult time for the town as a commercial centre, but if the volume of trade returned to its earlier level, then so ought the town have returned.

It is reasonably easy to see how the town in Italy might have changed considerably between the first century AD and the fourth, but unfortunately that is one area, except for deserted towns like Luni, where we know very little in the material sense, for excavation has just not been done. The model would be one in which the Italian town grew substantially on the profits of Empire and then had to retrench drastically when the profits of trade merely within Italy was far too restricted to support the urban superstructure constructed in the times of prosperity. This might apply to the South of Gaul, but the North of Gaul is probably in the same position as Britain. Here the model falls, because it is assumed that it is not till after the reversal of the direction of trade in the third century that Britain and North Gaul ought to have attained prosperity, and therefore proper prosperous urban centres. The periphery of the Empire ought to have acted in the same way as the core earlier on, and exploited the areas outside - Soctland, Ireland, Scandinavia in the case of Britain, so that the Good Life spread to the farthest reaches of Ocean. None of this happened although there is a striking amount of evidence that Britain in the fourth century was in fact more prosperous than at any other time. To the conservative, or is it Conservative?, economist the idea of increased prosperity with decreased urbani-

zation is anathema; to the open-minded it is an interesting irregularity.

Several points have come up in this discussion which need to be brought out more openly. One assumption of the influence, trade, prosperity, town, model is that the town is only a centre for trade, and that any area of the world is equally suitable for the development of towns, given the prerequisite of trade. The other point is the pastoral idyll by which the natural native succumbs, perhaps through original sin, to the nastiness of trade and towns; this will get us into difficulties when the tide of towns recedes, for we will need to make a preference for the natural way of life stronger in the long run than greed and fashion. Put less emotively, what is the difference between the fashion for, and attractions of, town life in AD 150 and 350? Differences there must be, if fashion and choice had anything to do with the growth of towns through the second century, for they did the opposite in the fourth century.

One point that has come out of the study of settlements in Scandinavia and the Netherlands such as Dorestad is that in the period between about AD 500 and AD 800 towns were in short supply, yet affluent trading camps or trade settlements were set at strategic points within a non-urban settlement pattern. Orthodoxy has it that these settlements, which now include Hamwih in Britain were killed off either directly by Viking aggression, or by the diminution in trade which the unsettled times resulting from Viking raiding induced. We might learn from this that towns and trading settlements are not synonymous; it may be that either can

Trans

exist without the other, and it seems clear that urban features will not necessarily appear in a nucleated trading post. We could add to this the observation which stands out so clearly in the survey of towns in Europe published some years ago, that town life was somehow not a natural part of North West Europe until well into the ninth or tenth century AD. The towns that do occur before then were limited to the area controlled politically, commercially, and culturally by the Roman Empire, and the surrounding natives did not fall prey to the urban idea like their cousins who were to fall under Roman control. This may be to do no more than to extend Groenman-van Waateringe's very useful thesis that the Romans could only conquer those who were ready to be conquered, and failed miserably, as in Free Germany, where the natives were unable to co-operate. This would then give us three groups either of social organizations within North West Europe, or three geographical areas, or both, in some sort of interdependence. The first group in Southern Gaul were ripe for conquest because they had already formed themselves into the urban mould: in this case conquest, however bloody, was really no more than federation. The second group which included Northern Gaul and Britain was in an intermediate stage by which their organization was good enough to assist in conquest but not far enough developed to sprout towns independently. The third group were not even well enough developed to conquer and the Romans did well to leave them alone to mature for a further thousand years. I am sceptical of that last division for two reasons. First it seems to conflict with the comparative ease of conquest, subjugation, and consequent exploitation of Africa by Europe in the 18th. and 19th. centuries. Second, towns seem to grow naturally in NW Europe from 900 AD onwards whether in Poland, Britain or Austria. Leaving, as always, Barbaricum to take care of itself, we can follow the events of the Romanized area.

We have arrived at about the year 300 with two conflicting models. One equated trade, prosperity, and towns and sees all three marching together, growing through the second century and collapsing in the third. A second sees a turn round in trade in the third century so that the fourth century, in many areas was no less prosperous than the second, but that prosperity was in the hands of the provinces rather then Italy, the periphery rather than the core, and the same volume of goods travelled much smaller distances. We should now add in the possible un-naturalness of urban life and institutions to NW Europe, and the recognition that nucleated settlements may be trade centres without being urban institutions.

This suggests a view of the town in Roman Britain as a trading settlement within a classical facade. This description satisfies me, for it is the first time that I have been able to express in terms that I could understand, my reservations about towns in Roman Britain. Each town is a trading settlement, sometimes purely for local trade, but in many other cases for trade wider afield, and each town has the trappings appropriate to a Roman town, brought from the area in which towns were endemic. But these settlements never became urbanized. Inscriptions are rare, yet in Gaul it is almost a basic definition of town life that you inscribe your beneficence and your achievements for all to see. Monumental urban buildings on which the life of a real town ought to depend are started, but they often seem not to reach completion and proper, official, urban use. We await with interest the reports on the basilicas at Silchester and especially London and Caerwent. On the other hand, some baths do seem to be used for many years, and mosaics do catch on. But the urban density of an Ostia is never reached, in the same way perhaps that the 19th.C. British town was never as densely populated as the contemporary French or Italian town. And worst of all, the threads of urban life, which ought to have carried the towns of Britain from the successes of the early third century to the prosperity of the fourth snap. If prosperity is the major determinant in town life then the towns of Roman Britain ought to show forth the old model of a thriving Roman Britain until the avalanche of Saxon conquest. I started by asserting that this model, whatever is in its place, is now firmly agreed to be wrong. If the thread of urban life has snapped well before AD 400, well before any avalanche, the simplest explanation to me is that the original thread was either weak or illusory.

This leaves me with a further problem, for the disjunction of trade centres from town facades, and the crumbling of those facades take place at a time when Romanitas in Britain, or many aspects of Romanitas, are in full flood. The Roman country house was thriving, floored with mosaics that would grace a house anywhere in the empire. Silver in use was up to the standard of any in the empire, the British em-

peror Carausius has better Latin on his coins than emperors elsewhere, and burial seems to have come into the empire wide fashion. It is not that the classical facade seems to be slipping off Britain as a whole through the fourth century, simply off the trading nuclei established in the early empire. There seems to be a phase of de-urbanization before the phase of de-Romanization, which no one doubts in the fifth century. Though the second process is extremely interesting, it is the first which concerns us at present. I will not for the moment bring the small defended areas of towns in Gaul into the argument because we still do not have many examples of firm published evidence on the presence of absence of continued occupation outside those walls in the fourth century. It may be that they show this process of de-urbanization at work in Gaul more clearly and quantitively than in Britain.

We are reduced to asking what was the difference between the second and third and fourth centuries which encouraged towns in the earlier period, and failed to encourage them in the later period. Fashion, commercial success, and the pull of town life can hardly have changed enough in the time to account for such failure; we ought perhaps to remember this when discussing the growth and spread of towns. The state administration can probably be absolved from any great change of heart, for it is highly unlikely that, for instance, the imperial government gave grants for urban development in the first century which were lacking in the fourth. And in any case the towns were developed, they simply needed keeping alive. This could explain a lack of new towns, apart from the obvious lack of space in the settlement network into which to slip them, but it is a poor explanation for the non-continuance of established centres. Another possibility is the change in taxation by which urban life in the early empire was on a low level of tax which mounted heavily in the later empire. This could adversely affect town life, yet, if it were firmly established I would expect it to continue and to find some way round the new extortions. In one way this is the story of the Later Roman Empire; new extortion followed by new exemptions. We can perhaps get one stage further forward by making another descriptive statement in place of analysis. Through the third century and into the fourth some people, and perhaps institutions, in Britain found that the classical facade to a limited number of trade centres was an unnecessary and foreign burden whose discontinuation caused several financial benefits and no obvious drawbacks. Even this causes problems because one thing that does seem to have drawn attention and inevitably money is the town wall. The attention to town walls in the fourth century by the building of stone towers, not bastions, has been used to show that the town was thriving; and this has been maintained in the face either of evidence of internal decline, or in the total absence of evidence. Perhaps a Civitas, in the sense of an area of government, was willing to spend money in the establishment and maintainance of a central refuge, just as elite bunkers seldom lack funds. As the adherents of fortifications always insist on their close alliance with the administration, which in the4th C. had got hold of most city revenues, I do not

need to worry further, for this in itself always gives ample scope for the flourishing of illogicality, inertia, and mass hysteria.

It may be that by this time the whole discussion has been mined and countermined. De-urbanization is hard to understand because it never happened (Comment 5: Matthew Johnson says that he wrote that in an essay for me at Cambridge several years ago, and it has taken rather a time for me to rediscover it for myself. Absolutely fair. Now he mentions it, I seem to remember thinking what a good essay it was, and he is right that it has taken some time to take root. Perhaps another example of how you can only accept ideas when you are ready for them. I take this opportunity to apologize to all other friends and students for appearing to lift their ideas. Wherever I am aware that I got the idea from someone else I have have tried to say so. If you would like to point it out I will acknowledge it properly the next time.

But I cannot help saying that students do also do things the other way round. They can hear something, and go away and let it germinate, and come back with my idea as a fully fledged new discovery. So it probably works out fairly in the end. I don't think I have ever tried to take such an idea away from anyone unless I had actually put it in print earlier). Thus it is not suprising that we find difficulty in understanding how people could turn their backs on something so obviously good as town life, if, in fact, they never really sampled it at home. If the trade centre and Civitas capital in Britain was never more than a trade centre and administrative head-office with the trappings of a Latin town, then the process of urbanization never happened in Britain and there was nothing at that level for people to turn their backs on or to reject. The Briton never turned against town life because, apart from visits to Arles or Placentia or even Rome, he never really knew what it was. What fell apart, after an initial phase of (with hindsight) misplaced enthusiasm, were the trappings. They were turned over to more productive uses - though what to do with a theatre or amphitheatre no Briton ever seems to have worked out - and those that did not become productive dropped out of use and fell down. We know so little about administrative and honorific town life in Britain simply because there was so little to know.

So, like a half-scale version of political conquest, urbanization reached those parts of the whole administrative unit called the Roman Empire, which were ready to be urbanized or which had already taken the first steps, and the rest went through the motions; those parts could not be reached. Depending on your point of view it is fortunate, or a disaster that our knowledge of the archaeology of Roman towns is best in areas where I suggest that urbanization never really took. Thus Britain and North Gaul are fairly well served with reports on urban excavation, but the ?continuous? density of town life further south in Gaul and Italy, means that there have been far fewer opportunities for urban excavation, that these are only now being seized, and few have therefore come to publication.

This all suggests that the 'towns' of Roman Britain and North Gaul were never the only settlements devoted to trade and exchange and secondly that the fortunes of their classical facades should no longer be taken as indices of trade and prosperity. The Briton worked with a network of markets which may have already been set at the time of the Roman conquest in AD 43. Indeed it might well have been the existence of this trade network, among other things, that made the conquest possible. Some of these nodes may well have attracted the attention of the military, which would in turn lead to a fort, and when the fort moved on the node might, or might not, take on the outward appearance of a Romanized settlement. But only some of the nodes would take on this Romanized carapace - other would continue at the Blasted Oak on the third Thursday of each moon and beside Gunga's Well, which might in time take on a Romanized from and turn into a stone temple with a hole in the middle. The temple gradually dropped out of fashion and new religious fashions came in, so that node changed; the nodes with carapaces changed as no one found any reason to keep up the carapace, though they remained nodes, and the blasted oak eventually fell down, but by that time there was a group of farms around known as Blistok.

Should we distinguish between what the different trade nodes dealt in? I think it has little future, yet, since it is one of the few points of these ideas that could be tested against the material it might be worth putting down. Let us divide goods and services up into Samian and carrots. Samian comes into Britain from Gaul, but carrots are best grown on the spot. A trader, perhaps foreign, might be more at home in a node with a Roman shell, so there might in AD 150 be more Samian than carrots in 'towns'; whereas carrots grew near all nodes and were marketed at all, even if there were no Samian stalls. In the third century when Samian declined and British pottery replaced it there was less reason to go especially to the 'towns', particularly perhaps when the pottery industries had placed themselves with an eye to the present and future in the middle of the country markets, and the change in status might have been that the Blasted Oak nodes thrived and 'town' nodes, being less well sited in some cases for the 'natural' population, declined. At present we lack any detailed information on markets in Roman Britain, and a study of markets elsewhere would be a great help at least for comparison. And we also lack any conception of the relationship between carrots and Samian even in the heady interprovincial boom of the second century.

Coins seem to help these ideas. In the period up to about 260 they are of a rather high value compared with the daily transactions concerning carrots, and they are more concentrated in towns and army centres. After 260 there is a great surge in coin use throughout the province and the later small coins are lost more in the countryside, small villages, temple sites, and even villas, than in the town. But the towns still have a decent coin loss through the fourth century, and are still losing coins when the supply stops around 395-402. The simplest picture that can be drawn from the coins is one in which towns have something approaching a monopoly early on, but by the fourth century there is something approaching at least equality between town and country, possibly with the country leading after 330.

Trans

The vital area of study here would seem to be modern France, for it has now produced three leads. The first is the one that I have outlined earlier suggesting that the South of France belongs to the naturally growing towns while the North of France belongs to the imposed style of towns. The second and third belong to two different periods of coin use which show some sort of dividing line between the South and the North of France. There is the production of Barbarous Radiates which seem to belong to Britain and the North of France, perhaps down to the Loire; and there is the use of the large and small denominations of the period 378 to 388 where Callu has seen two different areas joining somewhere in Gaul. These are just points which spring immediately to mind without search so that perhaps the search for further divisions, and topics in which there is no divide, would be useful.

Have we any further lines of argument on the newly defined process of ruralization? It is now reduced, in the North of France and Britain to a failure to keep up the Romanized trappings of certain trade nodes; this dereliction leaves the relics of Civitas administration in an administrative village, needing a few offices and a few good dwellings, in a rather large Romanized space, surrounded by an administrative necessity, defence. I think this corresponds remarkably well to the actual material evidence available in the towns of Roman Britain for the fourth century. The point remains a centre, a central place, or perhaps even a Central Place, and the population who would consider themselves as belonging to this point are either to be found in the good houses which are the estate centres in and around the administrative village, or at the gate villages with one view back into the town for possible refuge, and the other out into the country to farm. Not surprisingly, burial continues at the administrative point, and the area remains under the control of the locals, and relatively free from redevelopment for some time. Where small parties of newcomers can be seen, as perhaps at York or Canterbury they stay out of the old centre. And now we see, or think we see, that where new trading posts spring up, the Wics, they are beside the old centres, rather than in them.

This leaves us free to look at the rather different question of de-Romanization. The material cultural markers in Britain and Gaul in 360 are overwhelmingly what we call Roman. If this term needs definition I would suggest "material with a demonstrably higher density of distribution inside the frontiers of the historically attested Roman Empire than outside". A few things, produced in Free Germany, for export only, will slip through this net but they can be examined one by one where necessary. In 460, both, so far as we can tell at the moment, in North Gaul and Britain there are fewer cultural markers, and these are less easily classified as Roman. This is what I mean by de-Romanization. Unfortunately since most archaeologists working on the second to fourth centuries are overwhelmed by Roman material (definition as above unless otherwise stated) their methods are determined by that material, and hence when the material ceases they fall flat on their faces. I am an excellent example of this, in my speciality of coins, for I can lay down firm lines for dating, and make out a good case to support my claims up to 402; thereafter I shrug my shoulders and say "Who knows".

What are the aspects of de-Romanization? In Britain there is the cessation of coin supply, and the concomitant end of coin use - however strong that had or had not been before; rectangular stone buildings using mortar seem to come to a sudden end; mosaics finish, the very widespread use of pottery seems to end with the cessation of centralized production. It may be that the loss of interest in the classical facade of some trade nodes is an early symptom of this process and, whether this is true or not it ought to alert us to the possibility that these are not necessarily a package of aspects of a single event, but could be cumulative events taking place at different speeds throughout the fourth century. Buildings seem to go on later, into the fifth century, whereas the production of pottery even to the end of the fourth century has been questioned. The pottery problem is particularly acute for it concerns our main source for dating when coins are absent, rare, or residual. Young in his study of Oxford pottery noted that by the middle of the fourth century all innovations had been made and thereafter nothing new happened, but production concentrated on the old forms. He suggested that this was an industry settling down to efficient, uniform, production. Mike Fulford on New Forest Pottery found the same sort of thing, but wondered whether production really did continue for that long after the repertoire became uniform. Chris Going, more from the customers end in Chelmsford pushed the question of the length of manufacture in the later fourth century and suggests that the absence of almost any local attempts to make up the lack of centralized supply means an absence of demand rather than an absence of supply. Buildings are notoriously difficult to date except for the examples and the method of Prof. Frere at Verulamium where stone construction can be shown to continue well into the fifth century. Coins pose slightly more of a problem.

During the fourth century in Britain there was substantial supply of small value coinage. I have suggested that the state would only supply copper coinage to recapture gold and silver paid out, mainly to state functionaries. The level of copper coinage in Britain is higher than in Italy or the South of Gaul but is approached by the Danube area, another area of high troop concentration. But at certain periods of the fourth century the mint seems to have produced little coin, and at others it only produced coin of high value. At those time Britain made up the deficit by producing copies of the regular coins. This did not happen during the low supply of 380 to 387, and it did not happen when supply ceased either around 395, or finally in 402. Since coins were used and lost in substantial numbers between 388 and 402 I favour the idea that coin use depended on the army and the state servants, many of whom were taken out of Britain by Magnus Maximus between 383 and 388, and that the absence of copies depends simply on the absence of the copiers, the state employees both civil and military. After 402 no one remaining seems to find any need at all for small copper coinage, and cannot get hold of any gold or silver coinage,

apparently, so the whole subject lapses.

This I see as parallel with the 'towns'. I have suggested that after an initial phase of enthusiasm these declined, through the failure in support by traders, to the level of administrative villages, and it was in that form that they weathered the fourth century. The failure to concentrate trade in the towns prevented the development of urban life and institutions, but the administrative remnants kept the ideas alive, and it was the cessation of connection with the empire wide system of administration somewhere early in the period 400 to 410 that removed the only incentive left to keep up the facade. There had not been town life for say 150 years by 400, only low level life in 'towns', so when the administrative prop was removed, together with its bait of gold and silver, only estate centres survived, and they quickly went off the Roman way of life. But why?

There are two main possibilities, choice or compulsion. Compulsion is much easier to understand and deal with. The last of the Romans, holed up in the towns, even though, in general there are just as late signs in villas, if not later, were attacked by the invading Saxons, and Picts and Scots if necessary and either killed off, or driven into the Welsh fastness and mountains, or brought under the yoke of Germanic domination. This fantasy was particularly popular from the Franco-Prussian war to the aftermath of the Second World War. Now that we have got over the Second World War we can probably do without this silly extravaganza. Though there are plenty of people who would like to revive this scenario it is indicative of something that they have been totally unable to collect together any fragments of evidence to support their case. This probably means that they are wrong. The whole atmosphere is further hindered by the Romanists more or less general agreement to pull the decline of towns back into the fourth century and the matching pull from Saxonists to keep Saxon styles of decoration firmly after the first decades of the fifth century. There is therefore, on current dating a gap of nearly fifty years between the decline of towns and the flourishing of Saxon fashions. But the decline of Roman fashions and the rise of Saxon fashions do seem to fit better together in the first quarter of the fifth century. The Roman decline has started earlier and the Saxon style did not really flourish until later, but there does not seem to be an overlap between about 405 and 440. Since there really is no evidence at all for compulsion then the alternative, although more difficult to follow, must be aired.

One problem with both ideas, choice and compulsion, is that these changes in fashion did not happen everywhere. In East Anglia and Kent and more easterly regions of central Britain the Saxon style caught on but in the West and centre West it did not. But in the places where the Saxon style did not catch on the Roman style did not continue. Thus in my home region of Cirencester, from which all thoughts, whether good or not, proceed things Roman stop somewhere at the end of the fourth century and nothing identifiable takes their place until perhaps the eleventh century. That the fertile Cotswolds were not deserted is shown by an excellent crop of 'Saxon' churches, some of them quite early and even historical

evidence of thriving occupation as, for example, at Withington. This is another nail in the coffin of the rape-pillage-and-plunder corpse, for the absence both of 'historical' records of the Saxon conquest, and the absence of the Saxon style or fashion leaves a general consensus that the Cotswolds did not join the Saxon sphere for many years after the Roman style ceased. They chose not to carry on with things in the Roman way, but they did not chose to take up the new fangled Saxon style. Jeans and transistor radios, as it were, were spreading into the upper Thames valley by the later sixth and seventh century, as the recently excavated cemetery at Lechlade shows. And once some of the top people had taken on these new trappings, including perhaps the language, it is not surprising that the people in general followed. The very top people at this time had Germanic names and presumably spoke German, just as the Normans had Norman names and spoke Norman French, and there may well have been some hiccups in land tenure as self-styled kings declared that they owned everything. This is my interpretation of the fact that the majority of early land grants all come from the king, and only later began to circulate amongst the next level down, including the church. And we are coming at this point in the seventh or eighth centuries to the time when the oldest hedges surviving on the Cotswolds seem to have been planted or started. And hedges, like cows, need constant attention to survive. In other words I find it impossible to fit any idea of major discontinuity into the Cotswold area between about 600 and the present; and I see no evidence of that discontinuity nor do my sources, if I believed them, tell me of it, before that date. In the Cotswolds at least, and I see no reason why they should be substantially different from anywhere else in lowland Britain, farms nucleated and dispersed gently from the third century BC to AD 1500, and the Roman fashion came and went, and was not really replaced by any other obvious fashion until the blanket of the Christian middle ages fell.

Given, then, the trade network of nodes and markets which entered the Romanized period in Britain, and no doubt changed somewhat over 400 years, but then left the Roman fashion; and given the farms that produced basic needs of food and clothing, and accepting that in part of Britain at least there was no compulsion to adopt Saxon fashions and Saxon fashions were not adopted, why de-Romanize?

Coins seem to me to be more or less sorted out. I do not necessarily believe the story but there is a reasonable story which will stand for the moment. Coinage was always in Britain tied in to the elite, in the Iron Age, and those who had, in the Roman period. It came from the state through state servants based in Britain, and those same state officials made their own small value coins when the state failed to supply them, but all this was tied in to the Roman social system as based in the Empire, and the Roman economic system, empire wide, and when the links were broken early in the fifth century no more coins were supplied and the system in which they had circulated no longer had a privileged position from which to form a fashion. Coin use among the upper people stopped and there was no incentive from people in

general to do anything about it.

Pottery I do not understand. The sequence seems clear enough even if the dates are fuzzy. The major industries of the fourth century such as the New Forest, Oxford, the Nene Valley, and Shell Gritted ware cease to innovate after the middle of the fourth century. Levels on Roman sites which contain coins of the House of Valentinian, 364-78, contain the latest pottery types that are well known. Levels containing coins of 388 to 402 contain the same pottery, though whether it is residual or not, or old stock coming to an end we cannot tell. Levels above these last dated levels contain the same pottery which from its condition and size can now be seen to be residual, and there is virtually never any candidate for post-Roman pottery at all. Some sites show a few grass or chaff tempered sherds but they are seldom stratified and never numerous; in general there is no home made, or even local variety, which follows on the last products of the great fourth century wares. Pottery in Roman Britain did not break down, fragment, become locally produced, then home produced and finally trickle to an end, it stopped with a bang as the main production centres stopped. Chris Going finds it difficult to interpret this as anything other than a failure in demand because failure in supply, with continued demand, would lead to a series of backstreet potters, and a deposit of sub-Roman wares. I have to agree with him. Perhaps the answer, which he might have suggested in conversation, but if not, for which I am happy to take any credit or blame, is to push this drop in demand back in the fourth century so that the failure to innovate, and the concentration of each industry on just a few main lines was in fact the response to sluggish markets and decreasing demand by the middle of the century. We thus see in the later fourth century a series of business enterprises producing whatever seems to sell, and hawking their wares over an increasingly large market area to an increasingly uninterested set of customers.

Stone buildings with square mortared walls may take us a speculative leap further. Some of the last stone buildings that we see in the South of Britain are Prof. Frere's house in Verulamium, to me an estate centre, and the late villas of the Cotswolds, some of which are still going at the year 400 as far as coin finds indicate. In the North some of the latest stone buildings are forts such as Binchester, and military centres such as Corbridge. After the gap the first stone buildings in the South are often churches, and Somerford Keynes, near Cirencester, will do for the years around 690 to balance villas such as Froucester Court, and in the North we will have to rely on Benedict Biscop and his help from France to build churches after AD670 in the Gaulish manner. In between there is a gap. To understand the gap we shall have to make sense of either end, and one point that does stand out is authority in different forms; most obviously the army who could go on building in stone to the bitter end, or town walls such as London, and then the church. It may be that the estate centres represent the civil equivalent to the army, and this idea would be heavily backed up by the written sources for Gaul (Rutilius Namatianus, Panegyrics, Hydatius) who see the state taxation and the depredations of the governing classes as a major factor in the fall of the town and country. Those who can go on building in stone are those who have the power to squeeze both rents and services from the majority. All this is set against my own gut feeling that if I were building a house from scratch in a place like Cirencester with superb building stone and Roman quarry faces still visible (e.g. Cirencester Excavations vol.II 31-43) I should prefer to lever pieces of stone out bit by bit, rather than rely on wood.This feeling in the Cotswolds at least is irrelevant because after the Roman villa there is a gap in vernacular building in stone until the 13th century; and manor houses have few remains which date from before 1100, only the churches use stone.

This leaves us with a suspicion of a connection between stone building and the ability to organize other people. This is not nearly proved, for material can never 'prove' an idea, it can at best be consistent with it, but for those who want it there is a line to follow. Apart from a chronological link, that stone building stopped at the same time as several other Roman attributes, there is no direct connection between stone and coin, or stone and pottery, but I shall spread the net to see if the lead is worth following up. If we take stone building as a index of social organization and the dominance of the many by a few then we would have to suggest for the years after 400 a society in which there was considerably more equality than in the later Roman empire or in the early Middle Ages. On the surface this is nonsense, for the few people that we do know for the period 400 to 800 are kings and kinglets in number. Yet the story of Kingship from, say, Bede to the 11th.C. seems to be one of acknowledged kings turning their theoretical position into one that actually works in practice and can extort what ever Kingship wants. So the fact that we hear in sub-Roman Britain just as in 'Anglo-Saxon' England of kings and sub-kings, and chiefs and princes and bishops, does not of itself mean that local organization was built in such a way as to enable a Lord to force men theoretically his inferiors to work in his quarry. This idea runs counter to another that I proposed only a little time ago, in which the most obvious late Roman was the owner of great tracts of land, and perhaps the owner of great villas, and the most obvious men in early Saxon Britain were the great lords, so we might as well assume that they are one and the same and simply not recorded between 400 and 700. This may well need refinement. It may be that the appearance in texts of the late Roman magnate is a sign of the increasing break-up of what had been the Empire, and that there is a later stage in this process when the hierarchy is levelled even further, and that with the Saxon Lord we see the reverse process by which local hierarchy is being cemented, on which basis the national hierarchy of England can be built. My picture of markets in the Roman Empire is one by which nodes proliferate, bringing down the uniqueness of the town in each area and boosting the Blasted Oak; Prof. Glanville Jones has shown the exact opposite in Yorkshire in the period after 1100, in which a mess of markets is gradually brought to order and made to work for to the benefit of a few people and institutions.

Of course we cannot take, as it were, films of each side of our Great Divide, and then run them in reverse to illuminate the other side; even if the idea is correct, some processes will not be mirror images in decline and in return. But to focus on the point of least organization, and to take account of how it was reached and how changed back again, seems to me at least an interesting exercise, and certainly the right way to do it. So, for a little, we take the processes at present thought of as the end of Roman Britain and test them as aspects of increasing social equality; and we examine the material from the 5th. to the 9th.C. as evidence of increasing social stratification. I have put both of these in positive terms so that each reader may indentify with at least one. My personal account would be one of increasing equality, smothered by unpleasant go-getters who want the Saxon equivalent of double garages and fitted kitchens - or worse; but this might just possibly upset some delicate readers who would then throw the valuable theoretical baby out with the bathwater of optional flavour. The alternative is to talk as is often stupidly done of a break-down in late Roman society and the gradual emergence of civilization from the mess which resulted. I dislike even putting down this opinion because it epitomizes so much that is wrong with society as I see it at present, and hence must be a wrong view of the past. Now sentences like this in the middle of a supposedly academic text would be edited out by keen publishers, mainly, or explicitly, because they have no place in a scholarly publication, and I am lowering the tone to cheap invective. Implicitly, being publishers, they would be of the double garage variety, and would want to suppress such opinions. Yet in fact I am going beyond being scholarly to give every reader a plain unvarnished statement of why I think something, or why I refuse to work with certain models. In being as honest as this I am hoping that people who dislike my motives for investigating these areas of the past will be able to make allowances for the obvious bias and so use some of the basic ideas according to their own frame of reference.

So how do our material and theory fit together so far? Coins fit in well on the surface. Coinage cannot exist without authority, almost by definition, for the difference between a lump of bullion and a coin is that the coin bears the mark of the issuing or supporting authority. If the authority is national those coins will be usable, and usually acceptable, within that state and any other state that recognizes the first authority. If authority is only a city, then the coinage will be smaller and will often travel less far; and if it is a town or less there is probably little reason for producing coinage in the first place. Perhaps is is less the size of the authority, but the area over which that authority is known; this could be worked out in the medieval period. This concerns bullion. Copper coinage, or bronze or other base metal, is seldom worth its weight in metal, if it is to be practical, and hence its value has to be underwritten by some authority. To use such money is an act of faith in that authority, an act which the inhabitants of Free Germany were unwilling to make, for instance, in the fourth century, for although gold and silver travel across the imperial

frontiers, copper, in general , does not. In another sense, coinage not only comes from authority, but is OF authority; bullion in the Roman empire always remained in some rather mystical way part of the emperor, almost as if he had given part of himself to be negotiable, but kept authority over it, and needed it back. And this link to authority means that the coins circulate hierarchically from the top downwards. In Roman Britain we do not know how far down the scale coinage went, but the end of coinage strongly suggests that it did not get far below the level of authority and dealings with authority so that once the link with authority was broken neither money arrived, nor was needed.

Most other points can be subsumerd under the heading of Roman fashion, Romanitas, *in more Romano*. There are two ways of looking at this. Either we can look at what did happen and then relate our model to how we think it might have happened; or we can try to work out with the model what might have happened and see if it was what did happen. Roman fashions, in general went; society became more equal or the structure of society broke down, which ever you choose, and I choose the first. Does this mean that fashion is a characteristic of a well stratified society? There are many problems here. Perhaps one of these problems that I shall not set is the feeling at this point that one ought to go off to anthropological literature, or even that of sociology (publications, that is, not literature) in order to check out these random thoughts against current observations. There are two reasons why I do not do this, and so burden the text with technical terms which would turn any self respecting reader elsewhere. First I am not particularly interested. Second, even if I can find comments on three current societies where fashion is found to be linked heavily with a highly stratified society, this says absolutely nothing in strict logic about any past society whatsoever. It might be that if you survey the publications of the past fifty years and find that every discussion of fashion notes a stratified society that the two often march together, but it does not change the observations into a law of human society which says that fashion ALWAYS marches with a stratified society.

I am not even sure that we are really talking about stratified and unstratified societies. I have noted both in the late Roman period, and later, and in Saxon society kings, kinglets and chiefs, and I have assumed their social inferiors to exist, faute de mieux, because it makes sense. But I have also noted that the existence of rank does not automatically mean that the upper ranks have complete control over the lower ranks. I am interested in societies where the upper ranks do control the lower ranks, and those where they do not, and it may be only where we have lots of documents, or a good material record that we can distinguish between these two possibilities. To take things even further, I am not sure that even a material record can provide the proof. Does the present high rate of individual concern for e.g. Ethiopia show a stratified society? I would say not. Yet the existence of Stonehenge or St. Peter's Basilica at Rome are taken to show stratification.   In the case of St. Peter's there is little doubt that left to themselves the peasantry of Europe would not have built this wart, and Rome would

be much the richer. But does Stonehenge come in the Aid for Ethiopia, or St. Peter's variety? I would like to think that mass effort without stratified pressure is confined to immaterial good, and that white elephants like Stonehenge or St. Peter's are the result of stratified pressure. War memorials give me a moments pause, but, to date, all those have been built as the result of hard pressure or guilt from above, and they show it by their pointlessness. It therefore seems hopefully doubtful that any truly equal society would ever spend its effort in meaningless nonsense to be laughed at by future generations (or, through mediocrity, ignored).

So, judging by the absence of St. Peter's in the period of 400 to 800 in Britain, society consists of one in which labels of rank are known, but control of one human being by another was limited. This might be another useful index of Roman-ness. In the first and second century AD mini-white-elephants such as Fora, and Basilicas, were spread rather widely; by the third and fourth century AD these projects were receding back into the Mediterranean basin from whence they came. Thus centralized Romanitas managed the Baths of Diocletian in Rome, and even Diocletian's Palace in Split, but these are some of the last major civic or secular projects to succeed. Most of the later projects were managed by the church, or, in a rather restricted area by people like Justinian, with a heaven given right and ability to bleed the empire for his own purposes. Fora and Basilicas are a thing of the past in 4th.C. Britain, where the best that can be managed is the occasional town wall, or repair thereto, and a rash of country houses for the men who could get things done. Money, as judged by the position of new mosaics (and all the archaeological evidence shows second century mosaics either ruined, or covered over) was in the country house and successful farm whether like the Beeches House, Cirencester, inside the walls of a former 'town' or in the country side like Woodchester.

Received opinion on fashion before the 20th.C. is that it spreads from the top downwards. If you are studying architectural style, or dress, or jewellery or music you start either with the court or the top echelons of the church if you want to see the earliest examples of each type. Then the ideas spread out; masons, having brought the court up to date go out to lower customers until called back to start yet another circle. Where there is no top there is presumably no focus, and if one chieftain or village leader is not pre-eminent then no particular way of doing something is particularly to be copied. According to the fashion-concious this would be an unbearably dull life in which most people did, eat, wore, and lived in what they wanted, and anything out of the ordinary might or might not catch on according as people fancied it.

We are now at the position of seeing that Roman-ness might be associated with the big landowner and his extortion, and that is a very good reason for not following this fashion if you are one of the extorted. And the man-in-the-field might never have had very much to do with fashion, since he was living rather near the basic level anyway. As the land-owner came adrift from the empire wide organization, which would sometimes return run-away workers to him,

and, through taxation, give him control over the lives of his tenants who could not pay, he ceased to control people in an effective way and most of his Roman fashions, such as mosaics and stone buildings would not be attained. Money had gone rather earlier so that the most obvious incentive to relatively free peasants to do his bidding was missing. He presumably descends to that shadowy figure of the Dark Ages, the occupant of the Princely Residence; here he has a group of artisans who can provide him with personal fashion, perhaps such as brooches, so long as he feeds and cossets them; but they seem to be distressingly free to wander on their way to another Residence as the whim takes them. This is not only happening in the mists of Wales, for I had noted, in rather puzzled fashion, something similar taking place at the heart of the western empire in fifth century Ravenna. The emperor of the first or second century showed his wealth and power by building the Colosseum or the Column of Trajan. The fifth century emperor or empress concentrated on smaller jewels such as the mausoleum built by Galla Placidia or a copy of the Gospels or a book of the Old Testament superbly written on purple parchment and illuminated (e.g. the Vienna Genesis or Rossano Gospels). The top people seem to concentrate on producing beautiful things for themselves rather than on grandiloquent monuments for the masses. The Princely Resident seems to be doing exactly the same thing, in his own way. Have they chosen this, or are they simply allowing their wants to change in concert with what is available?

Does settlement pattern go hand in

hand with social layering? In other words are the clusters of people, nice and detectable round country houses and the large farms in Roman Britain a sign of an organized society? And the same around the proto-manor house of the more important man in the 8th. or 9th.C.? And if people are less detectable in between is this because they have dispersed because there is no great threat, and there is therefore no great reason to cluster together? This would certainly help in our material record, for a single wooden built house with few, if any, cultural labels is almost undetectable except in a formal open area excavation. Even when found, such cottages could well be labelled Iron Age or Medieval, and so not enter the appropriate record. It is only when people begin to cluster and occupy the same site for a time that we begin to see the earliest buildings in the sequence and date them stratigraphically rather then by their material culture. And it may be that they only cluster when there is some sort of hierarchy, and therefore some reason for control.

We have worked through urbanization, and found that it is not much help as a concept to describe the end of Roman Britain because Britain was never urbanized enough to make de-urbanization important, and the whole process happened far too early anyway. We have looked at de-Romanization and found that useful as a way in to the underlying process which seems to be the governing theme in life from AD 200 to 800, and that is decrease and increase in social organization and, more important, stratification. We therefore end up with an empire wide process of destratification which has rather different effects in Britain and the South and North of Gaul, and Italy and Africa. Where towns were firmly based they ??survived??, where, as in Britain they were novelties, little understood, they did not survive. If the town ?survived? in, say the South of Gaul or Italy, then almost automatically the smaller nucleated settlement survived as well. If the town did not survive in Britain then there is no direct evidence on the survival of any nucleated groups at all. It may be almost as if Italy was on grade 8/10 social organization in some intrinsic fashion, and Britain was on grade 4 when the slide began. The slide caused a fairly uniform drop of 3 points on the scale so Italy became 5/10, and Britain dropped to the basic 1/10. Where, what, and why was this slide?

I have described this change as Empire wide. Purposefully, in fact, so that I could draw attention to its blinkered presumption. While it may be useful to draw attention to the wideness of any movement by saying that it spans the whole Empire, it is just like a Romanist to do this without noticing that remarkably stringent and meaningless limits are being set at the same time. Do we actually know that our trend is not to be seen in Scotland, or Free Germany, or Denmark, or Eastern Hungary, or Romania after 270, or the Black Sea coast, and so on. There is for instance a well developed sequence in Denmark with phases of prosperity and outward-lookingness, and nucleation, and so on which I know of, but, like many Romanists, do not know. If the changes in Denmark show some similarity to the changes that I have suggested in Britain, then we have to start asking ourselves what units we should be working in, and where we can stand to see any overall picture without being either part of that picture, or, as for instance in China, part of another picture. If we are looking at general changes and movements then we can now see that the spatial limits of the Roman empire are just as irrelevant to our study as the temporal limits.

The historian of the empire has always wanted to study his subject as a unity. He has not insisted on isolation, for the barbarian raids on the West in the third century are obviously external, yet had a major impact, but he usually wants to find his moving forces within rather than as basic trends in a wider area of which the empire is only a part. I wonder, in an as yet unformulated way, whether the empire is a valid unit of study in a subject so basic as social structure. We might, for instance, be dealing with a period of climatic change which affected the temperate zone of Europe indiscriminately. I am not suggesting that we are, simply putting it forward as the type of model which might one day be seen to be valid. And also to annoy the geographers, who seem to have a thing about environmental determinism. Supposing the climate deteriorated, then this will affect the production of surpluses, and this in turn will affect social structure, and if that is not environmental determinism ...... So the decreasing yield of the farms will be first and most obvious in the more northerly parts, then it will spread south a certain way, but it may not have a deleterious effect beyond a certain point. Thus the climate of Greece could do with a little more rain and a little less hot sun, for my taste, and probably that of many crops, so long as the amount of frost did not appre-

ciably mount. So that what decreased yield in the North could increase yield in the South, As the yield in Britain decreased the surplus decreased and the landowner could no longer screw lots of tribute out of his tenants, try as he might, so he ceased to be different from his tenants except that he owned lots of not very productive land. The same problem would hit the Danish chief, or the German prince, and they would also lose their differentiation, and all this could be understood if the Roman Empire had never existed.

But it did exist, as a large block of land dividing up the area around it, and any process such as the one sketched above would have its particular effects on this organized area simply because it was organized more and differently from it surroundings. So our prime mover, which could well be environmental, though I am not particularly attached to this, causes sweeping changes which we can document and date more effectively inside the empire because of the ease of working with highly organized material, and what actually goes on on the empire is mostly effect, and little cause. To retreat from global theory to the Cotswolds, the climatic idea does not work very well because the country houses and farms seem to be the last thriving units, and if the changes of the third and fourth century are due to the decreased yield from the land it is surprising that their prosperity in this period seems to increase.

At least I have straightened out in my own mind a general theory of change between AD 200 and 800, and if I have not labelled for ever the Prime Mover in this, or the primes movers, I have opened the door to other ideas.

Trans

Publications

The background to Romanization

For a general background abroad you could start with *Oppida,* John Collis, Dept. Archaeology, Sheffield, 1984. This will give some general ideas about the later Iron Age in Europe, extensive bibliographies, and most important, ideas about what towns may or may not be, and the creeping urbanization of Rome. Partly from the other side, but from a remarkably balanced point of view you have Edith Wightman, *Gallia Belgica,* Batsford, 1985. This gives a survey of the area of Belgica before the Romans arrived, and then the process of starting up a province. Back in Britain then there are two reviews of the Iron Age to start with - always concentrated in the south, Ed. John Collis, *The Iron Age in Britain - a review,* Dept. Archaeology, Sheffield, 1977 with an important article by Christopher Smith on population. Don't worry if people tell you it is wrong or out of date or out of fashion; what matters is that he has put down his method and his ideas are therefore always testable, so they cannot be completely wrong. Ed. Barry Cunliffe and David Miles, *Aspects of the Iron Age in Southern Britain,* Oxford, Committee for Archaeology Monograph 2, 1984, is more recent, but more selective. Probably the most interesting is Richard Hingley, trying to interpret settlements and patterns; he is still partly incomprehensible here, but he is getting better, so keep a look out for later articles. A good article by Annie Grant on Animal Bones except that she has not got the courage of her convictions and bows to the Great and the Good when they do the

interpretation; they are wrong and her evidence is right - it is bound to be because it is basic evidence. Martin Jones on crops, and some nice new ideas from bronze, Peter Northover, and Iron, Chris Salter and Robert Ehernreich, metallurgy. But these are distilations, so you need to get back to some real archaeology. For the Iron Age proper I like Paul Drury, *Excavations at Little Waltham,* CBA Research Report 26, 1978; clear and straightforward and no nonsense. Pete Fasham, *The Prehistoric Settlement at Winnall Down, Winchester,* Hampshire Field Club Monograph 2, 1985, is more trendy and therefore gets you thinking in the ways of the future, but is a very good exercise in getting down on paper what he found. A lot of discussion and the specialist reports tell you far more about the business of archaeology and processes that were going on on the site, than about the Iron Age. This means that you need to learn the warning lessons here and keep them permanently in mind when you read other reports which never even wondered how the things they found came to be there. Finally to stand on the brink of the Romanization have a look at *Skeleton Green,* Clive Partrige, Britannia Monographs 2, 1981. The vital thing about this site is some late Iron Age occupation, badly tinged by Rome, then sealed under a layer of alluvium of flood silt, from the mid first century layers above. Good straightforward account of structures and lovely finds reports.

Now we come to the middle of the first century, when Romanization speeded up. An early attempt here to see what was going on was a conference organized by the archaeology and anthropology students at Cambridge in March 1979, which was the most enjoyable conference I have ever been to because it looked forward, most of the people there were young, at at least, young in mind, and those were only there by invitation, and anything went. The resulting volume, Ed. Barry Burnham and Helen Johnson, *Invasion and Response, BAR 73*, 1979, is unusual and stimulating; it actually requires you to think about the ideas it puts forward comparing invasions and responses in different parts of the world and different conditions. If you want a quick guide to any archaeologist's mind ask them their opinion of this book; if they haven't heard of it, tell them about it, but remember after that they are poorly informed; if they like it, talk archaeology and believe what they say; if they are grudging, or winge, or don't like it, talk gardening and get away as quickly as possible. The the brighter Britons were leap-frogged by the even more forward looking Dutch, and in English too. Ed. Brandt and Slofstra, *Roman and Native in the Low Countries*, BAR S 184, 1983, is the result of another conference which must have been yawningly hard to follow in places, but the published result is easier on the senses. The articles are from people who collect material information and people who have anthropological and sociological and systems theory ideas, and sometimes some of them inhabit, perhaps uneasily, the same head. Everything in in it good for you, even if only to show how other people think, but many of the articles in it are interesting, useful and enjoyable. If you want a model of how to write the perfect article, well, nearly perfect, read and analyze Willy Groenman-van Waateringe on 'The disastrous effect of the Roman occupation'. This is probably the place to mention her other superb article 'Urbanization and the North-West frontier of the Roman Empire', pages 1037 to 1044 in *Roman Frontier Studies 1979*, Ed. Hanson and Keppie, BAR S 71, 1980. I need to mention it here because the volume will not other wise concern us, filled as it is with military gunge.

After this things get bitty, and may turn elsewhere. Coins start off from *Coinage and Society in Britain and Gaul,* ed. Barry Cunliffe, CBA Research Report 38, 1981 with some useful surveys and a continuation of the argument between Collis and Rodwell on what Iron Age coins really are, and what they mean, and whether their distribution maps are real or useful. I side with Collis. Imported pottery in the first century is likely to be either amphora or samian. For amphorae there is David Peacock, and David Williams, *Amphorae and the Roman Economy,* Longman, 1986 to give the general background well before, and during the time that they came to Britain. For Samian the latest summary which seems excellent to me is *La Terre sigillée gallo-romaine,* ed. Colette Bémant and Jean-Paul Jacob, Documents d'Archéologie Française no.6. For the movement of making pottery into Britain then you have to go to Vivien Swan, *The pottery Kilns of Roman Britain,* RCHM supplementary series 5, 1984, because she is the first person to gather the information together and to realize that something could be got out of it.

As a Roman blot on the landscape I suppose that *Fishbourne,* Barry Cunliffe, Society of Antiquaries Research Report 26, 1971, is a good example, though the pedestrian nature of the report certainly does not give the author license to throw brick-bats at other Roman archaeologists for being dull. The growth of the stone building craze in towns relies on Walthew, *Britannia vi, p.189.* If you must have something about the army the there is Blagg and King, *Military and Civilian in Roman Britain,* BAR 136, 1984 where Colin Haselgrove shows that Romanization went on quite well without them, Martin Millett shows they had little effect on the siting of towns, I think they supported the unnecessary business of coinage which went as soon as they did, Simon James shows there were far less of them than we thought and Tom Blagg shows that they were culturally deprived and had little effect on art and architecture. Other authors go their own way, and you might find even find my summaries are biased.

NB. In abbreviations Antiquaries, Society of, is better given as Antiks, or Antiqus, or Antiqs than Ants because Ants suggests organization and activity.

Natural background

Most general surveys of the natural background, and by that I mean seeds, bones, pollen, soils and so on, not the paragraph at the beginning of every single excavation report on limestone, gravel and sloping subsoils which in the current squeeze should always be edited out, most surveys seem to loose interest before they get to the interesting part. There is the one great exception, but they only get there because they started late. *The environment of man - Iron Age to Anglo-Saxon,* ed. Martin Jones and Geoff Dimbleby, BAR 87, 1981. The superb thing here is that they started off with the firm intention of not being bamboozled by period specialists, so most of the articles cross the nonsense boundaries all the time. But it is no good stopping after you have read this because it all happened before 1980 in the early stages of the subject, and a lot has happened since. The trouble is, it will not be collected together again for some time so you just have to go through excavation reports till you find a nice juicy environmental appendix which has not been banished to microfiche; then use actual reports as examples and do not rely on boiled down summaries. But this will start you off on virtually everything from the filling up of dry valleys, which is far more interesting then it sounds, to the problems of the Black Earth, which are still problems.

On animal bones then you have to go through Mark Maltby, *The animal bones from Exeter,* Exeter Archaeological Reports 2, Dept. Archaeology, Sheffield, 1979 because it is a basic site report which actually gets some results, and you need to go through at least one at first hand. To correct the impression that every heap of bones has a fascinating story just waiting to be extracted then also read Maltby in Pete Fasham, *Winnall Down,* Hampshire Field Club Monograph 2, 1985. Tony King in *Bulletin of the Institute of Archaeology 15* for 1978, pp. 207 to 232, surveys Roman sites, and goes wider over similar ground in Blagg and King, *BAR 136,* pages 219 to 226. But animal bone reports are still developing, and they are working things like endless lists of butchery out of their system, so go through reports which are not even published as I write this and see a) what they are up to and then b) what you think they ought to be doing.

Pollen analyses tend to get tucked away and only reviewed occasionally, as in Turner, *J Arch Sci 6,* 1979, 285-90 where the Roman north-east gets put together from pollen. There is comment from David Breeze, once a hard-line militarist but now coming out well into the environmental world, for Bearsden, a fort on the Antonine Wall in ed. D Breeze, *Studies in Scottish Antiquities,* 1984, Edinburgh - not, of course that I have seen it, I am quoting it from elsewhere, just to be helpful. A paper on pollen in turves at Bar Hill, also a fort on the Antonine Wall is quoted from a quite revoltingly named *BAR IntS 266;* W E Boyd on turves from Bar Hill and Mollins. Another snippet from Scotland is Hanson and Macinnes, *Forests, Forts and Fields,* pp. 98-113 of ed. J Kenworthy Agricolas campaigns in Scotland, Scottish Arch. Forum 12, 1981.

The Black Earth or Dark Earth rumbles on, but the only survey at the moment is that in Jones and Dimbleby. On the other hand tree rings are going full blast and a useful way into these is Jennifer Hillam and Ruth Morgan in *The Roman Quay at St. Magnus House, London,* which really means New Fresh Wharf because St. Magnus House is just a business address, whereas New Fresh Wharf is a real excavation, London and Middlesex Arch Soc Special Pubs. 8, 1986. I suppose it is just possible that some nutty libraries might shelve them under the authors who are L Miller, J Scholfield, and M Rhodes.

Seeds and grain tend to occur in individual reports, so, once you have read the Jones and Dimbleby summary you will have to go round looking in recent reports, but add M. van der Veen, *Food for thought,* pp. 99-108 in Ed. R.F.J. Jones and the rest, First Millennium Papers, BARS 401, Oxford.

Dealing with Material

The subject tends to be either ignored, and material just gets dealt with, or people go into humourless depth and become unreadable and irrelevant. My article in *Bulletin of the Institute of Archaeology, 23,* Jubilee Issue, which gives some further ideas on the same lines as in the chapter here. Otherwise I trust in Ian Hodder, *The present past,* Batsford 1982, because he shows how bad dealing with material and interpretation have been in the past and present. The best article actually dealing with material and getting something out of it I have read is P A Mellars and M R Wilkinson in *PPS vol 46,* 1980, pages 19 to 44. Anyone who looks it up, sees that it is about fish otoliths, and thinks I have got it wrong, needs re-educating.

Pottery

Pottery publications tend to be terribly earnest, so, I suppose do pottery people when they are talking about pottery, but they can be very pleasant people otherwise. You can start either with Anne Anderson, *Interpreting pottery,* Batsford 1984, who will lead you in gently, mainly on Roman, with good drawings and maps and references for further reading, or with David Peacock, *Pottery in the Roman*

World, Longman 1982 which starts with making the pottery and ends up with the heap from excavation and its meaning. There is a firm ethnoarchaeological underpinning, but that is neither good nor, bad, just his way of putting it. When we get down to pottery in Roman Britain there is Vivien Swan, Shire Publications, *Pottery in Roman Britain,* 1975, which perhaps you ought to have started with anyway before you get onto the heavys.

After that things get difficult because what we are after is not so much blow by blow accounts, but thinking about pottery and doing something with it., What to do with it is set out in the formal manner by Chris Young, *Guidelines for the processing and publication of Roman pottery from excavations,* DOE Occasional Papers 4, 1980. Simple straight forward and lots of further references. Where you go from there is probably best expressed in Chris Going, *The Mansio .... Caesaromagus* (=Chelmsford) *.... Roman Pottery,* CBA Research Report 62, 1987. Up to page 105 is a pottery report, and pages 106 to 120 try to do something with it. A summary of different sets of thoughts and problems is found in Martin Millett ed., *Pottery and the Archaeologist,* Institute of Archaeology Occasional Publication 4, 1979. Then there have been volumes of papers which have some good things in them such as; Ed. Alec Detsicas, *Current Research in Romano-British Coarse pottery,* CBA Research Report 10, 1973, especially Rigby, Greene, Hartley, Peacock, Dannell, Bryant. Ed. John Dore and Kevin Green, *Roman Pottery Studies in Britain and beyond,* Papers presented to John Gillam, BAR S 30 1977, especially Hartley, Rigby, Peacock, Darling, Greene, Breeze, Bidwell, Pub

Dannell, Young, Fulford. Ed. Anne and Scott Anderson, *Roman Pottery Research in Britain and North-West Europe,* Papers presented to Graham Webster, BAR S 123, 1981 especially Gillam and Greene, Swan, Geoff Marsh the best - he actually thinks about it. Interesting that quite a lot happened between 1973 and 1977, partly, I think because of delays in publication, while 1977 to 1981 did not apparently give enough time to recharge batteries.

Ian Hodder did try to inject some thoughts into pottery with a discussion of marketing and marketing models in *Britannia V,* p.340 to 359, and, with Mike Fulford did possibly the best piece of work on pottery yet done when they looked at the distribution of Oxford Ware, *Oxoniensia 39,* p.28 to 35. The important point is that they produced results, put them on a diagram, found that looked much to scattered, and then rather than give up asked WHY. They got a result.

Coinage

The basics are now well covered, C H V Sutherland, *Roman Coins,* Barrie and Jenkins 1974. Mattingly, *Roman Coins,* 1928 originally, but brought up to date every so often. J P C Kent, *Roman Coins,* Thames and Hudson, 1978. Andrew Burnett, *The coins of Roman Britain,* British Museum Keys to the Past, 1977. John Casey, *Roman Coinage in Britain,* Shire Archaeology, 1980. John Casey, *Understanding Ancient Coins,* Batsford, 1986. Andrew Burnett, *Coinage in the Roman World,* Seaby, 1987. Me, *Coinage in Roman Britain,* Seaby 1987. Me and Simon James, *Identifying Roman Coins,* Seaby, 1986.

Moving on to further interpretations there will be *Coins and the Archaeologists*, Ed. John Casey and me, appearing in 1988 from Seaby. This will be a second edition with some additions of a few lines each, a few changes, and one complete rewrite of Irregular coinage and copies by George Boon, which will be authoritative for some time to come. Meanwhile there is the coin report from *Colchester Archaeological Report 4*, ed. Nina Crummy, distributed by Oxbow Books, 1987. This is vital reading because it has the first major article by Robert Kenyon on his work on Claudian copies, and this will supersede all that has gone before. It has pointers and a report by John Davies on his work on Barbarous Radiates, and that will be that for some time to come. And Mike Hammerson has abstracted from his thesis some thoughts on Constantinian copies, while reporting on these coins at Colchester.. It also includes some of my latest thoughts and method, and a complete list of excavated coins from Colchester. Bastien and Metzger, *Le Trésor de Beaurains, (dit d'Arras)*, Arras 1977. BAR 4 equal Coins and the Archaeologist. OK?

Settlements

A farmstead. The perfect one is going to be Owslebury, so watch out for it when it appears; some interim reports and oddments, but nothing permanent so far. Otherwise very difficult: try *Winnall Down*, Pete Fasham, Hampshire Field Club Monograph 2, 1985, and G Lambrick and M Robinson, *Farmoor*, CBA Research Report 32, 1879. But there are no houses. Quite, if there are houses they tend to be posh and called villas.

Farmsteads and villas should start with Froucester Court, Glos., in *Trans. Bristol and Gloster. Arch. Soc.*, 89, H S Gracie, pp.15 to 86, and *TBGAS 97*, H S Gracie and E G Price pages 9 to 64. The third report, by Eddie Price, in in preparation and will concentrate more on the farmstead of the early period. The problems of what is a villa can be followed through G Webster and co. Barnsly Park, *TBGAS 99*, pages 21 to 78, part II *TBGAS 100*, pages 65 to 190, and part III *TBGAS 103*, p.73-100. Then comes John Smith's reinterpretation in *Ox.J.Arch. vol. 4 part 3*, pages 341 to 351, and the Webster reply in *Oxford Journal Arch. vol. 6 no.1*, p.69-90. I don't think the reply makes much of a dent in John Smith's case as it concentrates on details and relies on What we all Know, but if you are bothering with this at all then you have to read through the whole lot in the right order and make up your own mind. Another reinterpretation by John Smith is on Marshfield, Kevin Blockley, *BAR 141*, 1985, and appears in the *Oxford Journal Arch. 6/2*, 243 to 256. Chedworth can be followed through Roger Goodburn, *Chedworth Roman Villa*, National Trust Guide, 1979 and Graham Webster, this time as the trouble-maker instead of John Smith, *TBGAS 101*, pages 5 to 20. The villa or small town of Gatcombe in Somerset is much more difficult since Barry Cunliffe's main publication in in the *Proceedings of the University of Bristol Spelaeological Society*, vol.11 part 2, 126 to 160, while the Brannigan side is in Gatecombe Roman Villa, *BAR 44, 1977*. Nettleton, W Wedlake, Society of *Antiqs. Research Report 40, 1982*. Portchester, vol.1 Roman, Barry Cunliffe, *Antiqs. Res. Rep. 32, 1975*.

Ian Hodder's settlement work: in ed. David L Calrke, *Models in Archaeology,* Methuen, date not given on offprint. And on trade patterns also, i.e. in addition to anything I have mentioned before, *World Archaeology, vol.6 issue 2,* 170 to 189. Apuleius, *The Golden Ass,* Penguin have a good translation, for what goes on in amphitheatres. Page refs not given because it will do you good to read the whole thing. And the *Satyricon* of Petronius. Central Places are discussed in *Central Places, Archaeology and History,* ed. Eric Grant, Sheffield, 1986.

There is very little on the subject of towns which I approve of so the only things I am willing to recommend are a few basic excavation reports so that you go back to see what the evidence actually is rather than read secondary sources which are totally constrained by one erroneous model or myth. As always, the most truthful is Frere, *Verulamium I,* Soc. Antiqs. Res. Rep. 28, 1972, *Verulamium II,* Soc. Antiqs. Res. Rep. 41 1983, and *Verulamium III,* definitely not Society of Antiqs, but cheaper and quicker, looking just the same, Oxford Archaeology Monographs 1, 1984. Also Alec Down, *Chichester Excavations, vols 1,3 and 5,* Phillimore, 1977, 1978, 1981. *Southwark,* ed. Bird, Graham, Sheldon, Townend, Joint Publications of Lond. and Mssx. Arch. Soc. and Surrey Arch. Soc. no.1, 1978. *Colchester Archaeological Reports 2,* Nina Crummy 1983; *3,* Philip Crummy, 1984. And K Kenyon, *Jewry Wall, Leicester,* S. Antiqs. RR 15, 1948 and D Atkinson, *Wroxeter,* Birmingham Arch. Soc. 1948, reprinted 1970, are out of digging fashion, but they do give some of the basic informa-

tion. Of course there are lots more, but they tend to be special features, eg. Exeter Bath House, Cirencester military, Cemetery, villa inside the walls, the Baths at Bath, which are not really to do with towns, except that they are in them, or just outside. For small towns try *Staines,* K R Crouch and S A Shanks, Joint Publications of Lond. and Mssx. Arch. Soc. and Surrey Arch. Soc.no. 2 1984, or Martin Millet's *Neatham,* Hampshire Field Club Monograph 3, 1986.

For nonsense arguments and some good sense (Hassall, Mertens, Blagg, Baatz) on defences and towers see ed. J Maloney and B Hobley, *Roman Urban Defences in the west,* CBA Res. Rep. 51, 1983. Goodchild 1953 I quote as I cannot remember where it comes from "The dating of Roman city walls in Britain as established by stratigraphic excavation normally varies between the reigns of Hadrian and Septimius Severus. It still has to be decided whether this is an accident of history or a consequence of divergent archaeological interpretation." Still just as true. Following on from that good sense is Mike Jarrett, *Antiquity, 1965,* volume 39, 57-59, which is far too good sense to be followed because it spoils the story lines, but it has been re-iterated by the latest survey Julie Crickmore, *Romano-British Urban defences,* BAR 126, 1984. A good gathering of information on The Military Defence of British Provinces - later phases, is Derek Welsby, BAR 101, 1982. Suburbs which is called extra mural settlements, since the use of the word suburb pre-judges what is outside the walls, Simon Esmond Cleary, *BAR 169,* 1987. Get at John Smith's other work on villas through his articles I have already quoted.

Cemeteries

Lankhills, Winchester, *Winchester Studies, vol 3*, part 2, Giles Clarke, 1979. Others also ran: Trentholme Drive, *Min. of Works Arch. Reps. 5*, Stationery Office, London 1968. Cirencester Cemetery, *Ciren. Excavations vol. 2*, McWhirr, Viner and Wells, Cirencester 1982. Most important part the bones by Calvin Wells. Poundbury, in preparation, watch out for it. Commentary: Bones, bodies and disease, please note that hyphen, it does tend to get left out and it ruins the message. Calvin Wells's book was *Bones Bodies and Disease*, Thames and Hudson 1964, specially good on Human Sacrifice. My paper, *Ox.J.Arch. 1/3*, 347-58, is un-ease over the treatment of bones and bodies. Not I hasten to add any of this sentimental nonsense about bones belonging to the person who exhibited them during life, still less to any descendants who have no claim on them whatsoever and should be shut up, just that the most is not being got out of them. In habit, to live inside, therefore exhabit, to live outside, which is just what you do to your bones. As an example of foreign analysis doing much better than British, up to Lankhills, V Lanyi Die spätantiken Gräberfelder von Pannonien, in *Acta Archaeologica Hungarica 24 for 1972*, pages 52 to 213. Do not be put off by the German because a lot of it can be gained from just looking at the diagrams where most of the information is summarized. Keith Hopkins, *Population Studies 20*. Grave alignment: first read C Wells and C Green *Norfolk Archaeology,35*, page 425 ff. where it all seems absolutely obvious and sensible. The read Giles Kendall *Arch. Journal, 139 for 1982*, pages 101 to 123 where it all falls apart again and should be heard of no more. But you must actually read both of them, and in that order, if you are going to say anything about it. And Calvin Wells's best bone report is North Elmham, *East Anglian Archaeology, vol.9, 1980*, 247 to 374. Yes, I know it is Anglo-Saxon - so what?

Deduction, analysis and thinking

Peter Abelard, *Ethics*, edited and translated by D E Luscombe, Oxford Medieval Texts, 1971. Otherwise this is something everyone has to do for themselves from scratch, with the help of R G Collingwood, various publications.

Interpretation

Some starters in Ian Hodder, *The present past*, Batsford, 1982. This chapter. Then DIY.

The End

Me in *World Archaeology, vol. 12, part 1, 1980*, pages 77 to 92. No one has bothered to reply because no change is needed in the status quo. Probably best taken in Frere, *Britannia,* latest edition. Simply to demonstrate that my ideas have changed, me in *TBGAS vol. 75, 1956*, page 203; *vol. 89, 1970*, p.11 to 14, *vol. 94, 1976*, pages 92 to 100, and the Reece and Catling, *Cirencester*, BAR 12, 1975, and me in *Archaeological and Historic Cirencester*, ed. A McWhirr, p.61to 80, esp. 70 to 73, sorry, BAR 30, 1976. Jeremy Evans, *Scottish Arch. Review, vol. 2 part 2*, 144 to 149; my reply, 149 to 153 with an excellent phrase about milking stools. Me on archaeology in a historical period, In*Scot. Arch. Rev. vol 3 part 2*, 113 to 115. Extramural occupation in general, Simon Esmonde Cleary, *BAR 169, 1987;* Silchester in particular, Mark Corney, in Mike Fulford, *Silchester Defences,* Britannia Monograph 5, 1984. The Silchester "church", Frere, *Archaeologia 105, 1975,* esp. p.297. Prof. Frere's late houses at Verulamium, Ver.III, 1983. pages 212 to 228. The Frere quote (1981) is in *The Roman West in the Third Century,* BAR S 109, King and Henig, ed. p.390. The 1975 quote for me is in BAR 12. For Frénouville, Christian Pilet, *BAR S 83, 1980.* Collingwood on ticklishness, *An essay on metaphysics,* Oxford 1940. The third century as slack water, me in *BAR S 109,* Roman W. 3rd. C., 27-38. Luni excavations, A Frova, ed. *Scavi di Luni,* Roma, 1973, *Scavi di Luni II,* Roma 1977. Dorestad, W A Van Es and W J H Verwers, ROB publications, *Nederlandse Oudheden 9, 1980.* Towns in Europe, M W Barley, ed. *European Towns,* London 1977. King and Callu on coins in ed. C King, 4th C., *BAR S 76, 1980. Central Places, Archaeology and History,* ed. Eric Grant, 1986, Sheffield. Newcomers at York and Canterbury, First Millennium Symposium Papers, BAR S401, ed. R. F. J. Jones and company. Pottery: Young *BAR 43, 1977,* Fulford *BAR 17, 1975,,* Going *CBA Res. Rep. 62, 1987.* Pay of state functionaries, me, *Coinage in Roman Britain,* Seaby, 1987. Withington, H P R Finberg, *Roman and Saxon Withington,* Leicester Dept. of Local History, Occasional Papers 8, 1959, republished in some of his books of essays. Saxon cemetery at Lechlade being written up. Grants in early post-Roman

Society Wendy Davies, *An early Welsh micorcosm,* Royal Hist. Soc. Studies in History No.9, London, 1978. Me on owners of great tracts of land from Roman to Saxon, ed. Alan Saville, *Archaeology in Glostershire,* Cheltenham, 1984, 181-90. Art and artisans for private enjoyment in the Later Empire, me in ed. Henig. *A handbook of Roman Art,* Oxford 1983, p.244-8.

Postscript to The End

I have just re-read my Scot. Arch. Rev. 2/2 for the first time for a long time and an surprised to find that virtually all the ideas in this End are there in embryo; all that had happened here is the working out of them at greater length. That was 1983, this is early 1988, so it has taken four years to come to the boil.

Postscript to Publications

It became obvious very early on in compiling these that they are inadequate. What is needed is a critical, very critical, bibliography of each subject with assessments of what has been written back to 19xx and a list of good things before then; at present they are really no more than expanded footnotes to enable you to get back to the original of what I have quoted. They are not there to buttress my case, just out of fairness to say, "I got the idea from here" or "This is what I think, go to the original and see what that said". I think this might be worth trying to do; suggestions for inclusion, either for praise or castigation welcome if written down.